Modern Approaches to Manufacturing Improvement:
The Shingo System

Modern Approaches to Manufacturing Improvement:
The Shingo System

SHIGEO SHINGO

DR. ALAN ROBINSON
University of Massachusetts at Amherst
Editor-in-Chief

Foreword by
Norman Bodek, Publisher

Productivity Press
Portland, Oregon

Productivity Press
P.O. Box 13390
Portland, OR   97213-0390
Telephone: (503) 235-0600
Telefax: (503) 235-0909
E-mail: service@ppress.com

Library of Congress Catalog Card Number: 89-43673
ISBN: 0-915299-64-X

Cover design by Hannus Design Associates
Printed and bound by Edwards Brothers
Printed in the United States of America

Library of Congress Cataloging-in-Publication Data

Shingō, Shigeo, 1909–1990
    Modern approaches to manufacturing improvement: the Shingo system/
Shigeo Shingō: Alan Robinson, editor-in-chief: foreword by Norman Bodek.
    p.   cm.
    Selections from the author's The sayings of Shigeo Shingō, A revolution in manufacturing, Zero quality control, and Non-stock production.
    I. Production management. 2. Quality control I. Robinson, Alan (Alan G.)
II. Title.
TS155.S4554   1990   658.5—dc20   89-43673

02 01 00 99 98 97   10 9 8 7 6 5 4

Dedication

To Margaret, Phoebe, and Margot Robinson
A.R.

Contents

Publisher's Foreword

When Dr. Shingo visited our Cambridge office this past summer, he remarked that he thought he could show the Pentagon how to reduce U.S. defense spending and thus help reduce the federal deficit. This, of course, gave us all a good chuckle. Although his statement seemed a lofty one, we didn't doubt that he could do what he said. Not for a minute. We've been associated with this remarkable man for the last seven years or so, during which time our translations of his books have been enthusiastically consumed by tens-of-thousands of managers and engineers throughout the world.

So, like Professor Alan Robinson, who has done a fine job editing this book, we believe the next logical step is to introduce Dr. Shingo to the managers and engineers of the present and future rather than a small cadre of Pentagon officials. This book was Professor Robinson's idea. He discovered Dr. Shingo just a few years ago and here describes how he came to recognize the importance and relevance of his writings:

> The need for this book emerged when I decided to develop a series of lectures on Japanese methods for my BBA and MBA classes on Operations Management. I was overwhelmed by the response from my students, many of whom reported in their course evaluations that these lectures had been the highlight of the course. The need for a single source for the broad and often complex span of ideas included in the lectures became apparent to me — not only from the amount of work I had to do to develop my lectures from scattered materials, but from the students' eagerness to learn more than I was able to cover in the short class time available.

Why is this book important? You must realize that what you are about to read is material carefully selected from the writings of one of the two co-developers of the Toyota Production System — the first Just-in-Time system. The product of the insight that only such a person could possess, the readings are extremely practical and clear explanations of some of the most important ideas about modern production management.

Professor Robinson informs me that most business schools still teach the concept of economic order quantity (EOQ) — the most economic quantity of a product to be made during a single production run. With Dr. Shingo's Single-Minute Exchange of Die (SMED) technique, however, setups that took hours can be reduced to minutes and seconds, making it entirely possible to reduce the EOQ to one!

Similarly, you are probably at least familiar with Statistical Quality Control (SQC). SQC, to be sure, is a great improvement over past inspection techniques. But SQC still tolerates *some* defects. Dr. Shingo, on the other hand, has devised tools and techniques for eliminating defects *completely*.

As I mentioned before, Dr. Shingo was one of two persons responsible for development of the Toyota Production System. His partner in this endeavor was Taiichi Ohno. And an unusual partnership it was indeed. Mr. Ohno was the manager and Dr. Shingo was the teacher. Dr. Shingo's writing reflects this; he knows how to explain things. His style is lucid and very entertaining. He anticipates counter-arguments to the material he presents, and he offers abundant data — as well as accounts of personal experience — to convince you of the soundness of his ideas.

Dr. Shingo has written twenty-three books and is currently working on his twenty-fourth. The selections presented here are taken from four of Dr. Shingo's recently translated books: *The Sayings of Shigeo Shingo: Key Strategies for Plant Improvement*; *A Revolution in Manufacturing: The SMED System*; *Zero Quality Control: Source Inspection and the Poka-Yoke System*; and *Non-Stock Production: The Shingo System for Continuous Improvement*.

Modern Approaches to Manufacturing Improvement is self-contained and intended to be of interest to specialists and non-specialists alike. Teachers of management and business operations will find the book useful as a supplementary resource at both the undergraduate and graduate levels. Practicing managers in all functional areas will discover in it ideas for personal and corporate improvement and can use it as a starting point for wider reading in the source books and literature on Japanese manufacturing. Professor Robinson has also taken care to make the book useful to the general reader who wants firsthand information about the reasons for the success and rapid growth of industrial Japan.

I'd like to thank Alan Robinson for making publication of this book possible. Many thanks, also, to project editor Barry Shulak; our production team of Esmé McTighe and David Lennon; cover designer Dick Hannus; and our friends at Rudra Press: Gayle Joyce, Michele Seery and Jane Donovan.

Norman Bodek
Publisher

Modern Approaches to Manufacturing Improvement:
The Shingo System

1

Editor's Introduction

Shigeo Shingo's Contributions to Manufacturing

So much of what we call management consists of making it difficult for people to work.

Peter Drucker

Shigeo Shingo has made substantial contributions to the rapid growth and success of Japan's manufacturing sector since the end of World War II. Although he is not yet as well known in the West as other industrial figures such as Akio Morita (co-founder of Sony), Soichiro Honda (founder of Honda), Konosuke Matsushita (founder of Matsushita Electric), and certain members of the Toyoda family (founders of Toyota Motor Corporation), his influence on the history and techniques of manufacturing is significantly greater. Not only did he co-develop (with Taiichi Ohno of Toyota) the Toyota production system (better known as the first Just-in-Time production control system), he invented the SMED (Single-Minute Exchange of Die) system for setup time reduction and the *poka-yoke* concept of "mistake-proof" or zero-defect manufacturing. As a recognized leading expert on productivity improvement, he is known as "Dr. Improvement" in Japan.

It is well known that children deal better with an object if they know its name. For example, when young children are asked to draw objects on a tray presented to them, they tend to draw only the objects they can identify by name. The principle seems to extend to adults. Shigeo Shingo has trained himself over his long career to see things that others do not or cannot see. He has applied his rare intelligence not only to the solution of problems, but to building

3

methodologies, and assigning "words" to his own fresh theories so that the rest of us can make them part of our vocabulary, thus, part of our cognitive repertoire.

Background

The concept of Just-in-Time (JIT) originated with Kiichiro Toyoda, the first president of Toyota Motor Corporation, which was created when Toyoda Automatic Looms spun off its truck division in 1936. When the company built its new plant in Koromo in 1938, Toyoda also planned that it should have a new production system: what he called "Just-in-Time." Eiji Toyoda, now president of Toyota Motor Corporation, wrote of this in his autobiography:

> We were then using a lot production system, but Kiichiro's idea was to switch over entirely to a flow-type production system. He reasoned that this would eliminate large stocks of materials and parts, doing away with the need for warehouses. Cutting back running stock would also reduce capital outflow. If, once this production system got under way, we were able to sell our finished product before payments were due on our materials and parts, we would no longer have any need for operating capital.
>
> What Kiichiro had in mind was to produce the needed quantity of the required parts each day. To make this a reality, every single step of the operation, like it or not, had to be converted over to his flow production concept. Kiichiro referred to this as the "just-in-time" concept.[1]

When war broke out between Japan and the United States, it became impossible to use the new JIT system at Toyota. Each month Toyota was ordered by the military to make a certain number of trucks, and was allotted materials by the Japanese government with which to work. The problem faced by the infant JIT system was that the orders and the allotments came from two different agencies and were therefore uncoordinated.

After the war, when Kiichiro Toyoda was no longer president of Toyota, Taiichi Ohno, a Toyota plant manager and vice president, revived the idea of Just-in-Time, and over the course of the next two decades, championed its development at Toyota. Taiichi Ohno used an interesting analogy to communicate his philosophy of what was named "the Toyota production system." He likened the company to a

---

[1] Eiji Toyoda, *Fifty Years in Motion*, Kodansha International, N.Y., 1987, p. 57.

ship which floats on the "water" of inventory. This water covers up "rocks," each of which represent production problems, such as quality problems, vendor problems, process imbalances, delays, and unreliable machines that break down often. If the water level is high, then the ship will not hit the rocks, that is, no problems will appear. If the water level is lowered, then rocks appear and the ship will hit them. Since water (at least for the purposes of this analogy) is expensive, to lower costs the company should continuously lower the water until a rock appears, at which point water should be added back into the system while all concerned study how to remove, or pare down, the rock. Gradually, the engine of production is "leaned out" until it runs smoothly and with minimal waste.

Dr. Shingo made vital contributions to the paring down of the two most significant and difficult rocks. First was the rock of the high cost and long times needed for setup operations (to reconfigure or "set up" a machine to do a new task). Second was the rock of quality problems and defects.

The Benefits of the SMED System

Dr. Shingo's SMED system permits many kinds of setup operations to be performed in minutes rather than hours. When several workers and many hours (often more than 20) are required to set up a machine, it makes good sense to amortize the high cost of setup by producing in large batches. But if, as Dr. Shingo points out, the time and resources needed for setup operations can be dramatically reduced (and, possibly, even made insignificant), the rationale for lengthy production runs is largely removed. Low setup times and costs are key requirements of any system that is aimed at minimal inventory and low overhead. They allow for the profitable low-volume production of many products, and make it possible for high-volume production to be achieved economically through many short production runs. In addition to lowering work-in-process inventory, smaller batch sizes reduce lead time and process variability, because they cause products to flow more uniformly, rather than in intense and long spurts. With smaller batch sizes flowing uniformly, scheduling and planning overhead decreases automatically — as do problems of materials handling — since the product flows more evenly and in smaller and therefore more portable quantities. Also, defects are quickly spotted and removed.

In the readings on SMED contained in the third and final section of this book, Dr. Shingo in each case explains clearly, and in an easily implementable way, how to reduce setup times drastically in many situations, and what the consequences of these reduced times will be. The average reduction in setup time reported in a 1986 survey of 120 companies applying the SMED system was ninety-eight percent.

Poka-Yoke: Assuring Quality at the Source

The other important "rock" addressed by Dr. Shingo is that of poor quality. The concept of poka-yoke [pronounced POka YOkay] is at the heart of zero-defect manufacturing (also known as Zero Quality Control). A poka-yoke is a device or practice that guarantees that an error, once its cause is known, will never recur. As you read Dr. Shingo's exposition of poka-yoke, in which he accurately observes that "money and resourcefulness offset one another," you will see that poka-yoke devices are characterized by three attributes: cleverness, simplicity, and inexpensiveness. I came across a good example of poka-yoke while on a team researching a case study on the DCM-Toyota Ltd. truck plant in the northern Indian town of Surajpur. In order to prevent workers from sometimes forgetting to tighten certain critical bolts on the vehicle, wrenches were kept in a bucket of brightly colored paint. When a bolt had been missed, it lacked the noticeable splash of color, thus reminding the worker that it should be tightened.

Many companies still use methods of *monitoring* or *controlling* quality (such as Statistical Quality Control), even when it is possible for them to use simple tools like poka-yoke that *assure* quality. The distinction between *control* and *assurance* is one that Dr. Shingo will make clear in the readings on Zero Quality Control in Section Two. As you will see, Dr. Shingo is not the world's most avid fan of Statistical Quality Control.

A System of Continuous Improvement

The JIT system constantly strives for improvements in productivity. Waste is exposed by the persistent lowering of inventory, and is then eliminated. Are the resulting improvements worth the time and trouble? Usually they are.

In *Kaisha: The Japanese Corporation*, James Abegglen and George Stalk, of the Boston Consulting Group's Tokyo office, estimate that labor productivity is almost *three times* higher in a factory with JIT than in an equivalent one without it. My students were confronted rather starkly with the consequences of these increased levels of productivity during a recent field trip in the Boston area.

The plant we visited had a mock assembly line, which had been set up that day to run first in the classical way, and then in the JIT way. The students acted as workers, inspectors, and managers. After twenty minutes of hard work in the classical format, the line was switched over to JIT. Half of the students were asked to step back from the line, while the other half rotated into new jobs so that the comparison would be fair. This new and leaner configuration produced twice as many finished goods with half the number of workers as had the classical system. Not surprisingly, the question then arose: "In the real-world, what would have happened to the workers who were not needed any more?"

The answer, of course, is that they would be reassigned to work that is more productive. Ideally, that is what should happen, but a traditional obstacle to productivity improvement (certainly a favorite area for labor-management dispute in both Japan and the United States) has been precisely the tendency for companies to cash-in on such improvements by firing workers. A good way to ensure that improvement will never happen, of course, is to lay people off for improving.

Differences in Japanese and Western Approaches to Production Management

I am asked often by students to articulate the essential differences between modern Japanese and Western thought and practice in production management. I believe that there are four:

1. Japanese Companies Are More Active About Process Improvement and Simplification Than Their Western Counterparts

A colleague of mine was recently taken on a plant tour of a well known automobile company in England. The tour was being conducted by a vice president of the company. This man was most anxious to please a Japanese corporate vice president who was also on tour — to examine the possibility of a sale of all or part of the British company to the Japanese company. As the tour progressed through the plant, the Japanese visitor was politely complimentary until the guide turned to him and asked if he would like to see the plant's fully-automated warehouse, where all the storage and retrieval was done by robots under the control of a central computer. With a wave of his hand the Toyota man indicated that this would not be necessary. In fact, he was not interested. Under Toyota management the warehouse is not needed.

During his visit to the School of Management at the University of Massachusetts, Dr. Shingo told me a similar story. He was touring an American plant under the guidance of an overbearing plant manager who marched him into a fancy automated warehouse and asked him patronizingly, "Do you have such warehouses in Japan?" Dr. Shingo replied, "No, we are too poor to afford such nice warehouses; we must use our *brains*."

During a recent tour of a catalog-merchandise warehouse that covered forty-five acres, my students and I were impressed with the amounts of goods in storage, the extent of the belts and conveyors and their high operating speeds and sorting rates. In general, we were awed by the level of automation and technology. Afterwards, during the panel discussion with plant staff, one of the operations managers alluded to the company's projected high-growth rate of the warehousing division for the next ten years and suggested to my students that it might therefore be an excellent place for them to work after graduation. To my great pleasure a student then asked if the company would have *any* warehouses at all in ten years, given the unmistakable trend toward lower inventories and short lead times (when a shirt ordered over the telephone would be *manufactured* and mailed within forty-eight hours, instead of *retrieved* and mailed in the same time frame). This young man's question somewhat dampened the manager's recruiting pitch.

In his introduction, Dr. Shingo explains the difference between processes and operations. Unfortunately, this difference is widely unrecognized. But it lies at the heart of the simplification and improvement of production systems and accounts for much of the Japanese success in production over the last twenty years. A process is what the product experiences; it consists of a collection of operations. Since operations are what machines and workers perform, it can be very easy to lose sight of the process amidst all the more visible operations. When trying to improve, it is important to keep the distinction between operations and processes clear:

- An automated warehouse is an *operations* improvement: it speeds up and makes the operation of storing items more efficient. Eliminating all or part of the need for the warehouse by tuning production better to the market is a *process* improvement.
- Conveyor belts, cranes, and forklift trucks are *operations* improvements: they speed and aid the act of transporting goods. Elimination of the need for transport in the first place is a *process* improvement.
- Finding faster and easier ways to remove glue, paint, oil, burrs and other undesirables from products are *operations* improvements; finding ways not to put them there in the first place is a *process* improvement.

Japanese companies have tended to be more process-oriented than their Western counterparts, who have tended to focus instead on operations. It is precisely this difference that prompted the following observation from Robert Hayes and Kim Clark in an article written in 1985:

> This American mentality has also kept us from exploring the impact of changing the basic structure of problems. If one is confronted with a highly complex factory environment—lots of production stages, lots of products, lots of flow patterns, lots of inventory locations, and so forth—one can deal with it in one of two ways. One can either attempt to develop a highly sophisticated (and usually computerized) information and control system to manage all this complexity, or one can set about reducing the complexity. . . . We have spent over a decade and millions of dollars developing elegant Materials Requirements Planning systems, while the Japanese were spending their time simplifying their factories to the point where materials control can be managed manually with a handful of kanban cards. [2]

2. The Japanese Have a More Enlightened Attitude Towards Employees

New United Motor Manufacturing Incorporated (NUMMI) of Fremont, California, is a joint venture between Toyota Motor Corporation and General Motors that was started in 1985 to produce the Chevrolet Nova, the Toyota Corolla, and (later) the Geo Prizm. For

---

[2] *Interfaces*, 15 (1985) p. 13.

General Motors, the venture offered the opportunity to learn about advanced Japanese production techniques as well as to gain experience in dealing with the Japanese. Toyota was attracted by the chance to get familiar with American workers and suppliers, and to adapt the Toyota Production System to an American environment.

The production site chosen was an old General Motors plant in Fremont, California, that had been closed permanently in 1982. Before the closure, the plant had one of the worst labor and quality records of all the GM plants. At the time of closure, absenteeism exceeded twenty percent (sometimes the plant was unable even to start up on time because of a lack of workers), and there were sixty disputed firings and a thousand unresolved grievances. When the plant was shut down, five thousand workers lost their jobs.

In the words of the UAW/NUMMI contract the main aim of the new company was "to promote harmonious worker-management relations and create higher productivity." The Chief Executive Officer was Tanaka Toyoda, a member of the founding Toyoda family of Toyota, and the son of Eiji Toyoda, then CEO of Toyota. The plant manager was also from Toyota. The plant itself was to be run by the Toyota production system (historically the first, and now one of many forms of JIT) and managed in the Toyota style. The company committed itself to hiring most of its workers from the five thousand original GM workers laid off when the plant was closed.

The contract is a very interesting document, and not only because it is short and plainly stated, in a category of writing not noted for terseness. In it, management agrees that workers can be laid off only in times of severe economic distress, and then only after management has taken pay cuts and arranged for previously subcontracted work to be done in the company. In return, the union allows the number of job classifications to be reduced from sixty-four to four (restrictive job classifications are a classic union defense against layoffs and arbitrariness — but introduce tremendous waste). The word *kaizen*, the Japanese for "continuous improvement," is used a number of times in the contract, and NUMMI is committed never to lay off workers when productivity is raised. Workers are referred to as team members: teams are completely responsible for their area of production with a senior member as team leader. The workers visit suppliers, buy parts, share the work to be done amongst themselves, and are the ones who decide which improvements should be made.

Naturally, this experiment has been closely watched, since it offered a test of the efficacy of the Japanese management style when applied outside of Japan, which was quite well controlled for factors such as culture, the political system, the business environment, and the workforce. Was it successful? Dale Buss, an auto analyst for the Wall Street Journal wrote in 1986 that NUMMI

> has managed to convert a crew of largely middle-aged, rabble-rousing former GM workers into a crack force that is beating the bumpers off Big Three plants in efficiency and product quality.[3]

3. The Japanese Appreciate the Power of Continuous Improvement

Masaaki Imai, a prominent Japanese management consultant, says that when kaizen, or continuous improvement, is properly deployed, it's a powerful competitive weapon:

> Kaizen is everybody's business. The kaizen concept is crucial to understanding the differences between the Japanese and Western approaches to management. If asked to name the most important difference between Japanese and Western management concepts, I would unhesitatingly say "Japanese kaizen and its process-oriented way of thinking versus the West's innovation and results-oriented way of thinking."[4]

An early kaizen program was put in place at the National Cash Register Company in Dayton, Ohio, in 1894, and was fully developed by the turn of the century. It involved, among other things, a well-implemented paid suggestion program (by the early 1940s an average of three thousand suggestions were received each year); company-run night courses for workers and managers at all levels; an hour of "employee development" time each day paid for by the company; fitness programs including a mandatory morning exercise period; company-owned parks and resort areas for employee recreation; and the real opportunity for advancement. The results of all these efforts were high quality, innovative products, and high profitability brought about by having all 11,000 minds "on duty," rather than just those of management.

---

[3] Dale Buss, "Gung Ho to Repeat Assembly Line Errors," *The Wall Street Journal*, March 27, 1986.

[4] Masaaki Imai, *Kaizen: The Key to Japan's Competitive Success*, Random House, NY, 1986.

It is of more than historical interest that many Japanese credit the American Training Within Industries (TWI) programs with introducing kaizen into Japan after World War II. TWI was one of the first emergency services set up by Congress after the fall of France in 1940. It was to provide training and consulting services for U.S. industry during its anticipated rapid expansion.

TWI played a vital role in this expansion, which did indeed turn out to be rapid. For example, Willamette Iron and Steel Co. of Portland, Oregon went from a prewar payroll of 320 to one of 16,500 by 1945. By the end of the war TWI had trained millions of foremen, supervisors, and managers.

It was only natural that TWI would be called upon, in the months following the signing of the Pacific treaty, to repeat its magic in Japan. The U.S. Military Occupation Authority felt it imperative, to avoid mass starvation, that Japanese industry be reactivated in a hurry, and well. After TWI was deactivated in 1946, ex-TWI staff were invited to Japan on a private basis to continue the training programs until as late as 1952. According to Lowell Mellen, who directed the postwar TWI programs in Japan, at one point in 1951, over one million Japanese foremen and supervisors were being trained by TWI instructors[5]. Although TWI was extensive, the most important aspect of it for worker empowerment was then termed "Job Simplification." Ideas for this, TWI taught, should come from the *workers*. Indeed, a written improvement suggestion was required for graduation from the Job Methods Training Course, which was one of the three main TWI courses offered at the time.

Leading companies in Japan have practiced kaizen for over forty years now. One of the aims of the Canon Production System (implemented in 1975 in response to difficult times at the company) was to tap the creativity of its employees via a strong kaizen process.[6] Canon's success was reflected in the high rate of participation in the company's suggestion system. In 1985, employees submitted almost 900,000 improvement suggestions, an average of seventy-eight per person (the highest number submitted by any single individual in

---

[5] Since the philosophy of TWI was to train people to train others, it must be assumed that many more Japanese took TWI courses than were officially documented at the time.

[6] Canon's experience implementing kaizen is well-documented in *The Canon Production System: Creative Involvement of the Total Workforce* (Cambridge: Productivity Press, 1987).

that year was 2,600). Canon paid out the equivalent of $2.2 million in prizes, but realized over $200 million in savings as a direct result of the suggestions.

Interestingly, this performance put Canon's suggestion program in only thirteenth place amongst Japanese companies. In first place was Matsushita Electric Corporation, with 6.5 million suggestions. How can a company that doesn't have such a program compete with a company that does?

Japanese workers have always had an enthusiastic attitude towards the improvement process. One of the other aims of the U.S. Military Occupation Authority after the war was to break up the traditions of fascism and paternalism in Japan. To this end they introduced into Japanese labor relations "industrial democracy," which legalized strikes, barred company managers from being officials in the company union, required secret ballots for elections, and so on. An interesting phenomenon developed. In labor disputes Japanese workers, instead of striking, often simply took over "production control" from management. A 1948 U.S. Army memorandum stated that the workers often

> forcibly entered mines and plants, operated them, collected payment for goods produced, paid wages and kept profits, while at the same time making no attempts to arbitrate or conciliate the dispute.[7]

In his book *U.S. Labor Policy in Postwar Japan*, Mr. Sung-Jo Park describes how, in 1946, discontented workers at the Kobe Steel Co. threatened a production control campaign against their management. Their goal was to finish in four hours all the work, which used to require eight hours plus an hour of overtime, and to use the remaining time for machine repair and recreation. The rebellion was put down by dismissing the leaders.

There was considerable debate for several years as to whether or not this technique, called "production control" was legal under Japanese law. The unions had a good argument: if strikes were legal, then surely a less aggressive action, that is, taking over the factory and running it more productively, was also within the law. The courts upheld the workers' position for a while, until the Trade Law was revised.

---

[7] Memorandum, Headquarters IX Corps, Office of the Commanding General, June 17, 1948.

The first section of this book, entitled "Improvement," contains excerpts from *The Sayings of Shigeo Shingo* and *Non-Stock Production* in which Dr. Shingo outlines his approach to the improvement process. He discusses the already described differences between processes and operations, and gives numerous real-world examples of improvements he has devised and implemented. In addition, he presents some general principles to follow when solving production problems. Most importantly, perhaps, he gives practical tips on the human side of improvement.

Improvement means change, and, he says, change can be threatening, unless it is properly introduced so that everyone can support it. Like John Patterson of NCR, for whom the words "it can't be done" were grounds for dismissal, Dr. Shingo heaps scorn on what he calls "*nyet*" engineers (*nyet* is Russian for "no"), who use their experience and position to reject — smugly and without hesitation — useful changes. Improvement starts, of course, with dissatisfaction about the way things are.

4. Japanese Companies Have a Better Understanding of the Pervasiveness of Invisible Waste — and How to Eliminate It

When an action adds cost without adding value to a product, it is called waste. The study of waste and ways to eliminate it is central to the history of manufacturing and service. The study of Operations Management, now a popular undergraduate business major, is largely about techniques and tools (some of which can involve relatively sophisticated mathematics, statistics, and computing) for the elimination of waste. In *Sayings*, Dr. Shingo writes,

> Unfortunately, real waste lurks in forms that do not look like waste. Only through careful observation and goal orientation can waste be identified. We must always keep in mind that the greatest waste is waste we don't see.[8]

A good example of the incremental and perfidious nature of this waste is bank roundoff fraud, a well-understood but very difficult to detect form of embezzlement. It is relatively easy to program a computer to shave automatically a fraction of a penny each month from

---

[8] Shigeo Shingo, *The Sayings of Shigeo Shingo: Key Strategies for Plant Improvement*, Productivity Press, Cambridge, Massachusetts, 1987, p. 18.

every account and place it into an account belonging to the programmer (but kept under an assumed name, of course). Such missing minute fractions do not generally bother a depositor with a normal psychological profile. If the bank has 50,000 accounts, pilfering of this nature will net several hundred dollars each month, not bad pay for a few judicious keystrokes. Overall, certain types of waste might seem insignificant or be difficult to spot, but they can still prove in the end to be very substantial.

The Toyota production system divides waste into seven categories:

Waste of producing defects. When defects are produced, either the company must correct the problem, or be willing to accept the annoyance or loss of a customer. It is quite expensive to irritate and lose a customer (typically it costs much more than if the problem had been detected before the customer entered the picture). As W. Edwards Deming, a quality control expert well-known for his prominent role in the industrial successes of postwar Japan, points out,

> The most important figures needed for management of any organization are unknown and unknowable.[9]

How many customers are lost when one badly-treated customer tells his or her friends about the bad experience with the company's product? The potential numbers are huge. To illustrate: All of my departmental colleagues and a number of students in my classes have been avoiding a particular local car dealer since the time when *one* colleague found that work that he had paid for had not been done. Each of us, myself included, have warned off friends as well. The cost to the company of that one disappointed customer is difficult to pin down, to be sure, but nonetheless it is substantial.

In Section Two, you will read about poka-yoke, or the art of mistake-proofing operations. It aims to guarantee that once the cause of a defect is found and understood, that type of defect will never occur again. Poka-yoke can be clever and fun, and is applicable to service as well as to manufacturing. A low-inventory system such as Just-in-Time cannot function if defective parts are passed along, for instead of simply discarding the defective part and reaching for a

---

[9] W. Edwards Deming, *Out of the Crisis*, Cambridge University Press, Cambridge, England, 1986, p. 20.

good part out of inventory, the worker is forced to issue an order for a new part, and wait until it comes to him. Quite quickly, the whole assembly line will shut down.

Waste of transportation. Every business thinks carefully about the layout of its facilities. The facility layout (where offices, machines, reception areas, storage areas, loading and unloading docks, and the like should go) and the necessary transportation mechanisms are the "invisible overhead" of the business.

Five years ago, I was invited to examine a problem involving elevator congestion at a large railway company. The company had just bought a twenty-nine story skyscraper and had transferred its headquarters staff into it. I arrived early in the morning, to see the problem for myself. Already, a long line of people extended out of the lobby and was snaking around the building.

The manager said to me, "You can see our difficulty. The elevator system is completely overloaded."

The situation had become a labor issue, for the average waiting time for an elevator was *forty-five minutes* during the morning rush hour. The trouble was caused by the layout of the building, originally designed for low-density occupation, not for the numbers of employees currently assigned to work in it.

The task facing me was an exercise in rooting out and eliminating many different kinds of invisible waste. A number of issues needed to be addressed:

- Each elevator car could carry fifteen people, but on average only twelve were travelling on each elevator. Placards instructing people to move to the back, together with a memo to all employees explaining the situation, raised the average carload to fourteen people, a seventeen percent increase in capacity.
- Reprogramming the doors to open and close faster, and to begin to open while the elevator was within a few feet of stopping resulted in a few seconds saved per stop. Since each trip required six to ten stops, and each of the six elevators made fifteen trips during the morning rush hour, the speedup resulted in twenty more trips being made each rush hour, a significant increase in capacity.
- Our data also showed us that during the morning rush hour a large percentage of the traffic was between higher floors, and

of this most was nonessential and even social in nature. The elevators were reprogrammed so that during the half-hour morning rush an elevator could not be called except from the lobby. The increase in capacity was, again, significant.

The total waste in the system, although cumulatively large enough to cause long waits, was the sum of many different kinds of smaller invisible wastes like those mentioned above, which had to be identified, and then eliminated. When that was achieved, the delays disappeared.

Waste of overproduction. If more goods are made than are ultimately sold, then the materials, labor, transportation, storage, and salvaging of these goods are wasted. Overproduction is often planned, to hedge against unforeseen demand or defects. Dr. Shingo and others have written much about the waste of overproduction, which they attack primarily through the reduction of lead time, or the time taken to produce the product, once an order for it is received. Any improvement in productivity will help to lower lead time, of course, because more goods are made with the same effort. As described earlier, one of the most significant of Dr. Shingo's contributions is the theory of SMED, whose aim is precisely to lower setup times, and hence also inventory and lead times.

Waste of waiting. I recently saw a good example of the waste caused by waiting when I was in a large general warehousing facility. The warehouse was over eighty feet tall, with parts stored on shelving extending all the way up to the roof. "Order pickers," whose jobs were to assemble orders of parts from the warehouse, circulated with "shopping lists" that they filled from bins on the bottom shelf, the only shelf within reach of a person standing on the floor. When an order picker discovered that a bin was empty, he or she was supposed to go and find a materials handler, who with his forklift truck could replenish the bin with new parts lifted down from the shelves above, and enter this movement of parts into the computerized inventory system.

The warehouse had many order pickers, and I was told that more were needed. My observation was that the existing order pickers were hardly used; they spent a good portion of their working time waiting around for materials handlers to give them the parts they needed.

Why not, I suggested, put a flashing red light on each bin which can be switched on when a bin is nearly empty, so that a roving forklift truck operator can fill the bin before the picker shows up. Good point, I was assured; but it would be too expensive to implement. How much do the delays to the hundred or so order pickers cost (whose ranks the company wished even to augment)? As Dr. Shingo likes to say, "money and resourcefulness offset each other."

Waste occurring in processing itself. In an entertaining paper published in 1955, Dr. Omond Solandt recalled some stories from the early days of Operations Research, which originated in the study of efficiency in British Army operations in World War II. One of them is very amusing:

> I remember another occasion when we started doing time-and-motion studies on the gun drill for the 25 pounder. In this case we took movies of the gun unit going into action. Everything looked quite good, except that there was one man who spent a long time just standing still doing nothing. When we looked back over the drill to discover what he was supposed to be doing, we found out he was in fact holding the horses! The horses, of course, had disappeared about twenty years earlier, but this task had not been eliminated when the gun drill had been rewritten.[10]

Waste may not always be so obvious. Indeed to those who are involved in it every day, waste in processing can be treacherously invisible.

Waste of movement. Waste of movement has been well studied since the inception of "Scientific Management" at the turn of the twentieth century. Frederick Taylor (the "Father of Scientific Management"), Lillian Gilbreth (the "Mother of Scientific Management") and her husband Frank Gilbreth all advocated careful study and scientific observation of work (using, for example, time and motion studies, performance ratings, allowance factors, and so on), determination of the best way to do the work, and then good training and setting of appropriate work standards for the workers. The tools and techniques that they and others devised were very powerful, and could be used most effectively to raise productivity. It is unfortunate that, as with any powerful tool, Scientific Management was also

---

[10] Omond Solandt, "Observation, Experiment, and Measurement in Operations Research," *Operations Research*, 3, 1955, p.3.

applied in "speedups" (Upton Sinclair has some moving scenes portraying the cruelty of the speedup in his classic book *The Jungle*) and in eliminating jobs, and so acquired a bad name for itself.

As Frank Gilbreth once said, however, the aim of Scientific Management is to "work smarter, not harder." The detail with which movement is studied seems surprisingly small to those seeing it for the first time: At Nissan Motor, any suggestion for improved work design that saves at least six tenths of a second is seriously considered by management. If the work is repeated often enough, say 500 times per day, this time per day saved becomes minutes, which can then be put to more productive use.

Waste of inventory. People are usually horrified when they discover how high the actual cost is of holding inventory. A rule-of-thumb carrying cost for a unit of product is commonly around one quarter of the product's value per year, with some arguing that the estimate should be much higher. Thus, for example, the direct cost of holding a car worth $15,000 will be about $3,750 per year. Interestingly, this cost is usually spread around so much that it qualifies as "invisible." No one sees it although the company pays it every day. Removing this form of waste can be quite difficult, particularly since it covers "rocks," and makes life easy. Dr. Shingo, in fact, has likened inventory to an addictive drug: the more you have, the more you will need.

A Word About the Master

Once, while sitting at dinner, Dr. Shingo said to me, "It is a wonderful feeling indeed to be the first to discover things as simple and easy to understand as SMED and poka-yoke." While it is true that there were some poka-yoke devices at Henry Ford's River Rouge plant in the early 1900s, and people had fretted about long setup times years before Dr. Shingo, no one had thought as deeply about either idea, or realized what their power and general applicability might be.

I hope that you enjoy what you read in this book, and go on to read other things by this remarkable man. He is an excellent teacher who answers questions with wit and sometimes the inscrutability of an Eastern guru. At the above-mentioned dinner, many of the guests noticed that Dr. Shingo (who is 82 years old) ordered several bowls of salad dressing for his small side salad. He caught me looking quizzically at these, and spoke rapidly in Japanese to his interpreter. The interpreter said, "Dr. Shingo wishes *sensei* Robinson to know that when you get to be his age, you realize that it is not the salad that is important, but the dressing. That is all he eats anymore."

Itadakimasu. Enjoy the meal!

2

Author's Introduction

Fundamental Flaws in European
*and American Production Philosophies**

In my lectures, I sometimes ask how many in the audience know
how to ride a bicycle. Nearly everyone's hand goes up in response. I
then ask how many know how to make any necessary repairs on a
bicycle. This time far fewer hands go up. From this demonstration,
we may conclude that the ability to ride a bicycle and the ability to repair a bicycle are different. Yet it seems to me that, unconsciously, we
mistakenly assume that knowing how to ride a bicycle means knowing how to fix one. It is important to understand, therefore, that to be
able to repair a bicycle, one has to understand the structure of the
bicycle, the functions of each part, and the functional relationships
among all the parts. The question of production is similar. The fact
that someone is engaged in production every day does not necessarily
mean that person knows how to fix the system when it breaks down,
for instance, when defects occur or efficiency plummets.

For that, one needs a proper understanding of the structure of
production, what the functions of each element of production are,
and how the various elements relate to one another.

---

* This chapter contains excerpts from *Non-Stock Production: The Shingo System for
Continuous Improvement* (Cambridge: Productivity Press, 1985) and *Zero Quality
Control: Source Inspection and the Poka-yoke System* (Cambridge: Productivity
Press, 1986).

European and American managers are busy studying and experimenting with kanban, Just-In-Time (JIT), and other features of the Toyota production system. Without an understanding of the system's basic concepts and implications, however, truly effective innovation in production management will not be achieved.

I would like to suggest that the basic concepts underlying conventional production systems — European and U.S. systems in particular — are flawed by substantial misunderstanding. This misunderstanding lies at the heart of Western production thinking, and progressive Japanese companies that indiscriminately imitate Western production practices are making the same mistakes.

The appearance of the Toyota production system has stimulated some change in this area. One cannot escape the impression, however, that this change reflects a superficial infatuation with a new gimmick, that the Toyota system is not seen as the basic conceptual revolution that it is.

The manufacturing improvement we see now is transient, superficial, and insubstantial. It cannot pull out the diseased roots of obsolete ideas to make room for a totally new production philosophy; it will not lead to innovative production systems.

MISUNDERSTANDING THE RELATIONS BETWEEN PROCESS AND OPERATION

The phenomena of *process* and *operation* have not always been distinguished clearly because they blend together when operations are carried out by a single individual.

The Impact of Division of Labor

Division of labor means that in cutting materials, for example, worker A works successively on different objects, perhaps first on pins P_1, P_2, P_3, etc.; then on bushings Q_1, Q_2, Q_3, etc.; and then on R_1, R_2, R_3, etc. (*Figure 2-1*).

When a lot of 100 pins cut by worker A has accumulated, the items are transferred to worker B, who tapers the tips of the pins. Next, they move to worker C, who grinds the pin tips. In this way,

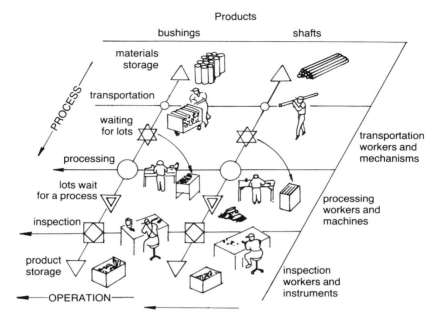

FIGURE 2-1. Two Streams of Production

items flow in succession to different workers, each of whom processes them as required.

Clearly, there is a distinction here:

- *Process* refers to the flow of products from one worker to another, that is, the stages through which raw materials gradually move to become finished products.
- *Operation* refers to the discrete stage at which a worker may work on different products, that is, a human temporal and spatial flow that consistently centers around the worker.

As these concepts evolved, however, people inevitably became captivated by directly observable human motion — that is, *operational* movements. Some concluded that production consisted exclusively of operations; others who were aware of the process as a separate concept disdained its role in production.

In 1921, however, F. B. Gilbreth reported in the *Journal of the American Society of Mechanical Engineering* that production phenomena include the flow leading from raw materials to finished product

— the phenomenon of *process* — and that processes are themselves composed of four phenomena: *processing* (or *machining*), *inspection*, *transport*, and *delay*.

Today, in Europe and the United States, the relationship between process and operation is typically defined as follows:

- *Processes* are large units used in analyzing production.
- *Operations* are small units used in analyzing production.

The West, therefore, ended up imagining that *processes* and *operations* are nothing more then overlapping phenomena lying on a single axis. As a result, even in Japan certain books on production management explained process and operation as classifications dependent merely on the size of units of analysis.

We can see where this led. Some people thought that production as a whole would improve once you improved operations, the smallest units of analysis. Others developed the obscure notion that if operations were improved, processes — as groups of operations — also would improve.

A little quiet thought will persuade anyone that processes lie along a y axis representing the flow from raw materials to finished goods, and operations lie on an x axis representing the flow in which a succession of workers works on items. This is precisely what I reported to a Japan Management Association (JMA) engineering conference in 1945 and later in my book *Lectures on Production Engineering Part I: Outline of Production Engineering* (Tokyo: Japan Management Assoc., 1949). "Production," I maintained, "is a network of processes (the y axis) and operations (the x axis)."

In my opinion, the argument was self-evident, yet my position proved to have little appeal. At the time, the mainstream of production managers still adhered to the idea that processes referred to large units of analysis and operations to small ones. There was no real awareness of the independence of processes.

Of course a good many people did believe that a process was a flow from raw materials to finished product. The problem lay in their poor understanding of production as a network of intersecting x- and y-axis phenomena. People called for operational improvements to raise the productivity of operations, but no one mentioned process improvements to raise the productivity of processes. There was no clear understanding, moreover, that in improving production, process improvements are of the first order, while operational improvements are secondary (*Figure 2-2*).

Since that time, I have published several books about improving production management. At the beginning of each of these books, I have repeated my claim that production is a network of operations and processes.

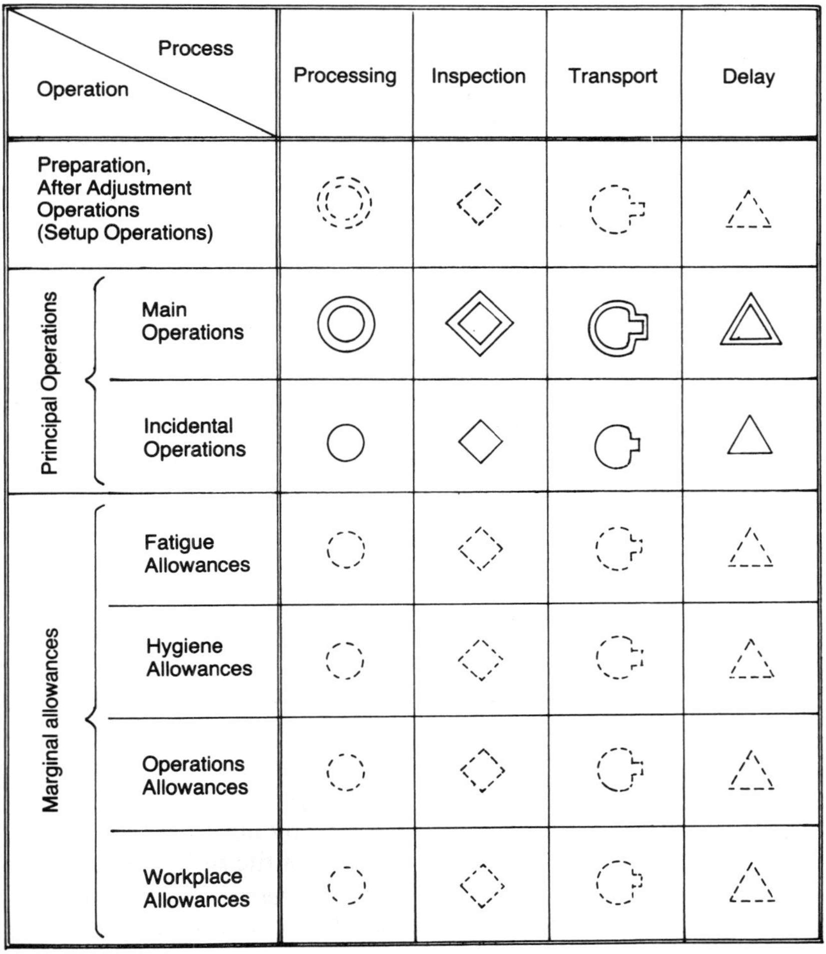

Operation \ Process	Processing	Inspection	Transport	Delay
Preparation, After Adjustment Operations (Setup Operations)	⟮⟯	◇	⟨⟩	△
Principal Operations — Main Operations	◎	◈	⬭	△
Principal Operations — Incidental Operations	○	◇	⟲	△
Marginal allowances — Fatigue Allowances	○	◇	⟨⟩	△
Marginal allowances — Hygiene Allowances	○	◇	⟨⟩	△
Marginal allowances — Operations Allowances	○	◇	⟨⟩	△
Marginal allowances — Workplace Allowances	○	◇	⟨⟩	△

FIGURE 2-2. **The Production Mechanism**

During the course of many trips to Europe and the United States in recent years, I have felt in discussions about production improvement that I was still not getting this point across. For a while I did not understand the problem. In the fall of 1986, however, I spoke with the engineering division manager at FACOM in France.

"Why," I asked him, "does your company use a machine-type layout, which groups the same kinds of machines together? Isn't that a disadvantage since it increases the need for transport?"

"That's not a problem," he replied. "We have chain conveyors set up between processes."

I explained to him that such conveyors represented an improvement in transport *operations* rather than in *transport*, but his expression told me that he did not understand what I meant.

"Look," I said, "improving transport itself would mean redesigning your layout so you don't need any transport at all. It's true that mechanical transport is preferable to human labor if you must transport things somewhere. All machines do, though, is make the work of transport easier — they improve *transport operations*.

"What it boils down to is that no matter how short the distances involved and no matter what methods used, acts of transport have an inherently negative value in terms of production."

This explanation seemed to make sense to the engineering division manager. Later I learned that French universities taught only a homogeneous machine layout in which identical machines were grouped together.

This brought to mind a talk I gave in Washington, D.C. early in 1986, where an enthusiastic questioner in the front row identified himself as a professor and told me that U.S. universities also teach only homogeneous machine layout.

"I've always described processes and operations as lying along the same axis," he said, "but now that I've heard your explanation about a network with x and y axes, I realize you're right."

Thus the difference between Western production philosophies and the new Japanese production philosophy lies at the most basic level, at the conceptual points of departure of the two approaches.

Production constitutes a network of processes and operations, phenomena that lie along intersecting axes. In improving production, process phenomena should be given top priority.

I am convinced that to understand this principle is the most important task presently before us. We must shift away from our conventional preoccupation with operations; we must come face to face with process phenomena and give serious consideration to *process improvement*. Now more than ever I want to argue clearly and forcefully that distinguishing process and operations is the key point for developing new production systems.

The Toyota production system represents a pioneering attempt at a new production philosophy, but no fundamental innovations in production can come about merely by imitating the superficial aspects of the Toyota system.

Processes and Operations in Harmony

The Conflict Between Processes and Operations

We have explained that production is composed of processes and operations. These two elements are occasionally in conflict with one another.

When, for example, rush orders call for shutting down machines to wait for goods to come down the line, machine work rates are sacrificed for the sake of process demands and processes are given priority over operations.

If the situation is reversed and, because of relatively similar setups, a worker has moved up an order that could just as well have been taken care of later, then items that ought to be processed will be delayed and delivery deadlines will be missed. Since in this case operational convenience has led to process delays, operations have taken precedence over the process.

We can, therefore, think of processes as actions that serve customers and operations as actions performed for the sake of plant efficiency. It follows that putting too much emphasis on either one is undesirable, and this is why confusion would arise on the shop floor without the intervention of managers. Front-line supervisors placed at the intersections of processes and operations must constantly seek to keep these opposing demands in harmony with one another.

Operations Supplement Processes

When we describe production activities as networks of processes and operations, we are referring to matters of structural organization. It is process functions, in fact, that attain the principal goals of production, while operations play a supplementary role.

It follows that, no matter how effectively operational functions are performed, production as a whole cannot achieve much success if process functions are inadequate. As long as there are errors in the organization of processes, product flaws will result no matter how perfectly operations are performed. Overly generous precision tolerances for parts will mean excessive play in assembled goods and numerous defects in finished products. Similarly, inappropriate processing procedures will necessitate the expenditure of unnecessary worker time and effort.

These extremely clear examples of process errors make it easy for people to see that process functions take precedence over operations functions. In real-world production activities, however, what we actually see are operations functions, and process functions leave only a faintly visible impression with us. This is because they are hidden by operations and we must make special efforts to be aware of them. Once we accustom ourselves to looking at production activities solely from the point of view of operations, the operations perspective takes over and we end up overlooking process-side deficiencies.

Undue stress laid on operations will cause numerous process-side inefficiencies to crop up. Consider the following cases:

- Concentrating solely on operations, we group similar machines together. In process terms, this sort of homogeneous grouping entails increased transportation, which in turn does nothing but raise costs.
- Single-minded efforts to push machine capacities to the limit will generate process-yield imbalances, and interprocess delays will increase.
- Conducting large-lot production to counter machine time lost to setup changes will increase inventory.

Overemphasis on Operations Characteristics

In 1972, I went as a consultant to the F-M Corporation in the United States. While there, I noticed that machine layout followed a homogeneous arrangement, large-lot operations were being carried out, and huge quantities of stock were visible everywhere. When I asked an IE engineer why his company did not adopt flow operations, he replied simply that if it did, it would not be able to balance its machine capacities.

The following year, when a delegation from the French firm Citroen came to visit the Washing Machine Division of Matsushita Electric, one member of the group asked how long it took between the first processing stroke on the body of a washing machine and completion of the finished product. "About a week?" the visitor guessed.

"Not at all," was the Matsushita plant manager's reply. "In general, it takes about 2½ hours."

His dumbfounded guest was profoundly impressed when he actually visited the plant and witnessed the process that turned out finished washing machines in 2½ hours.

Following the tour, the delegation leader, Mr. Mermet, described his impressions in a particularly striking way. He said that there were many cases in which Citroen's individual machines were far more efficient than the ones he had just seen. In terms of process flow, however, his own firm lagged far behind Matsushita.

Synchronization and Full Work Control

In West Germany, I visited Oslam Company, which produces light bulbs used in automobile headlamps. There were two automatic assembly machines, one used for the first half of the process and the other for the latter half.

As *Figure 2-3* shows,

1. Machine no. 1 was operated by workers A and B, and machine no. 2 was operated by workers C and D.
2. Worker A inserts a part in machine no. 1.
3. After machine no. 1 finishes its operation, the half-finished product is placed in a box. Worker B carries the box to a temporary storage area.
4. Worker C retrieves the half-finished product from the temporary storage area and inserts it in machine no. 2.
5. Worker D stores the product finished by machine no. 2 in the finished goods storage area.

I asked the plant manager, "Why don't you connect machines no. 1 and 2?"

He answered, "We thought of the same thing. But machine no. 1 can handle 5,500 pieces per day, while machine no. 2 can handle only 5,000. Because they aren't of equal capacity, we didn't connect them."

"How many do you need to process per day?" I asked.

"5,000 per day is enough," he replied.

I said, "Use a full-work control method. Create a pool between the two machines. When machine no. 1 has processed 100 pieces, stop it. When the pool drops down to 10 pieces, restart machine no. 1."

Three months later, the president of company S reported that productivity was improved 20 percent by using full work control.

The intermediate roles of workers B and C were eliminated, along with the temporary storage area. This example again shows that only the quantity required need be produced, and the operating rate of a high-capacity machine may be reduced if that will increase the overall benefit.

People frequently adopt a myopic view and believe that the operating rate of a machine should never be reduced. What is more important is to take a global view and pursue the overall benefit.

Numerous plants in Japan have learned from and followed in the wake of the industrialized nations of Europe and America, and many plants have uncritically and unconsciously adopted the one-sided

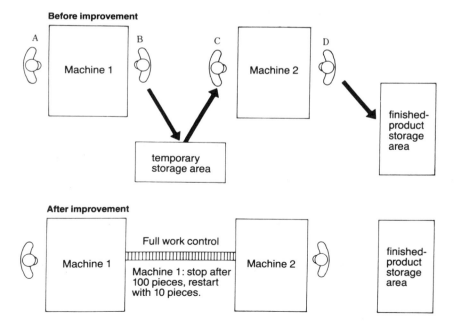

FIGURE 2-3. **Synchronization and Full Work Control**

Euro-American production philosophy that emphasizes operations. As a result, it seems to me, many one-sided, operations-oriented production approaches have been used by Japanese plants.

In any event, we need to be aware that:

- There are two functional sides to production: processes and operations.
- It is in the nature of operations functions to supplement process functions.
- Because operations functions loom large in our sight, we tend to have eyes only for issues of operational efficiency.
- Improving productivity requires that we consider both process efficiency and operations proficiency as we work to achieve harmony between the two.

AN INADEQUATE APPRECIATION OF TWO DELAY PHENOMENA

On the subject of process delays, an American production handbook states only that there are two types — "controlled storage" and "temporary storage." What I refer to as "delays," however, are two qualitatively different types of phenomena:

Process delays. These involve delay of an entire lot between processes; for example, when one lot arrives at a process before work has been completed on the previous lot.

Possible reasons for process delay include lack of synchronization, poor timing (which allows items to arrive ahead of schedule), variations in the size of adjacent lots, and convergent processes (where the output from several processes flows to a single process).

Lot delays. These occur when, for example, in a 1,000 piece lot, 999 unprocessed items wait while the first item in the lot is being processed, 998 unprocessed items wait while the second item is being processed, and each processed item waits while the remaining items in the lot are processed. *Lot delay* occurs when individual items wait to fall in step with entire lots. This is what some people used to refer to as "process delays" (for long waits) and "temporary delays" (for short waits), with the result that these temporary delays were confused with all lot delays. In the United States temporary delays are sometimes described as "temporary storage," but we may still think of these as a kind of process delay.

It seems fair to say that the distinction between long and short delays is vague and troublesome. How are we to decide whether a 30-minute delay is counted as long or short? We will never know how to go about making improvements as long as our perception of the problem is this superficial.

I take a different approach and ignore the time element. I have divided delays into *process delays* and *lot delays*. A lot delay is a delay for the purpose of synchronizing the entire processing lot. In a lot delay, even if there are 1,000 items in the processing lot, the delay will disappear when each lot to be transported to the next process contains only one item.

When we try to reduce delay, improvement is possible only when we distinguish process and lot delay on the basis of the nature of the delay rather than the length.

Of course, not all delays occur in the production process: for example, raw materials delays and finished parts (or product) delays. Such delays may be seen as process or lot delays that involve the relationship between the raw materials supplier and the production plant or between the sales market and the production plant. Similar improvement measures may therefore be developed.

SHIFTING HUMAN TASKS OVER TO MACHINES (MECHANIZATION AND PRE-AUTOMATION)

No one would disagree that the industrial revolution in England in 1778 marked the beginning of tremendous innovations in production and that the root of this revolution lay in the concept of division of labor or labor specialization.

Through division of labor, work tended to become simpler, more concrete, and more mechanical. This tendency, combined with the introduction of various forms of power, led to mechanization which became a major force in promoting advances in the nature of work, such as:

- mechanized machining
- mechanized tool feeding
- mechanized attachment and removal of workpieces

- mechanized switching of tools (as in machining centers)
- mechanized numerical control (NC)
- programmed computer support
- robots

In Japan, however, as in the West, a visitor to a production facility often finds that while machines are working automatically, workers stand by the machines "supervising" them. Why? Because even though the agency and power functions of the human hand have been mechanized, we have neglected to mechanize another important human function — the intelligence to detect abnormal situations. Shifting this function to machines frees workers from having to stay near their machines. Yet many European and U.S. plants actively and intentionally fail to take this step.

This function is what I call pre-automation; in the Toyota production system it is referred to as autonomation.

THE SCIENCE OF WORK AND
THE APPLICATION OF HUMAN ENGINEERING

In the 1890s, many American workers were paid on a day-wage basis. This system was not very efficient because it meant workers were paid according to how many hours they were present in the plant, not how much work they did. This led to the development of a piece-rate system.

Under this system, workers' pay was based on how many items they produced. This motivated them to work harder, but when wages rose even higher than anticipated, managers decided their piece rates were too generous and lowered them. Disappointed at first, workers began working even harder and their wages rose again. Inevitably the price per unit would be lowered once more.

After several such productivity surges and rate reductions, many workers lost interest in working and productivity plummeted. When tougher standards were established in response to higher productivity, workers began to limit output through organized slowdowns known as soldiering.

Frederick W. Taylor, who became a manager at about this time, seriously doubted that soldiering was good for the country, the companies, or even the workers themselves. He asked himself why the phenomenon had arisen in the first place. The problem, he decided, was that the setting of standards was too arbitrary. In Taylor's view, only unscientific standards allow brief spurts of enthusiastic effort to send output soaring. He determined that setting high, stable standards on the basis of scientific research would enable managers to pay higher wages to workers *and* reduce the cost of products. His now famous dictum was: "High efficiency, high wages, and low cost."

Taylor advocated a three-step technique called *time study:*

1. Understand the status quo through time analysis.
2. Improve operations through intensive study.
3. Use the standard times required for improved operations to determine wage scales and production values.

In 1898, Taylor conducted his famous pig-iron hauling experiments at Bethlehem Steel following a detailed study of human fatigue and rest. In these experiments, a trial method was adopted in which hauling work was performed only 42 percent of the time. A worker would haul fifteen bars of pig-iron for seven minutes and then rest for ten. While previously even the best haulers could move no more than 12.5 tons per day, they could haul 47.5 tons with the new method. This made it possible to increase workers' wages by 60 percent — a perfect example of high efficiency, high wages, and low cost.

During the same period, F. B. Gilbreth developed *motion study* and argued that human motion is composed of 18 elemental movements, or "therbligs."

Gilbreth came up with a number of theories concerning economy of motion and the relationships between human motion and work posture. He maintained, moreover, that "time is merely a shadow of motion," that time is nothing but an effect. (Something takes a long time to complete because the motions used to do it take a long time.) Thus, he argued there could be no reduction in time unless profound improvements were made in the (causal) motions themselves and the work conditions that necessitated those motions.

Many theorists, unfortunately, did not understand such "human engineering" insights or were entirely unaware of them. They ignored theories of fatigue, which recommended that work be performed sitting down rather than standing up, and claimed that work should be carried out while walking. They forgot that walking is preferable only in limited situations and argued that standing and walking are preferable to sitting.

Although Taylor argued for the establishment of standard times based on time analysis, many U.S. producers, in response to pressure to establish standards, set times without actually studying time. They simply accept the status quo (the times required for current operations) and then set mean standard times by leveling, by taking worker skill and effort levels into account. Attention is focussed on techniques related to time *setting*, such as work factors (WF) or method time measurement (MTM), and on the simplification of statistically-based analyses of the status quo, such as work sampling and snap sampling. Conceptual approaches and activities basic to work improvement are often forgotten. The industrial engineering (IE) techniques used in Japan to promote daily work improvement are seldom used.

Clearly Europe and the United States excel in the development of basic technologies. There are very few in the West, however, who focus on daily improvement — with total worker participation in the area of manufacturing and production technology. In my view, this has a tremendous impact on the relative productivity of Euro-American and Japanese workplaces respectively.

UNDERSTANDING MANUFACTURING AND PRODUCTION TECHNOLOGY

In Europe and the United States, interest is generally concentrated exclusively on manufacturing technology and little is known about production technology. For example, how many people would agree with me immediately if I were to assert that producing fish cakes is exactly the same as producing automobiles?

The Evolution of Manufacturing Technology

In any kind of production we must first identify the basic technologies that determine *how* products are made, that is, all the manufacturing conditions necessary to produce a particular product. At this stage, making automobiles and fish cakes is by no means the same, because the factors we must investigate to establish those conditions are vastly different.

We must also study various fabrication techniques:

- mechanization
- pre-automation
- multiple machine operations
- labor techniques

Basic Technologies

The initial problem in production is understanding the basic (or specific) technologies that determine how items are made. By *basic technologies* I mean the variety of factors we consider in the following areas, for example:

- *Machining:* tool composition, blade shape, depth of cut, cutting speed, and chip removal — for example, breaking up chips or using "magic cut" methods (compressed air used to apply a cutting oil mist) to remove cuttings in drilling and tapping
- *Forging:* forging temperature, die shape, precision forging techniques
- *Casting:* fusion temperature, quantity and quality of flux, casting die shape, properties of materials, precision casting
- *Welding:* current and voltage values, properties of welding materials, type of flux
- *Plastic and diecast forming:* fusion temperature, pressure, compression speed, vacuum forming

Processing technologies such as these need to be studied and improved in terms of specific applications. Once the problems posed by such basic technologies are resolved, attention must be paid to the following other techniques:

Mechanization

Generally speaking, these technologies shift main and incidental operations from humans to machines; for example, tool feeding, product attachment and removal, switch operation and blade exchange.

Pre-automation

These techniques improve principal operations. The use of sensors to detect abnormalities in main and incidental operations eliminates the need for human monitors to watch machines. Physical and mental fatigue can be reduced significantly, because all workers have to do is respond to automatically detected problems. This is the pre-automation I advocate.

The next step, of course, is true automation, which frees workers from machines entirely because the equipment is able to respond appropriately to any abnormalities that may occur. This level of automation, however, calls for high levels of technology, and equipment is very costly. Pre-automation, on the other hand, can secure around 90 percent of the effects of true automation for about 10 percent of the cost.

Multiple Machine Operations and Motion

Shifting operations from workers to machines naturally frees up workers' time, which permits a single worker to run more than one machine. Where more than one machine of the same type is involved, this is referred to as *multiple machine operation*. The term *multi-process operation* applies when a worker is responsible for several different kinds of machines in the process flow.

These situations inevitably require a worker to walk back and forth between several machines. Since such walking is intrinsically wasteful, distances must be minimized and abrupt changes in worker position eliminated. For example, human motion is characterized by certain facts:

- A sitting position always requires less energy than a standing position.
- Fatigue is lessened when a worker can trade off among various muscle groups rather than using the same ones all the time.
- It is very tiring to change constantly between a standing position and a sitting position.
- Appropriate combinations of work and rest periods and suitable allowances for weariness are major safeguards against fatigue.

Interestingly, the recent growth of multiple machine operations has led to increased walking. This trend is defended by people who do not consider shortening distances, because they think "walking is good for you" and by those who claim that standing is preferable to sitting even for stationary work. Such opinions, however, clearly demonstrate ignorance of human engineering principles.

Labor Techniques

Here, considerable thought should be given to applying Taylor's theories on work and fatigue and Gilbreth's principles of motion economy. For example, problems often arise in handling heavy objects.

Suppose you have to transport an item weighing 100 kilograms. Using sliding friction would yield an effective weight of 10 kilograms because the coefficient of friction is 0.1. The coefficient of rolling friction, however, is 0.01, so this approach would amount to handling 1 kilogram, a considerable reduction in effort. As this example shows, we need to think about improving the phenomena that constitute the objects of labor.

Improvement and Safety in Marginal Activities

To improve rest breaks, for example, reduce physical and mental fatigue. Consider shorter working times, come up with low-fatigue work motions, shift human labor to machines, match labor to rest, improve comfort in rest areas, and set up small gardens near production areas or at least plant flowers in rest areas.

To improve personal hygiene breaks (for rest room visits, drinking water, wiping away perspiration, and so on), increase the length of breaks by adopting pre-automation methods, improve the environment with air conditioning, and provide drinking fountains and smoking areas, for example.

To improve work breaks (for clearing away cuttings and adding oil, for example), automate scrap removal and oiling. To reduce shop breaks (due to machine failures, materials delays, and so on), employ better management methods.

To improve safety, rather than relying on the psychological campaigns of the past, install safety devices which, for example, make it impossible for workers' hands to come into contact with rotating parts of machines. Japan has a lot to learn in this regard; Japanese safety campaigns lag far behind Western programs. It is time to abandon safety campaigns that merely tell people to be careful.

The techniques described above are known collectively as *fabrication techniques*. On a larger scale, basic technologies plus fabrication techniques can be referred to as *manufacturing technology*. Industries that have gone no farther than to solve the question of how products can be made can be called manufacturing industries.

At this level of manufacturing technology, it is not yet clear how making fish cakes is like making automobiles. We are still in the realm of specific operations, which must differ. As we move into the next stage, however, making fish cakes and making automobiles gradually become identical.

Growing Toward Production Technology

In the real world of production, things do not stop at the manufacturing technology stage. Once we start asking how to make things faster, cheaper and in larger quantities, we have advanced to the production technology stage. We must adopt a process-oriented perspective and investigate the following techniques to improve process:

- *basic techniques* for processing operations
- *quality control techniques* for raising and sustaining quality levels
- *layout techniques* to improve transport
- *synchronization* and *one-piece flows* by using scheduling techniques for dealing with delays

When we look at production at this level, making cars and making fish cakes begin to look alike. Understand that in addition to our choice of production systems, a variety of production improvement techniques are available at this level, including:

- *Management techniques* that help determine how best to carry out planning, control (and eventually implementation), and monitoring.
- *Improvement techniques* for improvement in these specific areas through, for example, the application of a scientific thinking mechanism (STM).
- Thorough application of *industrial engineering (IE)*.

Indeed, in terms of production technology, making fish cakes is identical to making cars, because at this level all these factors must be addressed no matter what product we are producing.

RESPONDING TO THE EMOTIONAL
SIDE OF HUMAN NATURE

In 1960, Douglas McGregor of the Massachusetts Institute of Technology published his famous book on the "*X-Y* theory" of management (*The Human Side of Enterprise* [New York: McGraw-Hill, 1960]). Simply put, McGregor argued that managers have two views of workers. According to the older, traditional view (*theory X*), people basically dislike work and will do whatever they can to avoid it. According to a more positive management view (*theory Y*), people see the application of their minds and bodies to work as perfectly natural and want to be productive.

In the 1700s, as industries and the labor force to support them expanded rapidly, managers tended to treat workers as theory *X* people, lazy, resentful, and unmotivated. Oppressive management practices — arbitrarily lowering unit rates is just one example — led to adversarial relations between management and workers, the formation of labor unions, and a long period of often violent struggle, which added fuel to the growth of theories such as socialism and communism.

More recently, welfare systems have evolved in the name of respect for human dignity. Yet rather than aiding the truly needy, welfare is often doled out indiscriminately, with the result that higher and higher taxes must be levied to cover the considerable costs involved. Sweden is a model welfare state, but even workers who have just graduated from school are taxed at a rate of 35 percent of their income. One university professor told me that the government took 85 percent of his salary in taxes. I wonder if these systems do not end up eroding the will to work on a grand scale.

In the United States in the 1920s, the Hawthorne plant experiments may have demonstrated the theory *Y* side of workers human nature, but American industry neglected to nurture it. It is truly regrettable that promotion of *Y* characteristics in workers never went beyond the superficial application of such concepts as management by objectives and zero defects (ZD) campaigns. Substantial progress in raising productivity in the United States and Europe can never be expected to materialize absent more far-reaching improvements in human relations at work.

By contrast, as a result of Japan's lack of natural resources, the Japanese worker traditionally has been seen as the only resource that can secure national prosperity and individual happiness. Furthermore, lifetime employment, a monthly wage system, company unions, and other measures that promote the Y side of human nature are responsible to a large extent for what is known as "Japanese-style management."

In the United States, many firms have implemented effective lifetime employment, profit-sharing, employee stock plans and other activities designed to promote the theory Y nature in workers. Moreover, some of these and other U.S. companies are having tremendous success with the aggressive use of IE-based strategies for improving productivity.

On a visit to T Auto Body in April of 1987, Mr. Okajima, the executive in charge of production, told me the following story:

"When a group of management and union officials from GM showed up in our plant not long ago, we learned that, in carrying out new policies, GM has recently been doing whatever it can to bring labor union representatives to meetings to express their views freely at the deliberation stage. Whenever anything new is introduced, moreover, similar meetings are held where detailed plans are presented and reactions actively solicited. In addition, consultants are reportedly present to help with any necessary adjustments. These efforts have resulted in a striking improvement in labor-management relations; unions have become active participants in company policies and the company as a whole has been energized by the process."

As practices of this sort spread among American companies, the old adversarial atmosphere will dissolve and an atmosphere of cooperation will begin to form that can only energize labor-management relations and promote fundamental improvement.

IS STOCK A NECESSARY EVIL OR AN ABSOLUTE EVIL?

In recent years I have had numerous occasions to visit the United States and Europe and to observe a number of production plants. I have come across many plants where, as described above, operational efficiency is stressed to the neglect of process efficiency. In other words, I have seen a number of cases in which homogeneous machine layouts mean extra transportation or stock accumulates all over plants because batch systems or process systems have been adopted in the hope of pushing machine capacities to the limit.

The general attitude toward such stock is that it is a "necessary evil," but it seems to me that there is almost no sense of guilt involved: that 90 percent of the emphasis is on the "necessary" part and only 10 percent on the "evil." Some people even claim that stock is necessary!

To be sure, the presence of stock has the effect of mitigating or resolving a variety of production problems. Indeed, it might be said to have a narcotic effect. By this we mean that stock can resolve certain problems very simply and effectively. For example:

- Stock permits an immediate response to unanticipated demand.
- The impact of long setup times can be lessened by increasing lot sizes and regulating the increase through use of the economic lot.
- Stock on hand immediately compensates for any defects that may occur.
- Inventory is also useful when machine failures halt production.
- Stock can guard against disruptions in production due to worker absences and so on.

In the new *non-stock* production system, stock is considered an absolute evil that must be absolutely eliminated.

The need for stock can be eliminated by adopting various measures:

- Rush orders can be handled by shortening, for example, a four-week lead time to two weeks.
- Single-Minute Exchange of Die (SMED) setups can reduce four-hour setups to three minutes or to a matter of seconds when combined with automation.
- Zero defects can be accomplished through Zero Quality Control (ZQC), that is, through source inspections and the poka-yoke system.
- Machine failures can also be eliminated through source checks and the poka-yoke system.
- Most work absences can be prevented from interrupting production by providing workers with multiple skills or by means of pre-automation.

When I say that stock has a narcotic effect I mean, first of all, that stock immediately and easily eases the pain accompanying a broad range of production problems. As with other drugs, increasingly large doses of stock are required to sustain the effect, and inventory grows gradually once a taste for the "drug" is acquired. Our tolerance for stock increases over time and we find we cannot feel secure without it.

There is another reason that companies adopt large-lot production, however. This stems from the confusion between high-volume production and large-lot production.

High-volume production refers to the production of the same type of item in large quantities. This mode of production brings expectations of improved efficiency and decreased defects, for it has the advantages that machines, dies, and the like can be depreciated quickly and that skills improve rapidly as a result of labor division and specialization. But it is the prerogative of the market to choose and control high-volume production — not that of the production plant. The only real choice the production plant has is whether to produce in large or small lots. Companies usually use large-lot production to cut their losses when setup times are long. As pointed out above, however, SMED methods have made this approach almost worthless, since it does nothing but increase inventory.

In any case, the traditional idea has been that although stock may be an evil, it serves a useful role. We are now making a 180-degree shift and asserting that stock is *absolutely* evil. Indeed, the absolute elimination of stock lies at the heart of the non-stock production system, a system that overcomes the factors traditionally thought to create demand for stock.

The important strategies in this process are to improve machine layout for drastic reductions in lead times and to produce in small lots that match orders. These improvements are achieved by adopting the principles of SMED. I think it is accurate to say that development of the single-minute exchange of die is the starting point for a worldwide revolution in production systems.

TOTAL WASTE ELIMINATION
AND FUNDAMENTAL IMPROVEMENT

There is no doubt that many people have thought about improvement, but it was Taylor and the Gilbreths — F. B. Gilbreth and his wife, Lillian — who, in the 1890s, developed a clearly-defined notion of improvement and established techniques to achieve it. Their methods can be described as follows:

- *Taylor:* Define the status quo analytically and temporally, and improve it through scientific reasoning — these activities are known as *time-study techniques.*
- *The Gilbreths:* Carry out motion analysis by breaking up the status quo into elemental units of motion called *therbligs.* Identify the purpose of each therblig, and find the *one best way* (in which work is broken down, purposes are tracked down, and better methods are devised) using techniques that accord with those purposes.

The Gilbreths' idea of one best way and their "motion mind" concept powerfully influenced many people. My own teacher, Horigome Ken'ichi, drilled these ideas into me, and they lie at the heart of my improvement activities.

All too often, unfortunately, quantitative methods that precede improvement — in other words, *means* — are thought to be *ends* in themselves. They include motion study, time study (facilitated by work-factor analysis and method time measurement), work analysis (facilitated by work sampling and snap sampling), and histograms and control charts for defining the current quality picture (aided by the methods of statistical science). More important than any of these for making improvements is an understanding of improvement itself and the conceptual approach and techniques involved in making improvements.

Especially in the United States, the setting of standards for contract systems has led to the replacement of time study with time setting. It seems that American management has lost sight of the original goal of doing away with waste.

In terms of the pursuit of goals (root cause analysis), too many improvements are aimed at superficial phenomena. In addition, just as the possibility of major reductions in setup times has been obscured by excessive concentration on the idea of economic lots, opportunities for fundamental improvements are continuously overlooked.

Ideas I have developed to address this problem include the following:

- ZQC (zero quality control) for zero defects, *i.e.*, source inspections and the poka-yoke system
- Process-based layouts for reducing transport to zero
- Pre-automation, for shifting human work to machines
- Techniques for drastic lead time reductions (conceived in the context of the Toyota production system)

These are all techniques for fundamental improvement in production systems. They are improvements that pursue basic goals, or root causes, and, in my opinion, they will play a significant part in future production system innovation.

Improvement*

* This section contains excerpts from *Non-Stock Production:
The Shingo System for Continuous Improvement*
(Cambridge: Productivity Press, 1985) and
The Sayings of Shigeo Shingo: Key Strategies for Plant Improvement
(Cambridge: Productivity Press, 1987).

INTRODUCTION

One of the conclusions of the 1989 study *Made in America* by the MIT Commission on Industrial Productivity is stated below:

> Another area in which U.S. firms have often lagged behind their overseas competitors is in exploiting the potential for continuous improvement in the quality and reliability of their products and processes. The cumulative effect of successive incremental improvements and modification to established products and processes can be very large and may outpace efforts to achieve technological breakthroughs.[1]

Please consider the following examples:

- At a large food processing plant with a group of my Operations Management students, I was watching the operations of a line which was filling and packaging "variety packs," each containing an assorted selection of a half dozen or so of the company's food products. Each worker on the line was responsible for inserting a different item into each pack as it passed him or her. Another worker kept the packers supplied with items by tearing open boxes of the constituent products and pouring them into large barrels next to the packers. The funny thing was that considerable labor was being invested on the company's main product lines less than 100 yards away to erect, fill, seal, and label the same boxes of components, only moments before they were to be taken over to the variety pack line, where they were to be torn open. A student asked if it was possible not to box in the first place those products which were to be needed immediately on the "mixture" line, so as to eliminate the waste of packing and unpacking boxes. She was told this would be difficult, if not impossible, because the variety pack line was a different administrative unit within the plant from the main product line, and for accounting purposes the variety pack line needed to "buy" finished goods from the main production lines. Thus the extra work to pack and unpack the finished goods from the main line, the wasted boxes, tape, glue, and labels were justified.

---

[1] The MIT Commission on Industrial Productivity, *Made in America: Regaining the Productive Edge*, MIT Press, Cambridge, MA, 1989.

- I recently had occasion to be in a foundry and fabrication facility which manufactured very large metal components for industrial use. In one process, parts moved from machine to machine down the length of a building 150 or so yards long. The parts to be worked on were delivered at the opposite end of the building from where they needed to start down the process, even though this starting point had a loading dock nearby. Several workers and quite a bit of equipment were engaged in moving parts down the building to the beginning point of the process. Why are things done this way? The answer: "It's been done that way for 20 years — it would be too difficult to change."

In the above examples there is, of course, no reason why the process couldn't be improved, and the workers switched to more productive functions in the company. Their morale would have improved, as well, for workers performing the wasteful tasks are the first to realize how unnecessary their labor is, "Why am I spending my life ripping open boxes that need never have been packed in the first place?" "Why I am I needed here—why don't they just dump this stuff at the other end of the building?" Dr. Shingo defines waste as "that which adds cost without adding value." Since everyone wants to add value (and be valued), the improvement process, far from being a threat, is a prerequisite for high morale and an integral part of any progressive employee relations program. A company that is not interested in improvement is never a pleasant place to work. Indeed, at one of the two companies described above, I asked one of the managers about the company's pension plan. The reply was scarcely inspiring, "Don't get me started on that — I'll just get mad and upset."

In the following section of readings, Dr. Shingo discusses the process of *improvement* or *waste elimination*. By using many actual examples, he shows that the barriers to improvement are attitudinal only: If improvement is truly desired, it will happen of its own accord. From these pages, you will learn how to see waste that others do not see and how to persist until it has been eliminated. Dr. Shingo describes how to make change attractive to those it affects, articulates specific steps to follow when attempting improvement, and offers quite an arsenal of tricks and ideas to solve real-world problems.

With training and effort, it is possible to involve all the workforce in making and implementing suggestions for improvement. At one of the companies mentioned above, plant management proudly told us that they had put in place a very successful suggestion program. In 1988 they had experienced 320 percent participation: each worker had on average submitted 3.2 suggestions. They are certainly on the right track, but compared to the 7010 percent participation in Canon's suggestion system[2] outlined in the Introduction, the good news pales.

How is it possible for a company that doesn't have such a program to compete against a company that does?

---

[2] Detailed in *Canon Production System: Creative Involvement of the Total Workforce*, also published by Productivity Press.

3
Basic Concepts for
Improving Production Systems

Improved production systems are built on new ideas and on the rethinking of basic notions. The initial step in understanding the new Japanese production systems, therefore, lies in correctly grasping their fundamental concepts.

Total Waste Elimination

In the fall of 1984, I gave a seminar in Helsinki. At a reception for me the night before the seminar, the chairman of the Council of Finnish Machine Industries, Mr. Sarasute, approached me and said:

"In your book on the Toyota production system, you claim that any setup change for any task can be completed in less than ten minutes. Is that really true?"

"Of course it is," I replied.

"Then I imagine you have to use very expensive devices."

"Not at all. We generally keep the cost below $250.00."

"I just can't believe that," Mr. Sarasute said skeptically.

"Look," I proposed. "I have to give my talk at 10 a.m. tomorrow. If you can find a suitable company for a demonstration, I'll visit their plant at 8 a.m. and have them prepare for a single-minute press setup."

Mr. Sarasute was able to make arrangements with the G Safe Company. I visited the company the next morning and assembled the engineers and shop foreman. I asked them to bring out two dies and had them perform a number of tasks, including:

- standardizing die heights
- installing stoppers for centering
- carrying out functional standardization of clamping sites

When my seminar was over at 3 p.m., we had a brief question-and-answer session and then 80 of us took busses to the G Safe Company. With all of us looking on, the setup was carried out and the first new product was run through after 6 minutes and 28 seconds. This operation had previously required an hour and a half!

I then asked the engineer in charge to explain what we had done, and he concluded with the words, "I understand completely!" It was very impressive. What's more, the only materials used were odds and ends already on hand, so the total improvement cost was a mere $87.00.

At a round-table discussion in the plant immediately afterwards, Mr. Sarasute asked me another question:

"In your book you say that 'the Toyota production system wrings water out of towels that are already dry.' Is that really possible?"

"All right," I said, "let's take a look around the plant."

By asking people why they did things the way they did and suggesting improvements, I identified about 10 things that could be improved. "We thought we had improved a lot," people in the plant told me, "but everything you've pointed out seems quite reasonable. Clearly, we have to do some more thinking."

At this point, Mr. Sarasute agreed that there is often more water to be wrung out of towels we think are dry.

On the way back from the plant, the interpreter, Mr. Kumada, a second-generation naturalized Swede, told me that they had a joke along the same line in Sweden.

"How does it go?" I asked. Here's what he told me:

A young man just finished squeezing a lemon over his food. The old man at the next table tells him he hasn't squeezed enough.

"What are you talking about?" the young man says. "I squeezed as hard as I could."

"You still didn't squeeze hard enough," the old man responds. "Here, let me show you."

The old man takes the lemon, and when he squeezes it, more juice comes out.

At this point, a young woman sitting next to him breaks in and says, "You're not squeezing it enough, either, grandpa."

"Impossible!" the old man replies. 'I've never lost a lemon-squeezing contest in my life!"

"Don't speak too soon," the young woman says. "Here, let me have the lemon."

She picks up the crushed lemon, squeezes it and gets still more juice out of it.

"I take my hat off to you, the old man tells her. "I'd never been beaten by anyone until I met you. How is it you're so good at squeezing the juice out?"

"I work in the Tax Collector's Office," she said.

This story demonstrates that plant improvement, like tax collection, demands an unrelentingly keen eye and persistent efforts to identify problems. Maintaining this attitude and tirelessly observing the job at hand to find problems makes it possible to wring water even out of dry towels. This is how we have to think about total waste elimination.

Improving Transport and Transport Operations

My visits to European plants have convinced me that Europeans do not distinguish between improving transport and improving *the means* of transport. Most people think that improving transport refers to things like using forklifts or installing conveyors. While these may represent improved means of transport, they do not represent improvements in transport itself. Improving transport means reducing or even eliminating it, and the only way to accomplish that is to improve layout.

Many university engineering departments teach only layout by machine type, which groups similar pieces of equipment together. Machine-type layout, however, inevitably requires transport between processes. Yet it has not occurred to people that interprocess transport merely increases cost, that it is a wasteful phenomenon that does not add to the value of products. I wonder why.

It seems to me that scholars and managers need to reflect carefully on why so many engineers and managers see improving transport and improving transport operations as the same thing and why they mistakenly believe that improvements in transport operations are the only way in which transport can be improved.

Economic Lots and Improved Setup Operations

According to the concept of the *economic lot*, if we plot costs on the *y* axis and processing lot size on the *x* axis, we observe that labor costs gradually decrease as lot size rises. On the other hand, large lots are accompanied by rising inventories. As *Figure 3-1* illustrates, the intersection of these two lines is known as an economic lot.

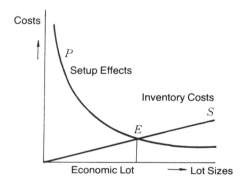

FIGURE 3-1. Economic Lot

No doubt, the notion of an economic lot is rational. Nevertheless, we must admit that it offers only a passive strategy for rationalization and leads only to superficial improvements.

It is true that increasing the size of processing lots reduces apparent labor costs. As *Table 3-1* shows, if setups take four hours and actual processing time per part is one minute, increasing lot size from 100 to 1,000 parts will cut apparent processing labor time from 3.4 to 1.24 minutes. With the old and new times in a ratio of 100:36, labor costs will have decreased 64 percent and less frequent setups will presumably increase the work rate.

This is why people in the production shop try to maximize lot sizes. If you increase the lot size from 1,000 to 10,000, however, you will cut labor time only by a ratio of 100:83 or 17 percent. Here we can see the significance of economic lots since, as lot size increases, the savings in labor time level off and the disadvantage of large inventories grows.

Setup Time	Lot Size	Principal Operation Time Per Item	Apparent Operation Time	Ratio (%)
4 hrs.	100	1 min.	$1 \text{ min.} + \dfrac{4 \times 60}{100} = 3.4 \text{ min.}$	100
4 hrs.	1,000	1 min.	$1 \text{ min.} + \dfrac{4 \times 60}{1,000} = 1.24 \text{ min.}$	36

TABLE 3-1. **The Impact of Setup Time**

This concept contains a fundamental flaw, however: It assumes that drastic reductions in setup times are impossible. The single-minute exchange of die (SMED), however, can reduce four-hour setups to three minutes.

As *Table 3-2* shows, once you have a setup time of three minutes in an operation where the actual processing time per part is one minute, increasing lot size from 100 to 1,000 will cut labor time from 1.03 to 1.003 minutes, a ratio of 100 to 97, a reduction of no more than 3 percent. At this stage, the negative impact of increasing inventory is far more significant.

Setup Time	Lot Size	Principal Operation Time Per Item	Total Operation Time Per Item (Including Setup)	Ratio (%)
3 min.	100	1 min.	$1 \text{ min.} + \dfrac{3}{100} = 1.03 \text{ min.}$	100
3 min.	1,000	1 min.	$1 \text{ min.} + \dfrac{3}{1,000} = 1.003 \text{ min.}$	97

TABLE 3-2. **Relationship Between Setup Time and Lot Size**

If what we have said is true, the whole notion of an economic lot collapses. Indeed, I understand that the term "economic lot" is no longer taught in courses on profitability accounting in Japanese universities.

Improvements guided by the economic lot concept are superficial. We must develop strategies aimed at more fundamental improvements, for example, drastic reduction of setup times.

A Japanese authority on skill engineering reported in a newspaper that Toyota Motors apparently needed 10 years to cut its four-hour setup down to three minutes. If you figured in the number of opportunities to practice during that period, the outcome, he said, was in line with calculations based on accumulated skill.

Toyota's achievement was not based on the accumulation of practice, however; it was the result of SMED — a fundamental revolution in awareness — and of faithful implementation of specific techniques that accompany SMED.

Finding Conceptual Blind Spots

Ashton T. Marcus is a senior vice president of Omark Industries and one of his firm's leaders in the implementation of stunning improvement activities, among them the reduction of a four-hour setup time to two minutes 40 seconds. Mr. Marcus came to Japan in 1981 and we had lunch together after one of my lectures in Tokyo. During the meal, he told me an impressive story.

"Setup changes on our 100-ton press used to take us hours," he began. "The worker in charge of the setup was the best and most skilled man we had, but even he needed two hours to make the changeover. Because of this, we vaguely assumed that two hours was the minimum time requirement for completion of changeover.

"In your book on the Toyota production system, though, it says that *any* setup can be carried out in less than ten minutes, so we put together a project team with a couple of engineers and shop foremen. Their investigation turned up quite a few areas of waste, and by applying the conceptual approach to SMED described in your book, we succeeded in cutting the time down to two minutes and 40 seconds in three months.

"This experience gave us the courage to take a fresh look at other operations and to apply SMED to them. Without exception, we reduced all of them to the single-minute range. As a result, inventory dropped considerably, and we were able to streamline the plant to a remarkable degree.

"We had started out with the assumption that nothing more could be done because a top-notch skilled worker said he needed two hours for the setup. We now realize that assumption was our blind spot.

"Another of our mistaken notions was that the ideal way to cut setup time was to automate adjustments of ram shut height. Now we know that the more basic and effective improvement would have been to eliminate adjustments altogether by standardizing die heights with patch plates."

Surely there are many more of these conceptual blind spots. The improvement described by Mr. Marcus is, indeed, a fundamental one.

QC to Reduce Defects vs. QC to Eliminate Defects

It was quite a jolt when I first learned about American methods of statistical quality control (SQC) in 1951. I had always vaguely assumed that the only kind of inspection was the so-called judgment inspection, in which defective items were distinguished from good ones. It was a shock to me, therefore, to learn about informative inspections, which are based on an entirely different way of thinking. During an informative inspection, you check for abnormalities and perform feedback and action; this allows you to eliminate the cause of the problem and reduce defects. My respect was heightened when I learned that this approach was backed by advanced theories of statistical science, and I became convinced that I could trust in SQC.

Some time later, however, Mr. Tokizane, managing director at Matsushita Electric, told me that he did not want a single Matsushita television set to be defective. After all, he reasoned, a single customer buys only one television set.

I readily agreed with him but then wondered why sampling inspections were being used in the production shop. Sampling inspections may be backed by statistical science, but they rest on the assumption that nothing can be done about, say, one defect in 1,000. I was struck by the contradiction between extremely rational, scientifically based techniques, on the one hand, and the perfectly reasonable demand that not a single defect be allowed, on the other. After much thought, I realized that although supported by statistical science, sampling inspections are ultimately only a rationalized *means* of inspecting; they cannot serve to rationalize quality assurance itself. This insight lessened my faith in SQC methods.

Later on, seeing the results of a zero quality control (ZQC) system liberated me from SQC entirely. ZQC applies the idea of poka-yoke devices to perform rapid, trouble-free 100 percent inspection. Instead of looking for defects that have already occurred, source inspections check for errors that may cause defects. Feedback is then carried out and immediate action taken to prevent the error from generating a defect.

Thus there are two kinds of quality control:

- Quality control to *reduce* defects
- Quality control to *eliminate* defects

Which is the better choice?

I had been bewitched by the claim that QC required the support of statistical science. Now, I keenly regret that it took me 26 years to free myself from the spell of SQC.

THE THREE STEPS OF IMPROVEMENT

Improvement work always involves three levels of inquiry:

1. Basic concepts
2. Systems to give shape to those concepts
3. Techniques for implementing systems

Too often, however, we start at the bottom and never go beyond improving techniques. For example, suppose we want to substitute an electric bolt driver for manual tightening of screw fastenings. This would simply trade a mechanical force for a manual one. On a more fundamental level, we might consider using clamps, cam methods, or insertion methods if our goal is merely to immobilize an object. On an even more fundamental level, however, we might ask why the item must be immobilized at all. For a press or plastic molding machine, perhaps all that is needed is an idea — a concept — about "integral forming" that can be used on the machine.

In short, we should not be satisfied with low-order improvements in techniques. By working back to higher systems or concepts, more thorough, basic improvements become possible.

We can use the same approach in thinking about the economic lot. In other words, assuming the necessity of the system or method of economic lots, various techniques are available for determining what conditions and what values should be specified. The idea — the concept — then, is that where setup times are long, increasing lot size has the advantage of reducing apparent labor costs. On the other hand, it has the disadvantages associated with increased inventories. Therefore, a balance between the two effects must be found.

By itself, this is an extremely rational approach. Yet we can also see that in presupposing long setup times, this concept neglects deeper probing and improvements.

A variety of systems are available to us, each of them an extension of its conceptual premises. We can improve systems and techniques all we want, but unless we make significant changes by thoroughly questioning and improving these basic conceptual premises, our splendid systems and techniques will crumble like castles built on sand.

Both in Japan and in the West, many people think that the Toyota production system is a kanban system. Taiichi Ohno, the great proponent of the Toyota production system, sees things differently, however:

"Why do people think of kanban as a shorthand expression for the Toyota production system?" he asks. "In the first place, a kanban is simply a tool for driving the system. The kanban system in itself does not raise productivity.

"Suppose a company imitates Toyota and adopts only kanban. It may, indeed, be able to set up a system using, say, 200 kanban where Toyota used only 50. This may persuade the company that it can do away with inventory in excess of 200 units. Yet the only real advantage here is that the firm has begun to control the level of excess — it hasn't really done anything to reduce inventory."

The point is that adopting a kanban system or some other system of control in itself will not do the trick. We cannot hope for thorough and innovative results without conceptual improvements. Unless we improve production systems so as to cut inventories drastically, we cannot approach a non-stock ideal.

Thus we can begin to achieve innovative overall improvements only by improving not our techniques but the higher-level systems they support and, still higher, the concepts or premises that justify them. This is what I mean by fundamental improvement. We need to look at current improvements — even through they yield certain limited results — and continually ask whether there are any corresponding higher-level improvements that can be made.

We should keep another point in mind. We must remind ourselves that the possibility of improvement is infinite in the sense that, for each group of concepts, systems, and techniques, there is a higher-level group of concepts, systems, and techniques.

NON-STOCK AS A SOURCE OF PROFIT

People used to think that only three factors could produce profit in production activities: (1) lower materials costs, (2) lower labor costs, and (3) lower indirect costs. Yet one extremely important factor to generate profit was overlooked: (4) higher capital turnover rate — that is, raising profits by reducing inventories. Experience confirms that getting rid of inventory lowers labor costs by approximately 40 percent.

People in the past have recognized that increasing capital turnover rates is a good idea, but they gave up on the idea because of the difficulty in implementing drastic inventory reductions. Since many executives and managers believed that a certain level of inventory was inevitable, stock production systems were soon accepted as natural. I believe this is why the existence of stock has not been a matter for concern and why inventory is tolerated in current production management.

By contrast, the Toyota production system regards stock as the root of all evil. With the objective of producing only what is needed, Toyota boldly set itself the challenge of building a non-stock production system that rejects inventories.

To further this goal, Toyota carried out exhaustive improvements centering on two specific policies:

1. Drastically shorten lead times
2. Avoid overproduction by producing minimal lots

To shorten lead times, the company made several thorough improvements, including eliminating process delays through synchronization, drastically shortening production periods by transporting items in lots of one (one-piece flows), and reducing lot sizes through the adoption of SMED, which shortens production periods as well.

Drastic reductions in setup times are a prerequisite for both the small-lot production needed to cut lead times and the small-lot production needed to avoid overproduction. I believe that SMED has succeeded in overcoming problems that were once considered insurmountable.

The myth that some inventory is inevitable is dying and production systems that tolerate inventory are becoming obsolete. Production systems that reject inventory are being developed, and the first of these is the Toyota production system.

CREATING DEMAND

In 1985, a reporter from *USA Today* interviewed me in New York. At that time, there was much talk about U.S.-Japan trade frictions, so I gave him my view:

"A member of a Japanese agricultural cooperative traveled to Los Angeles and noticed a billboard on the way to his hotel. 'Hey!' he shouted, 'They have Coca-Cola in America, too!' His travel companions had to struggle to stifle their laughter.

"This gives you an idea of how thoroughly Coca Cola has penetrated the Japanese market. McDonald's hamburgers and Kentucky Fried Chicken are also hugely popular wherever you go in Japan. Take things that appeal to the Japanese public, put a lot of effort into marketing them, and the Japanese will welcome American products. The president of another country recently visited Japan and demanded of the Japanese prime minister that Japan buy more of his country's wine and cognac. The prime minister is reported to have said that he would look into the matter. He reacted so coolly because the Japanese are not in the habit of drinking wine or cognac.

"The Japanese prime minister once suggested that one way to relieve trade friction would be for each Japanese to buy 100 dollars worth of American products per year. In response to this appeal, I attended a U.S. products fair at a department store but did not see anything that struck me as a great product. The products they offered were scotch and chocolate, and even though we already have both in Japan, I bought some scotch and took it home.

"Cars are another case in point. Japanese cars normally have the steering wheel on the right, but manufacturers make left-handed cars for export to the United States. Yet cars imported from America have the steering wheel on the left. Why don't Americans export cars that match local requirements? Maybe a few automobile buffs will buy them with steering wheels on the left, but most people will keep their distance. Of course, it might be different if we were talking about inexpensive, high-quality, high-performance cars.

"A recent survey indicated that most 'second cars' bought by American families are made in Japan. Several reasons for this preference were given: Japanese cars don't break down. They are easy to drive; fuel costs are low, and they are comfortable."

"I'm wearing a Seiko watch right now," I said. "Is there an American watch that beats Seiko in quality and price?"

"No," the reporter conceded. "Actually, I use a Seiko watch, too."

Then I noticed that the photographer who was taking pictures at the interview was using a Nikon.

"Why do you use a Nikon?" I asked him.

"Because it takes good pictures and doesn't break down."

"When products perform well, do not break down, and are inexpensive besides, most consumers will want to buy them.

Therefore, demand can be created by

- Identifying latent consumer needs and promptly developing new products in response
- Offering less expensive versions of existing products that perform better and are more reliable

You can fool around with political negotiations and policies all you want, but when all is said and done, true demand will emerge only when you create products that your target population really wants.

In the United States, Ford's strategy of mass production and mass marketing allowed the company to open up tremendous markets. Since only one model was being built, however, consumers gradually lost interest. The age of specialization had arrived. GM's Sloan responded to this change in the marketplace by anticipating needs with a full-line policy for luxury cars. As a result, Ford's strategy of mass-producing Model T's crumbled. When products do not meet the needs of the marketplace — even if they are inexpensive — they will not sell.

DELIVERY CYCLES (*D*) AND
PRODUCTION CYCLES (*P*)

An employee of a Japanese trading company recently transferred to Frankfurt, West Germany. After finding a partially-furnished apartment, he went to a furniture store to buy a chest of drawers and was told that delivery would be made in a month.

"Actually," he said, "I need it right away."

"A chest of drawers we make," he was told, "will be so strong that your grandchildren will be able to use it. Can't you wait one month for a chest that's going to last 50 years?"

Disappointed, the customer went to other furniture stores, but at each one the response was similar.

What the customer wanted — his *allowable purchase interval* (D) was delivery the same day. Yet, the supplier said that the manufacturing cycle (P) was 30 days. If furniture store B had said it could produce the item in 20 days, the customer would have bought his chest there and store A would have suffered an *opportunity loss*. To avoid such opportunity losses, we keep inventories of finished products that allow us to ship immediately. This practice, however, gives rise to the disadvantages associated with inventories.

By drastically reducing the production cycle (P), however, we can supply products within the customer's allowable purchase interval (D), that is, the period of time that satisfies the customer's desire to purchase the product. If we do not want to accumulate unnecessary inventory, all we have to do is to produce only the number of items requested in the demand cycle.

Some people argue that the notion of opportunity losses is faulty, but I disagree. Perhaps we should ask ourselves what contributes more to profit, returns from selling or the costs of keeping inventory. Indeed, the better approach is to head off opportunity losses — even without keeping inventory — by producing with a lead time that is shorter than the customer's allowable purchase interval. This seems an ideal way to proceed.

How long a customer will tolerate waiting for delivery (the allowable purchase interval) is a major production management consideration. I have been told that one of the reasons Japanese cars are so popular in the United States is that they are more easily available than domestic ones. The point is that everyone wants the shortest possible purchase interval.

The problem for producers boils down to a choice: Should they supply from inventories or can they satisfy the customers' allowable purchase interval with a non-stock system?

Consider a sushi bar where customers are not satisfied unless the food is prepared in a one-piece flow process. Similarly, one could argue that factory production has to be a one-piece flow process, because such methods are effective in shortening production cycles. On the other hand, when you have take-out orders, which may have somewhat longer allowable purchase intervals than those for customers in the shop, it is undeniably more efficient to make the sushi in lots. This, in fact, is the way it is done.

In summary, we must consider the following two issues in choosing the most advantageous policy: How long can the customer's allowable purchase interval be? And, is it preferable, from the producer's point of view, to carry out processing in lots that are as large as possible?

Some people take a shortcut and argue that all production, both processing and transport, should take place in lots of one, that is, in one-piece flows. However, a one-piece flow is a tool for shortening the production cycle in order to satisfy the customer's allowable purchase interval. And, while increasing the size of processing lots is effective when setups take a long time, there is no particular advantage to increasing lot sizes if setup times are drastically reduced.

It is a proven fact that no matter how short setup times become, their disadvantages can be eased by making processing lots bigger. At the same time, however, the impact of short setup times falls off rapidly as setup time decreases, so that by the time improvement has cut a four-hour setup down to one minute, increasing lot size becomes almost meaningless.

Production plant work and making sushi can be viewed in exactly the same way. Ideally, we want a production system that can maintain producer profits in the face of demands both from customers who want immediate delivery and from those who want to buy only one item. This requires drastic setup time reductions.

While conducting a survey at Mitsubishi Heavy Industries' Nagasaki Shipyards in the fifties, I set a world record by developing a production system that cut construction of the hull of the *World Independence* from four to two months. This production system spread rapidly throughout the Japanese shipbuilding industry and in no time at all Japan was producing ships faster than anyone else. Shipbuilding companies from around the world flooded Japan with orders and soon, over half the world's ship construction was taking place in Japan. At the time, West German shipbuilders constructed hulls for similar supertankers in seven months and British shipbuilders in ten. Ship owners who could take delivery of a completed ship from five to eight months earlier could transport that much more oil. It was perfectly natural, then, that shipbuilding orders streamed into Japan. At the same time, Japanese shipbuilders made tremendous profits because their capital turnover rates had improved.

In another case, the B Tire Company used to take 42 days to manufacture the dies for tire vulcanization. We were able to shorten lead times to four days. Just then, D Automotive Industries began marketing a new model car, which caused a large increase in tire orders. Because vulcanizing dies could now be completed in four days, the company was able to handle rush orders that previously would have been impossible to fill. D Automotive Industries was very grateful for this improvement, which enabled company B to win new orders and bring higher profits to the plant.

Such examples make it clear that the consumer's preferred allowable purchase interval is immediate delivery. A certain amount of lead time is tolerated because the consumer recognizes the need for production scheduling. In terms of gaining new orders, however, there is a tremendous advantage in being able to produce items of a given quality and cost with lead times five to ten times shorter than those of competitors. We must not forget that shortened setup times do more than merely satisfy consumers; they give an advantage to producers as well.

SPECULATIVE PRODUCTION SYSTEMS AND ASSURED PRODUCTION SYSTEMS

Apart from a certain amount of production on order, all current production systems in Japan and the West are based on estimates or speculation and no one seems to entertain any doubts about the validity of this approach. It is accepted as perfectly natural and the inventory such systems generate is accepted as a necessary evil.

But what is the purpose of production? Is it to make products that *may* sell or products that *will* sell? Obviously, we want to make products that will sell. In fact, however, current production methods incur significant losses by creating two undesirable phenomena:

- Items made too early spend a long time stocked as inventory
- Overproduction generates dead stock that eventually must be discarded

Why does this happen? The basic reason is that we have adopted speculative production systems that produce too much too early, on the chance that products *may* sell.

I believe that there are two more fundamental reasons. First, we are forced to produce according to guesses about demand because lead times are longer than customers' allowable purchase intervals. And second, we discovered we can manufacture things more cheaply with large-lot production.

How different things would be if we could cut one-month lead times to one day and shorten setups from several hours to several minutes, so that even with small-lot production the losses in labor costs would be insignificant.

Even with speculative production systems, of course, a certain amount of effort is put into minimizing inventories. For example, serious investigations probably take place in a number of areas:

- Statistics from the past are consulted about market trends
- Monitors are used for market research
- Sellers may make demand forecasts
- Market trend specialists are consulted
- Conditions closely related to demand are monitored, for example, weather conditions and foreign demand

Yet no matter how detailed this information or how earnestly we study it, the answers it gives us are speculative and will not match actual demand perfectly.

In periods of high economic growth with a sellers' market, consumers may be willing to put aside their dissatisfaction over items that are in short supply and our prediction may seem to have been accurate. But this certainty would be superficial; we would not actually have satisfied our customers.

When low economic growth creates a buyers' market, such demand forecasts will fall wide of the mark and speculative production will generate considerable waste. For example, suppose we market a new product. We distribute it nationwide and mass produce it in anticipation of strong sales. An unexpected sales slump would result in inventories of unusable items. Whether we try to sell them off at deep discounts or simply discard them as dead stock, we end up suffering considerable losses. This kind of situation occurs over and over again.

Take the case of oil heaters or juicers, so-called seasonal goods for which demand is concentrated in winter or summer. In the case of one winter product, the company collected information by studying the Weather Service's long-range forecasts and soliciting the views of farmers and fishermen. The company's sources agreed that the winter would be severe, so the company brought in temporary workers and increased production during the summer to build up inventory. When some unpredictable factor caused an unexpectedly warm winter, the firm was left with overstocks. The company was in serious financial straits for a long time thereafter, and managerial personnel from division heads down took responsibility for the fiasco and resigned.

Even for non-seasonal products, demand fluctuates in response to the state of the economy or current monetary policies. Demand is particularly unstable for export-dependent industries affected by policies and economic trends in customer nations. The resultant large inventories have a negative impact on businesses. Many producers give up in the face of what they perceive to be unalterable circumstances. It is reasonable to argue that there is no defense against such situations, but managers and employees will be hit hard if a business totters or, worse, is forced into bankruptcy.

For these phenomena, the root of evil is planning for demand on the basis of speculation. If this is true, then all we have to do is wait to produce until we are assured of demand.

When you think about it, the current situation for purchase intervals is that customers want immediate delivery about 95 percent of the time. This holds true for fresh foodstuffs and other grocery items, clothing, sports gear, general application machine tools, electrical appliances, transport devices, and so on. Take the case of suits or shoes. You used to be unable to get these items without putting in an order a few days in advance. Now, you can take delivery of ready-made items immediately and pick up "easy-order" goods within a few hours.

We have entered an age when delays are tolerated only for a limited group of made-to-order items such as specialized machine tools, ships, and aircraft. There are other products for which a certain delay is tolerated, but the producers with the shortest lead times will corner the market.

In this era of immediate delivery, the difficult thing is to produce and deliver items as soon as one is assured of demand. As mentioned earlier, some companies deal with it by keeping inventories of finished products. Yet this approach frequently leads to considerable losses for the company involved. As a result, nearly all firms carry out speculative production because they see no other way to deal with demands for immediate delivery.

This is not the best solution, however. A *semi-assured production system* in which production is carried out with the smallest possible inventory cushion while all efforts are directed at achieving assured production has been devised. Isn't this the fundamental meaning of the Toyota production system?

As Taiichi Ohno explained in his books, the Toyota production system was adapted from supermarket methods where, theoretically, products are displayed in minimal quantities and a replacement for a purchased item is delivered before the next customer arrives. This approach means that the system can satisfy the customer's zero purchase interval; the producer can guarantee a *production cycle* of *n* days; and the only inventory is what is displayed in the store.

This represents a radical departure from speculative production. Here, the idea is to produce basically in response to firm orders and to use minimal stocks to accommodate the customer's desire for immediate delivery.

The production cycle — that is, the speed with which quantities demanded by customers can be replaced — will have considerable impact on how much minimal inventory is displayed in the store. The quantities supplied, of course, must match whatever is produced to replace what has been purchased. It follows that lots must be as small as possible.

Some scholars have criticized the Toyota production system because it increases inventories by producing some unsalable goods for display in stores. This is a biased and short-sighted view of the matter. To be sure, the observation holds in some sense, but two points need to be kept in mind:

- Items are produced only to replace goods that have been sold.
- Unsold goods do not need to be replaced and, therefore, no further items are produced.

The only items produced are those that sell, and the demand for immediate delivery is satisfied. Moreover, the maximal reduction of inventories in stores drastically shortens production cycles, and production is carried out in lots that are as small as possible in order to cut quantities supplied to a minimum. This is the greatest significance of the system; ultimately, it achieves the smallest lots conceivable and manages to accommodate itself to an actual *assured production system*.

Let me emphasize once again that the basic idea behind a "supermarket" system is that of assured production, not speculative production. Non-stock production is the best method if customers accept a demand time of *n* days.

B Lighting Industries has a plant in Osaka where it has adopted a one-piece flow system from presswork to assembly processes. If an order comes in from Okayama City, 200 kilometers away, by 2 p.m., it is delivered to the outlet the morning of the following day. This quick response is possible because setup changes in presswork and assembly processes can be performed in two minutes and lead times are around one hour. Consequently, outlets that used to keep 65 days' worth of inventory on hand now have only 30 days' worth, and current plans call for reducing it still further, to about 20 days' worth. Last year the company's profit ratio was about six percent, but this year it has jumped to 13.5, the highest ever.

Another example is the Granville-Phillips Company in the United States where this year's profits for May were five times higher than last year's. Why? Because inventories of finished products and inter-process stock were totally eliminated. Some raw materials inventories still remain, but amounts have been reduced drastically. Setup times were cut from several hours to two minutes or less, and the traditional machine-type layout was improved so that machines were arranged by process. One-piece flows were instituted as well, all of which made it possible to shorten a four-week lead time to two hours.

Some people have characterized the Toyota production system as a pull system, but this reflects a superficial understanding. Categorizing production systems simply as push or pull systems is meaningless.

Pull-type production — where production is based on orders received — is inevitable (1) once you are committed to non-stock production, and (2) have therefore adopted assured production and (3) are, for that reason, producing only after orders are firm.

Clearly, this involves a fundamentally different approach to production from push production. The basic premise of push-type production is speculative production, where items are pushed through production from the source.

Here is a summary of what has been said so far:

Stage 1

In a seller's market, allowable purchase intervals (D_n) are constrained by manufacturers' production cycles (P_n) and fairly long. The process takes long because consumers accept it.

From the producer's vantage point, fairly long production cycles are accepted because there is no particular interest in shortening them. Assured production systems are used because goods are made to order.

Stage 2

The preferences of consumers come to be reflected in the marketplace owing to a gradual increase in producers. Over time, a buyers' market emerges and demands are made to shorten allowable purchase intervals.

From the producer's point of view, an increase in the number of producers leads to competition and the need to meet allowable purchase intervals (D_s). There is no known method for shortening production cycles, however, so manufacturers have no choice but to adopt speculative production systems. Consequently, production is arranged so that either work-in-process inventories accumulate between processes or stocks of finished products are generated.

Large-lot production is carried out as well to lower costs and prevent opportunity losses incurred by not meeting customer demand. This results in the generation of considerable inventories. Because the approach is regarded as advantageous overall, however, stock is tolerated as a necessary evil.

Stage 3

As the attitudes of a buyers' market take root, calls for shorter demand times became increasingly urgent and eventually consumers demand immediate delivery.

Producer's inventories grow steadily in response to these demands for immediate delivery, and the idea takes hold that speculative production is the only kind possible.

Stage 4

Mass production and mass marketing by producers restrict the number of product types and limit consumer choices. Nevertheless, low prices and immediate availability enlarge the consumer base, and the market takes on the appearance of a sellers' market.

For the producer, mass production has several consequences:

- Depreciation of machinery, dies, and so on, is more profitable.
- The use of dedicated machines improves productivity.
- Division of labor simplifies operations and raises productivity. Labor costs can be cut by employing low-wage, unskilled workers for production.
- Workers increase in number and, in turn, become consumers. The resulting expanded demand opens up further opportunities for mass production.
- Mass production of this sort that results from producers creating more demand leads to the adoption of large-lot production methods. Such methods make setup time reductions unnecessary or minimize apparent labor costs. Long production cycles are not much of a problem either, and speculative production systems are used as a matter of course.

Stage 5

Consumers grow dissatisfied with the lack of variety in products, and the buyers' market mentality returns. Wants gradually diversify and demand frequently changes in response to fluctuations in the economy and other factors.

For producers, the diversification of consumer wants and the instability associated with demands for varying quantities and times lead to increased uncertainty in speculative production. This gives rise to larger inventories. Considerable work-in-process is also generated by the excessive use of large-lot production believed to lower costs. Inventories are increased further to compensate for defects and machine breakdowns.

To offset these destabilizing influences, every effort is made to improve the accuracy of forecasts through such means as marketing seminars and more reliable market research. Attempts also are made to reduce inventories through the establishment of economic lots and other devices. Basically, however, the generation of stock comes to be seen as a necessary evil. As a result, drastic inventory reductions are not attempted.

Stage 6

The market becomes more clearly a buyers' market with diversified demand, and orders for small quantities of varied products and other destabilizing factors have greater significance with respect to product types, quantities, and allowable purchase intervals. Consumers become increasingly demanding in their delivery expectations.

Major losses are caused for producers when unsold stock must be discarded. Even if it is not discarded, the generation of inventory incurs considerable losses through handling costs, wasted storage space, increased interest costs, and lowered capital turnover. Because of these losses and neglected profits, managers become concerned about inventories. They investigate the causes of stock and come up with ways to make improvements at the source of the problem. In other words, they adopt several fundamental improvements: First, assured production takes the place of speculative production as a fundamental concept, a move that eliminates the losses inherent in guesswork. Then, efforts are made to minimize production cycles. This means the producer must:

- Eliminate transport by linking many machines in accordance with process flows.
- Drastically cut production cycles by adopting one-piece flows and eliminating lot delays.
- Avoid production of surplus products and minimize production cycles by processing in small, separate lots.
- Adopt SMED or one-touch changeovers to make drastic cuts in setup times.
- Use source inspection and the poka-yoke system to achieve zero defects and zero equipment failures.
- Make non-stock production possible by using a flexible manufacturing system that is sensitive to demand fluctuations.
- Use a *superproduction system* where immediate delivery is demanded.

The object is to carry minimal inventories while fulfilling demand for immediate delivery.

The features listed are characteristics of the Toyota production system and other recent revolutionary Japanese production systems. Japanese production systems are oriented toward *non-stock* production, and are based on the fundamental concept of *assured* production. The essence of these systems cannot be grasped through a familiarity with superficial production methods. In fact, such a limited knowledge may lead to losses and failure.

CONFUSING MASS PRODUCTION
AND LARGE-LOT PRODUCTION

As I have already mentioned, many people — among them some supposedly well-informed ones — seem to be confused about mass production and large-lot production. One reason for this is that the words designating these two systems are ambiguous. The distinction would probably be clearer if we changed the expressions as follows:

Mass production → production for large orders
Large-lot production → production in large processing lots

Production for large orders applies to production where the customer demands a large volume of the same product. Here, it is the customer who determines whether production is for large, medium-sized, or small orders — the producer has nothing to do with it. In contrast, regardless of the size of the order, the choice of whether to produce in small, medium-sized, or large lots belongs completely to the producer.

Producing for large orders offers a number of advantages.

- Purchasing machines, dies, etc. in large quantities provides opportunity for quantity discounts. This is also true for purchases of tools, gauges, etc.
- High-volume sales bring high profits.
- Operating rates for machines and tools are higher.
- Quicker depreciation of machines and dies brings higher profits.
- Large orders make it possible to carry out a thorough segmentation of tasks to simplify unit operations. The resulting rapid rise in skill levels increases productivity and labor costs drop because low-wage, unskilled labor can be used. In terms of company policy, it is desirable to offer employment opportunities to many people, and these measures will create new demand for people.
- Productivity rises because exhaustive division of tasks facilitates the introduction of tools and mechanization, and the use of specialized machines should further raise productivity.
- Finally, materials costs, incidental costs, and other collateral items are affected favorably.

By way of contrast, producing in large processing lots has the following merits:

- The proportion of setup time to processing time is minimized.
- Machine and die operating rates increase as the number of setups drops, and this elimination of lost time improves productivity.

When we produce for small orders, we generally choose to proceed as follows: If only 5,000 units of product A are ordered each month, for example, we may combine their processing into larger lots of 30,000 every six months. The trouble with this approach is that producing items ahead of time inevitably generates inventory. Moreover, since it is speculative production, there is a potential for dead stock or discarded surplus. The approach does reduce setup time losses and machine operating rates, however.

These advantages and disadvantages must be weighed before deciding on large-lot production.

In any event, the large-lot approach has very little appeal when single-minute setups cut setups of several hours down to several minutes.

Suppose the forecast demand for items A, B, and C is as follows:

- Item A: 120,000
- Item B: 120,000
- Item C: 120,000

There are several approaches to deal with this situation.

Approach 1: Large-Lot Production:

Produce 120,000 A in the first ten days of the month, 120,000 B in the second ten days of the month, and 120,000 C in the final ten days of the month. Usually, the demand for 120,000 each of A, B, and C will be dispersed evenly over the course of a month. Consequently, significant and long-term inventories of all three products will be generated. In addition, when forecasts are long-term, unusable items are more likely because the accuracy of estimates decreases.

These factors lead many companies to move to choose an alternate approach.

Approach 2: Leveled Production

Here, 40,000 units each of items A, B, and C are produced during each third of the month. This approach generates smaller inventories than Approach 1, increasing the likelihood of accurate forecasts. This is an example of leveled production, also called a segmented production system.

Approach 3: Divided Small-Lot System

For an operation running, say, 30 days a month, processing occurs in even smaller lots, for example, in lots of 4,000 units each of A, B and C a day. Using this system, called a divided small-lot production (DSP) system, would make it possible to cut back inventories and improve even further the chance for accurate estimates.

Approach 4: Mixed Production System

Lot sizes can be reduced even further if we use a mixed production System (MPS), in which one each of products A, B and C are repeatedly made in succession. This method has certain consequences:

- Because of its flexibility, fluctuations in demand can be followed closely.
- Changes in product mix can be dealt with by changing the order of production.
- Inventories can be eliminated or minimized because timely production is assured.
- Setup changes will have to be carried out all the time, however. To minimize setup times, try to make setup unnecessary wherever possible.
- One-touch setup changes must be developed.
- Frequent operational changeovers are needed to keep up with constantly changing products, making assembly errors likely. (The zero quality control [ZQC] system, that is, source inspection and the poka-yoke system, is especially effective here.)

Since the number of setup changes increases as we move from Approach 1 to 4, it is essential that we use the SMED system or one-touch setups — or even do away with setups completely.

In production system improvements, it is extremely important to distinguish between mass production (production for large orders) and large-lot production, for these are phenomena of inherently different orders.

In this connection, Ohno Taiichi, the creator of the Toyota production system, is certain that in the future, with its expected low growth, the Toyota production system will win out over American-style mass production. He also claims that the Toyota production system is the antithesis of American-style mass production systems. This argument is more persuasive when we make the distinction between *mass production* and *large-lot production*.

SUMMARY

The great domestic and overseas interest in learning from new Japanese production systems is a good thing, but real improvement will not result from superficial imitation of isolated techniques ("know-how") in these systems — true innovation cannot come about without "know-why." In this sense, the study of the new production systems can be undertaken successfully only after a proper understanding of their underlying concepts has been gained.

4

Stage One:
Problem Identification

Problem identification, the first step in making improvements, involves the following concepts:

- Never accept the status quo.
- Find problems where you think none exist.
- Work is more than people in motion.
- Perceiving and thinking are not the same.

NEVER ACCEPT THE STATUS QUO

People who are satisfied with the way things are can never achieve improvement or progress. Indeed, the first step in improvement is dissatisfaction with the status quo; it means always asking why productivity can't be increased, why stocks are necessary, or whether there aren't better ways to do things.

We often voice our complaints and dissatisfaction. According to Mr. Harada, managing director of the Sailor Pen Company, however, lack of dissatisfaction is of greater concern than complaints. A human being with no dissatisfaction will never make any progress. Problem awareness will never occur in the person who is utterly without discontent, who says he is satisfied.

Even among those who feel dissatisfaction, however, there are some who blame it on the fact that they must contend with high-diversity, low-volume production, or that they must produce in response to orders, or that plant equipment is outdated. In these people, who ascribe problems mainly to external factors and make no

79

move to resolve them through their own efforts, dissatisfaction has changed to complaining. By the same token, people are on the road to progress when, on their own initiative, they try to face such problems head on.

Figure 4-1.

It is a universal truth that those who are not dissatisfied will never make any progress. Yet even if one feels dissatisfaction, it must not be diverted into complaining; it must be actively linked to improvement. In this sense, we can say that *dissatisfaction is the mother of improvement*.

FIND PROBLEMS WHERE YOU THINK NONE EXIST

When I walk through a production workshop, workers never call out to tell me about waste or to raise questions about inefficient operations. If I just kept my mouth shut and walked through the shop, we would conclude that there were no problems at all. Obviously, this would be no good. Rather than zipping through the shop like a sightseer, looking only at the surface of things, it is better to spend an hour or even half an hour observing a machine that is thought to have no problems. If you have the attitude that there probably are some problems, you will inevitably find some. To accept the likelihood of problems is a challenge, but adopting this perspective will allow you to outpace ordinary companies.

When we seriously contemplate making an improvement, the first step is to *identify the problem.*

Is Eliminating Waste Nonsense?

When I visited company K, I noticed the slogan "Eliminate Waste" posted on the wall of the president's office. So I remarked to the president, "You must have many stupid employees here at your company."

"That's not true," he replied. Why do you say that?"

"But the poster there says 'Eliminate Waste.'"

"What's wrong with that? Isn't eliminating waste a good thing to do?"

"True. But don't you have that slogan posted because here at your company people don't automatically try to eliminate recognizable waste? Anybody who recognizes waste will try to eliminate it. The real problem is when people do not recognize waste when they see it."

I then told the president my story about bananas.

I had been asked to give a talk to women shift supervisors about improvement at an apparel manufacturer's in Taiwan. So I told them the following story: "Everybody says that bananas in Taiwan taste great. In Japan, bananas are imported while still green. They are ripened by steaming. But this spoils their taste. Because in Taiwan the bananas ripen on the trees, they smell different and taste great. They are also cheap. So, whenever I go to Taiwan, I look forward to eating bananas.

"However, the last time I went to Taiwan and bought bananas, I noticed something strange. One bunch cost only 200 yen, which was very inexpensive. Still, the fruit-stand owner charged for them by weight, including the banana peel."

"But being a cultured person, I don't eat the banana peel. I eat only the white inner part. Do you eat the banana peel?" I asked a woman seated nearby.

She laughed. "No, I don't."

I continued. "When I got back to the hotel, I weighed the bunch of bananas. It weighed 2.6 kilograms including the peels. I then removed the peels and weighed only the edible portion. That weighed only 1.58 kilograms — a mere 60 percent of the gross weight."

"Why do you have to pay for the gross weight when you can eat only 60 percent of it? Next time I go to that fruit stand, I plan to tell the owner that I want only the edible portion, that I don't want the banana peels. What do you think?"

One of the women replied, "If you do that, the owner will get angry."

I said, "Is that so? Since it makes no sense to anger the owner over a mere 200 yen, I won't ask for bananas without the peels. But the same cannot be said about the work done in a factory.

"There are two types of tasks performed in a factory: those that increase a product's value and those that merely increase the cost of producing it. In other words, there are tasks that add value (comparable to the edible portion of a banana) and tasks that merely run up the cost (comparable to the banana peel.)

"Marking off lines on raw fabric, cutting it, and sewing it are all tasks that add value. They are the edible portion of the banana. However, transporting the raw fabric, bundling fabrics together, and tying them up just increase the cost. Those tasks are the banana peel.

"When I revisit your company in three months," I said, "I'll bring a basket of bananas. As I watch you work, I'll give the edible part of a banana to the ones doing meaningful work and a banana peel to those performing only cost-increasing tasks. What do you think of that idea?"

I did return three months later, and I noticed that the size of the shift had dropped from 65 to only 17 workers.

Operations used to be performed in a *lot-by-lot* sequence, (*i.e.*, line-marking an entire lot, then cutting that lot, followed by sewing the lot). Now, the machines had been rearranged to reflect the overall *process* sequence: marking was followed by cutting, which was followed by sewing, piece-by-piece. This permitted an assembly-line setup that drastically reduced the transport of materials and consequent delays.

I also told the workers, "There are two important lessons to be learned from this story. The first is to separate all the tasks that add value from those that merely increase cost. Replacing manual transport with mechanized transport is one type of improvement. Even so, whether done manually or mechanically, having to move materials around remains a cost-increasing operation. Transport by mechanical means may reduce the amount of this loss, but a loss is still a loss. It is therefore important to optimize the plant layout so that the need to move materials around is either minimized or eliminated.

"Another thing. When you yourselves have bought bananas, you have always paid for the inedible peels, without question. You considered this natural. That's because paying for the peels, too, has become an ingrained habit. However, it is very important to develop an attitude that allows you to shed such habits and recognize the true value of work."

There is nothing intrinsically wrong with the slogan "Eliminate Waste," but in many cases a better slogan would be "Find Waste." Company M did adopt the slogan "Find Waste," and it solicited employee ideas for solving specific problems and on improvement in general. Over 500 suggestions were submitted. Many were adopted and implemented. The project was a great success.

It must be clearly understood that:

There are many examples of waste in the workplace, but not all waste is obvious. It often appears in the guise of useful work. We must see beneath the surface and grasp the essence.

Often, though, a company will try to implement an improvement program with an appeal to "Eliminate Waste" or to "Tell us what you think is wrong." But such improvement programs will usually not succeed unless they are accompanied by a clear understanding of what *waste* is and an alertness to possible trouble points in a seemingly trouble-free environment.

The Real Problem Is Thinking There Are No Problems

To identify a problem, one must be constructively dissatisfied with the status quo. People who are completely satisfied with it will not be contemplating any improvements.

Other counterproductive attitudes can be seen in the following statements:

- "There is no particular problem."
- "To have some problems is unavoidable. It happens in every company. We're just like all the rest; there's no need for concern."
- "We change our product line frequently. We can't spend too much money. Let's be content with the way things are."

People with these attitudes have become complacent and may not recognize a real problem when one comes along. More desirable attitudes include the following:

- Closely observe for one hour the operation of a machine you believe to be trouble-free, trying to discover hitherto undetected problems.
- Attempt to reduce to 0.15 percent or even to 0 percent the defect rate at your own plant, even though rates at other plants may be 1.5 percent or more. This is an attitude of striving to achieve the supposedly impossible.
- Even if model changes are frequent, analyze the tasks common to all models and seek to cut costs by fabricating jigs and tools that will remain usable regardless of model changes.
- Aggressively seek out problems.

Many companies imitate other companies to solve their problems. They send someone to tour another company's advanced plant and use the lessons learned there to discover problems in their own plant. This *is* a very effective method of solving problems that can be spotted relatively easily. Still, it is not always so easy to tour a competitor's plant. Even if it were, while this is a more or less sure-fire method, it virtually guarantees that your plant will permanently remain a second-rate imitation and will never make it to the top.

Other attitude problems include becoming aware of the need to identify problems only after one's parent company demands cost reductions, or starting to think about improvements only after a high defect rate has been noticed and pointed out by one's parent company.

Given those attitude problems, the credit for any improvements goes mainly to the parent company and is not shared by the plant benefiting from them.

The best approach is to dig out and eliminate problems where they were assumed not to exist. The greatest contribution you can make to the successful development of your own plant is to seek out problems aggressively and then to correct them. To do this, you must first divide all the tasks currently being performed into those adding value and those merely driving up costs. All the tasks that drive up costs can then be recognized as utterly wasteful. Do not passively accept such tasks as inevitable; look for different, better ways of getting the job done. The important thing is never to throw in the towel and declare resignedly that nothing can be done.

In life there are things that we refer to as "necessary evils." A familiar example: "One has to maintain a certain amount of inventory as a cushion in case a piece of equipment fails or develops a defect. This may be an evil, but it is a necessary one." But what happens is that too much emphasis gets placed on the *necessary* and too little on the *evil*.

Nevertheless, one must call a spade a spade, an evil an evil, and look for ways to eliminate such equipment failures and other defects. This helps to instill a problem-seeking attitude that leads to the implementation of basic improvements.

Never being content and always looking for ways to make things better are prime prerequisites for uncovering problems.

WORK IS MORE THAN PEOPLE IN MOTION

In the Japanese writing system, the character for *work* is composed of two elements, meaning, respectively, *person* and *move*. Indeed, there is a tendency to think that when people are in motion they are working. This is hardly true, however. At another level of analysis, the same written character is composed of three elements: *person* + *weight* + *strength*. This is the real meaning of work: "A person exerts strength on a weighty task."

Thus, rather than assuming that a man in motion is working, we must be sure to ask whether he is really exerting his strength on some task that will produce added value.

All substances on earth are composed of a mere 104 elements, for example, oxygen, nitrogen, and hydrogen; or gold, silver, and copper, etc. Similarly, Gilbreth, in his analysis of work, identified 18 basic elements of human motion (*therbligs*). These therbligs are organized as illustrated in *Figure 4-2*.

1. In the center are:
   A — Assemble
   DA — Disassemble
   U — Use
2. Around these are:
   TE — Transport empty
   G — Grasp
   TL — Transport loaded
   RL — Release load

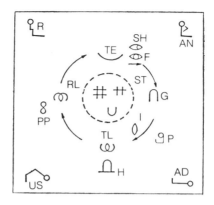

FIGURE 4-2. The 18 "Therbligs"

3. Subsidiary to these are:
   SH — Search
   F — Find
   ST — Select
   P — Reposition
   H — Hold
   I — Inspect
   PP — Pre-position
4. Outside these are:
   R — Rest
   PN — Plan
   UD — Unavoidable delay
   AD — Avoidable delay

From birth to death, the argument goes, humans simply repeat these 18 elements of motion. Obviously, there are infinite variations, depending on what is being held, and on the number and combinations of motion. Nevertheless, at the abstract level of motion, there are no more than 18 such elements.

Ranks in the old Japanese army were organized as follows:

Commander grade
   • general
   • lieutenant-general
   • major-general

Field grade
- colonel
- lieutenant-colonel
- major

Subordinate grade
- captain
- first lieutenant
- second lieutenant

My rank was that of a tank corps second lieutenant. Using a similar approach to evaluating grades of motion elements, we might obtain the following scheme:

1. *Assemble, disassemble,* and *use* are basically elements of motion that increase value — the generals — and can be labeled commander grade.

2. *Transport empty, grasp, transport loaded,* and *release load* are merely elements for transporting objects and, rather than increasing value, they generally increase only cost. Still, in many cases, work cannot be accomplished without these elements of motion, and although they are of low value, they are the most frequently occurring therbligs — the true field grade elements of motion.

3. *Search, find,* and *select* occur because objects are poorly arranged or mixed together. *Reposition* is due to faulty placement. *Hold,* moreover, is a therblig resulting from poor timing. *Inspect* is an element that occurs in order to ascertain whether *assemble, disassemble,* and *use* have been performed correctly. In addition, *pre-position* is an element of motion for positioning an object correctly for the next cycle. The value of all these elements of motion — corresponding to the subordinate grade — is a grade lower than that of the other therbligs. Such elements should be kept to a minimum.

4. A task should not be so fatiguing that it requires *rest,* nor should it demand that you *plan* frequently. Nor should *unavoidable delays* be frequent, nor, obviously, should workers slack off due to *avoidable delays.* Therbligs of this sort have no "officer rank" at all, so we may refer to them as second class privates.

Since there are four grades of motion, striving to eliminate everything except value-adding motion, *assemble, disassemble*, and *use*, is ultimately linked to the assertion that *work* means "people exerting strength to accomplish weighty tasks."

PERCEIVING AND THINKING ARE NOT THE SAME

Perceiving means recognizing phenomena by means of our five senses. *Thinking*, on the other hand, is our mental ability to pursue causes and purposes by objectively asking "why" about all phenomena.

Humans *perceive* via the five senses — sight, hearing, touch, smell, and taste. Looking up at the sky, we perceive that it is cloudy. Then there is *thought*: Will it rain or not?

Here is a little story that illustrates this point:

Foreman A walks into plant manager Ohara's office with a safety part and says that a defect has occurred. "What do we do?" he asks.

Ohara examines the part for a moment and then instructs the foreman to bring him the next defective item if the defect shows up again. Dubious because he has received no instructions on how to handle the matter, the foreman goes back to the shop floor.

A week later, the defect shows up again and the foreman immediately rushes to the plant manager's office. "We've got another defect," he announces. But when the manager asks him about the conditions under which the defect occurred, the foreman stammers incoherently.

"In that case," the manager says, "bring the offending part to me if the defect shows up again." The foreman quickly withdraws.

Ten days later, when the defect occurs again, the foreman visits the manager's office for a third time. "The defect was caused by play in a stopper on the machine," he reports. "We've fixed it so the defect won't show up again."

Here's what happened: The first two times, the foreman merely *perceived* that a defect had occurred. The third time, having understood what the manager had in mind, he *thought* about why the defect might have occurred.

Thus there are two positions we can take: merely perceiving — or thinking objectively about what we have perceived. Action comes about in response to cycling back and forth between perceiving and thinking, perceiving and thinking, and then finally, perceiving the solution. The more this cycle of perceiving and thinking is repeated, the closer we can approach the truth.

We must remember to ask ourselves, as we move from thought to action in the course of every day, whether we are merely perceiving or whether we have really thought about the matter in question.

The IBM Slogan

Some years ago, when I visited IBM as a participant in a study mission, I was impressed to see the slogan THINK posted everywhere in the plant. I asked a question of our guide after the tour. I had heard of IBM's famous slogan some time ago, I said, and I was truly impressed to see how prominently displayed it was throughout the plant. "But what on earth," I asked, "is THINK supposed to mean?"

I was given the following answer. Whenever a problem crops up at IBM, a worker doesn't go right in to the department head's office and report the problem without first thinking about it himself. The worker goes over the problem at least three times by himself and only then does he consult the department head.

The instant I heard this explanation, it struck me that at IBM, when you catch a fish, you do not take it right away to the department head and ask him how it should be cooked. You must first clean it, scale it, and wash it, and then ask how it will be cooked. Even today, the THINK slogan has left a deep impression on me. When a problem shows up, you should try to reach a solution by *thinking* about it yourself, at least three times, rather than immediately consulting your superior — as so many people do — after simply having *perceived* that a problem has occurred. This is the proper attitude — that you consult your superior only when the problem still seems insoluble.

5

Stage Two:
Basic Approaches to Improvement
(I) Understand the Status Quo

The first problem in what we call improvement is to get a grip on the status quo. The most magnificent improvement scheme in the world will be worthless if your perception of the current situation is in error. We have a tendency to think that fictitious "facts" are real. I mean by this that either we do not try to grasp the real facts and simply hypothesize facts using guesswork, or we inadvertently ignore changes over time and assume that things are the same as they used to be — we ignore changes that occur over time. Too frequently, such mistakes lead us to confuse fictitious facts and real ones.

Even when we have recognized real facts, we must:

- Grasp facts in greater detail
- Grasp facts quantitatively rather than qualitatively
- Think in terms of categorical principles and understand phenomena by clearly classifying them

To do this, we have to be able to analyze problems based on the "five elements of production":

1. *Object*: what?
2. *Agent*: who?
3. *Method*: how?
4. *Space*: where?
5. *Time*: when?

Also, we must not forget to "observe from both sides," in terms of:

- *Process*: the course of changes in the object
- *Operation*: the course of changes in the agent

It is also true that we cannot approach the real truth unless, rather than using our ordinary senses, we perceive in greater detail — using Frank B. Gilbreth's elements of motion, the 18 therbligs.

Moreover, even if a fact is true, its significance may be minimal. There is a saying: "A deeper truth lies behind every fact." We must relentlessly root out the truth no matter where it hides. Accomplishing this requires a detailed, quantifying, classifying approach.

I was once involved in a project to reduce the construction time involved in shipbuilding. We had developed a new production method, but when the time came to implement it, we faced strong opposition from one of the engineers: "It's all very good in theory, but it won't work in practice."

I asked him, "What is the problem?"

He replied, "The cranes do not have sufficient capacity."

I said, "Let's study the operation ratio of the four cranes."

We observed the operation of the cranes for a week. The results are given in *Table 5-1*.

	Loaded	Empty
Moving	25.4%	27.8%
Stopped	18.5%	28.3%

TABLE 5-1. Operating Rate for Cranes

I asked the engineer to come by and told him, "Only 25.4 percent of the time are the cranes actually carrying loads. Since a month is some 8 percent of a year, the cranes are actually operating only 3 months out of the year."

The engineer merely grunted.

We then went to the dock every day to observe the operation of the cranes. We discovered waste, eliminated it, and thereby solved the problem of the cranes' insufficient capacity. As a result, we set a world record for reducing the time required to build a ship.

In this way, major improvements can be achieved through detailed, quantifying, classifying observation and analysis.

"Is" Outweighs "Ought"

We often say things such as, "It *ought* to be working according to the standard operation," or "It *ought* to be finished." Yet over and over again when we check to see what is really going on, it turns out that things are not necessarily going the way they are supposed to. "Ought" refers to *guesswork* and not to *fact*. We must recognize that although a guess may have a high probability of being correct, that still does not make it fact. For important matters, we must always grasp the real facts — what *is* — rather than what *ought* to be.

"Feel" Is Not Ideal

A lot of work done on the shop floor is carried out by "feel." "Feel" is a kind of experiential, statistical awareness that succeeds at a fairly high degree of probability. It follows that as we increase our reliance on a worker's feel for the job we get to a point where everything ends up being taken care of by feel. Yet a feel for the job is ultimately vague; by its nature it cannot provide 100 percent reliability, and so sometimes, it is well off the mark. This is why I maintain that "feel" has to be on target three times in a row. Why are three tries needed? — A baseball pitcher has to get three strikes before he has done his job.

In plastic molding processes, maintaining suitable die temperatures is extremely important in stabilizing product quality. Yet D Plastics followed the following procedures:

1. Check temperature by placing a hand on the die.
2. Pinch the coolant line connected to the die to check flow rate by feel.
3. Open and close the coolant line valve by feel.

By switching to the following procedures, it became possible to eliminate chronic problems involving "whitening" of products:

1. Ascertain die temperature quantitatively by inserting thermometer into the die.

2. Fit a round plate to the valve and draw a scale on the plate so that the valve turns in increments of 1 degree Celsius.

In another operation at W Ceramics, plunger stroke size was determined by "feeling" the volume of glaze. This was changed so the stroke could be adjusted with a geared knob. A scale was drawn on the knob to allow quantitative control, and as a result, quality stabilized considerably with previous off-specification rates of 30 percent dropping to less than 3 percent.

Relying on feel exaggerates the gap between skilled and unskilled workers, because while skilled workers can rapidly determine the proper conditions, unskilled workers can never get conditions stable. Quality can be stabilized however, when "feel" is abandoned in favor of quantitative measures.

There Is Truth Beyond Every Fact

We use the word *fact* to designate things we perceive, but in many cases our perception is only superficial. Oversights and misperceptions are revealed when we look deeper and observe more rigorously. It is only by means of such detailed, rigorous observation that we can begin to get a grip on truth. In matters of improvement, we begin by *grasping truth*.

You Don't Understand Not Understanding?

For a human being, not to understand "not understanding" is a problem without remedy. If we don't understand what it is that we don't understand, we have no idea what to do about it. In other words, we can't see something if we don't know to look for it. When people aren't aware of this possibility, they may end up unconsciously overlooking problems.

The first step toward solving a problem is to clarify what is not understood, that is, to make a clear distinction between what we know and understand and what we do not know. By making this clear, we typically end up understanding about half of what was not known about the problem initially.

Next, the essence of what remains unknown is slowly revealed by the application of hypotheses and trials, until we can eventually arrive at a full understanding.

Time Is But a Reflection of Motion

There is a saying: "Time is but a reflection of motion." A person who says "This takes too long" or "We can do that faster," is talking about saving time. It would be meaningless, however, to ask workers just to speed up their work. They would merely become confused, would not know exactly what to do, and there would be no significant savings in time.

When we say a task takes too long, we really mean that certain motions are taking too long to perform. So it is really meaningless to complain just about their duration. The real culprit is the structure of the motions themselves; this is what causes them to take so long. It may be necessary to restructure the task to which the motions are tailored. Suppose a doctor visits a sick person and, taking his temperature, finds it to be above normal. Anybody would call the doctor an idiot if he were to cool off the thermometer and then announce to the patient that his temperature had dropped. The relationship between time and motion is analogous to the relationship between a thermometer and body temperature.

FIGURE 5-1.

There are too many incompetent managers, however, who content themselves with complaining about the effect, that is, the waste of time, without looking for its cause.

The saying "Time is but a reflection of motion" must be understood completely by all managers.

Accuracy and Precision Are Not the Same

Suppose one were to divide $1,000 among three people with an error of $10 or less. Under one *accurate* apportionment:

A gets $330
B gets $330
C gets $340

If we were to make a further division so that

A gets $333
B gets $333
C gets $334

the distribution would still be accurate, but it would be more precise.

In the same way, even when degrees of precision differ, they are all accurate as long as they satisfy allowable tolerances. Consequently, it is a mistake to think that the more precise something is the more accurate it is. Frequently, rather than demand unnecessary precision, one need merely achieve a degree of accuracy that maintains the required degree of precision. Seeking more precision than necessary is often wasteful.

6

Basic Approaches to Improvement
(II) The Pursuit of Goals

Improvement means the elimination of waste, and the most essential precondition for improvement is the proper pursuit of goals.

We must not be mistaken, first of all, about what improvement means. The four goals of improvement must be to make things:

- easier
- better
- faster
- cheaper

How thoroughly we pursue goals is affected by the quality of our improvement plans. This means, in any case, that it is impossible to be too thorough in pursuing underlying goals. Revolutionary improvement schemes can be developed by persistently tracking down these "source goals."

THE PURSUIT OF GOALS IN THREE DIMENSIONS

Eliminating waste means improving procedures that are too broadly or generally defined in terms of goals. It means asking *why* at every opportunity.

Just as grasping a physical object requires that it be seen in front, top, and side views, goals must be pursued along three dimensions, X, Y, and Z:

- *X*: focus your thinking
- *Y*: look for multiple goals
- *Z*: look for higher-level goals

97

Below are examples of the kinds of thinking needed.

Type X: Focus Your Thinking

At R Confectionery, in a process for melting the starch syrup base for caramel, 18 liter cans of syrup are placed in a heating oven. Its insufficient capacity could not keep up with production, however, and the company was looking around for a better way.

On a visit to the plant, I opened the doors of the oven and saw that the syrup cans were all overflowing and sticking to one another. Why, I asked, were the cans packed in so tightly? The official in charge of shop operations replied that they wanted to melt large quantities of syrup because of increased production and that recently, perhaps because of a change in the quality of the syrup, melting time had increased, so that they could only keep up by putting large quantities of syrup in the oven at the same time.

In response, I observed that heat can be transmitted in three ways — conduction, convection, or radiation — and that since the oven blew in hot air, it was essentially designed to heat by convection. Packing so many cans of syrup inside, however, meant that heat could only be transmitted by conduction. The cans in the center would therefore take longer to heat, and this resulted in longer heating times overall.

To remedy this, spaces were opened up to allow hot air to flow between cans, and a blower and an exhaust fan were installed to help the hot air circulate. As a result, per cycle capacity dropped to 60 percent, melting time was reduced by two-thirds — from 2 hours to 40 minutes. This meant a 180 percent net increase in melting capacity.

In this example, the key to improvement lay in following through with goal pursuit, by asking what was really involved in heating the syrup instead of assuming that all that was required was to pack in cans and blow in hot air.

Type Y: Look for Multiple Goals

Company T does electrodeposition coating. In the process, paint is mixed by blowing air into it to ensure uniform consistency. But this generates foam that overflows from the vats. The problem, therefore, was what to do about the foaming.

The solution being used, which was to apply an antifoaming agent, was effective but costly and time-consuming. I was asked to come up with a cheaper, simpler way of preventing foaming.

I asked Mr. H, the young engineer in charge, "What is foam?"

FIGURE 6-1.

He merely blinked his eyes, offering no answer.

I joked, "Perhaps bubbles are getting in your eyes." I continued, "A bubble is made up of two things. The first is air inside and the second is the film of paint forming the bubble's surface. Now, you are trying to dissolve the film of paint. Why don't you look for ways of removing the air inside?"

He asked, "But how?"

We went to the shop floor and brought back some foam. I put some of the foam on the palm of my hand and clapped my hands. The bubbles disappeared instantly.

The engineer protested, "Clapping your hands?"

I then asked him to get a washing machine. We filled the spin drier with foam, and turned on the machine. The foam disappeared immediately but no paint came out of the discharge hose. We did this three times. No paint came out of the hose. When we tilted the washing machine, a small amount of paint, maybe two or three tablespoonfuls, dribbled out.

This revealed that the amount of paint contained in three washer loads of foam amounted to no more than two or three tablespoonfuls. The rest was air. The problem of foaming was easily solved by passing the foamed paint through a fine mesh that punctured the bubbles.

The approach used to solve this problem is different depending on whether the purpose is to dissolve the paint film forming the bubbles or to eliminate the air inside the bubbles. Unless one is clear about the purpose, the result may be other than desired.

Type Z: Look for Higher-Level Goals

In drawing wire, the wire is dipped in lime water and then dried. This process took two hours at one plant; the people involved wanted to shorten this time.

I visited the plant and saw about a ton of coiled wire hanging on pipes and drying over oil burners. Not only did the wire take a long time to dry, but after the drying was complete, the hot wire needed roughly half an hour to cool down. Naturally, this created problems when expedited operations were required.

I asked the head of the wire-drawing department what he was doing in the operation.

"We're drying the drawn wire," he replied.

"Can't you do without drying the wire?"

"Not dry it?" he said. "No, no. It would be all sticky from the lime water and wouldn't be good for anything."

"Listen," I said. "What gets sticky isn't the wire at all. It's the lime water on the outside of the wire, isn't it?"

I immediately borrowed a portable dryer and managed, in a mere three minutes, to dry the lime water on the outside of the wire.

"How about it?" I said to the department head. "If we were to stand next to the drying oven and ask it how things were going, I bet we'd hear the wire inside calling out to say that it's too hot. 'All you have to do is dry the lime water on the outside of me!' it would shout."

This particular company official was a junior classmate of mine and he turned the tables on me:

"If we were to do silly things like that," he countered, "then we'd put you out of business."

He was right about that.

X — FOCUS

Listen to the Voices of the Machines

When we make the rounds of a production floor, we tend to walk through nonchalantly with as much detachment as tourists on a tour bus. This is not good. It is necessary to spend at least 30 minutes observing and asking why a particular machine produces defects. When you truly observe your work, you will naturally uncover problems. By persistently asking the question, "What is the true purpose of this job?" you will eventually become able to tune in to the true voices of the machines.

At a plant in Kumamoto that manufactures high-pressure hoses, Mr. Sakamoto, a section manager, said to me, "We have a problem with severing of the steel wires wrapped around the hose. The repair takes time. What can we do to shorten the repair time?"

I said, "What you should do is prevent the steel wires from becoming severed. You should listen well to the machines to find out why the wires are being cut."

Mr. Sakamoto said, "You mean *listen* to machines? How does one do that?"

"What you do is stand next to the machine and observe its operation for at least half a day. You'll eventually become able to tune in to the machine's voice."

Mr. Sakamoto did just that. When a steel wire became severed, he asked himself why. He told me, "A comb-shaped guide is used to wrap 16 steel wires around the hose. I realized that there were two places where the comb-shaped guide made a 90-degree turn. We replaced the bent grooves with more streamlined ones."

That reportedly put an end to the severing of wires.

Since then Mr. Sakamoto stands next to his machines and listens to them whenever a problem occurs. Says Mr. Sakamoto earnestly, "When one listens carefully to a machine's voice, one can hear it."

Paint the Air?

The S Fountain Pen Company's T plant is located in the countryside and surrounded by rice paddies. Waste from the painting booth consequently needs to be treated, but during periods of heavy rainfall, the paddies used to be contaminated by overflows of polluted water from the water treatment facilities. This provoked frequent complaints from neighboring farmers and each year the firm was paying out substantial sums to compensate them.

At this point, the company decided to conduct a fact-finding survey of the plant. The survey revealed that in the painting booth, pigment was sprayed onto 50 fountain pen caps, inserted on pins mounted on top of a revolving stand. Excess pigment was led off to a water screen and flushed to the bottom of the booth. From there it flowed into a waste treatment device where it was neutralized; drainage canals then took the purified water outside the plant. This meant that the least error in treatment could result in contaminated water being sent into nearby paddies.

When I asked the plant manager what the operation was for, he made a rather strange face — as though the answer were obvious — and replied that it was for painting fountain pen caps.

"That's right," I said, "but isn't it true that more than 50 percent of the paint is painting the air?"

"Painting the air? Well, I suppose you might say that, but...."

"Look," I told him. "If all you have to do is paint the caps, why paint the air as well? Isn't there some painting method that would allow you to paint only the caps?" The manager thought about this and when I visited the plant the next day a greatly improved process was already in place:

- An extremely small painting booth was constructed.
- The pen caps were supported by rotating rods, so that the caps can turn.
- A special sprayer was built with a nozzle that blew out only extremely small amounts of pigment. This nozzle was designed to move up and down automatically. It therefore painted only the caps and sprayed out almost no excess pigment.
- Five such sprayers were installed in a row so that painting could be done in groups of five.
- Exhaust air from the small painting booth was sucked out, and the entire unit was constructed so that such exhaust was extremely localized. In addition, a sponge-like urethane rubber filtering device attached to the exhaust channel absorbed all excess pigment.
- Urethane rubber that had absorbed pigment was replaced every day and incinerated.

As a result of these changes, no contaminated water whatsoever left the plant. Farmers from the surrounding region to whom the new setup was shown agreed that improvement had taken place and released the company thereafter from the payment of compensation.

It was moving to hear the plant manager describe the profound relief he felt. "Until recently," he said, "I always used to worry when it rained hard that contaminated water was leaving the plant. These changes have really helped, though, and now I don't have those worries."

Even so, many Japanese plants continue to "paint the air" in painting booths. What is more, technicians frequently do not even notice that anything is wrong.

Is Drilling Really the Best Way to Make Holes?

In many hole-boring operations a bit cuts through the entire hole section. For large diameter holes, moreover, a small guide hole is often drilled in the center and then a larger bit widens the hole.

Processing time can be reduced if a cutter with a cylindrical tip matching the hole diameter is used to cut out the circumference of the hole. The cutout pieces can also be put to other uses. Clearly, rather than drilling an entire hole, it is sufficient merely to cut away the hole's circumference.

Do We Really Cut Things with a Lathe?

After delivering a lecture at Citroen in France, I retired to an antechamber and thanked Miss Junko Ishii, my interpreter.

"Not at all!" she replied. "The interpreting part isn't that difficult; what's really draining is when there are gaps in the language."

"Gaps in the language?" I asked. "What do you mean?"

"For example, in your talk today, you used the phrase, 'cut things with a lathe.' But in French you can't use an expression like that."

"Why not?" I asked in surprise. "Nothing could be more natural than to cut things with a lathe."

"It doesn't work that way. You have to say that you mount tools on the lathe and then cut things with the tools. Since a lathe is simply a machine for turning things you attach to it, you can't actually cut things with just a lathe. Japanese has many gaps like this that can't be interpreted just as they are. You've got to think carefully about what they mean."

When I thought about it, I realized — and I still feel — that there are many such gaps in the way we express ourselves and that we frequently do not notice them.

After returning to Japan, I visited an electric company that had a problem of "lead wires coming out."

When I asked what that meant, I was told that after several lead wires were twisted together and soldered, vinyl caps were put on and fused with a soldering iron. It turned out that some of the wires would come loose due to vibration when they were transported by conveyor. Although, ideally, the vinyl caps should harden rapidly, in fact the process took a little time and this was why the wires were coming out.

"So all you have to do is cool the vinyl caps so that they harden quickly," I said.

"No, we're already doing that. We're using a fan to cool them, but the cooling is still too slow."

At this point I went to the shop floor to observe the operation and saw how they were cooling the caps with a fan.

"Tell me, Mr. M," I asked, "just what are you doing?"

"What do you mean? I'm cooling these vinyl caps with a fan."

"But surely you can't cool the vinyl caps with a fan," I said.

"Certainly we can," the worker replied. "They cool down, all right. The problem is that they take too long to cool."

"What I'm trying to say is that you can't cool them with a fan. What's really cooling them isn't the force of the breeze from the fan at all, is it?"

"Oh, well, I suppose not."

"The breeze from the fan is zero at the center of the blades and radiates out at the circumference. Your current technique is inefficient because only minimal air strikes the vinyl caps. It would work better if you were to concentrate the air coming from the fan and construct a guide to make it strike the caps directly. The caps could be cooled if the air were focused on them for a longer period of time.

The implementation of this improvement speeded cooling, and defects involving detached wires completely disappeared (see *Figure 6-2*).

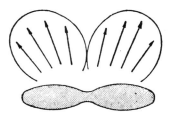

FIGURE 6-2. Air from the Blades of a Fan

As a matter of interest, we might ask whether our linguistic gaps are accompanied by more basic gaps in consciousness. If such gaps do exist, they will tend to cause problems.

Speed Alone Isn't Enough

When I graduated from school in 1930, Dr. Sugiyama, my physics professor, addressed the students: "You are all about to leave this school and go out into the world," he said. "When you do, remember not to concentrate merely on speed. What you've got to pay attention to is velocity. No matter what record-breaking speeds you may be able to attain as you swim along, you will never reach your goals unless you are moving in specific directions toward specific objectives.

"Speed is fine as far as it goes, but velocity requires a direction component. So as you're swimming, you've got to raise your heads from time to time and check to make sure you're moving toward your objectives."

Unless you are heading straight for your objectives, the most heroic efforts in the world will only be as effective as the component of work directly related to your goals. Indeed, when carrying out improvements, you will only be truly effective when you first set your objectives and then head straight for them.

Time Is Not the Same as Timing

We frequently say that something didn't get done on time. We probably ought to say that it didn't get done with proper timing.

I once saw a newspaper advertisement in which S Electric claimed it produced "a television a minute." How could a television be produced in one minute, I wondered. What the ad meant, of course, was that one minute was the time between the completion of the one television set and the completion of next, not that the television production process took one minute. The assembly of a television from start to finish might take four hours, but the space between television no. 1 and television no. 2 was one minute.

We see, then, that *time* and *timing* mean completely different things. Clocks, for example, possess different modes of expression. *Digital clocks* accurately express timing, whereas *analog clocks* help us gain an intuitive grasp of time. In the same way, the difference between time problems and timing problems must be understood in production. For example, delays are less a matter of time and more the effect of timing.

For example, one of the jobs at T Industries involved preheating mandrels used in insulated tubing. Where 40 tubes per hour had been produced in the past, the idea now was to increase this to 60 tubes per hour. The problem was the capacity of the oven for heating the mandrels — it would only hold 40.

I decided to visit the plant and observe the operation. Sure enough, the oven could hold only 40 mandrels. But as I watched the job being performed, I saw that they would use half the total number of mandrels — about 20 — and then feed new mandrels into the oven. When they used the remaining 20 mandrels, another group of new mandrels was supplied. At this point I talked to the workers.

"With the method you're using now," I said, "the newly supplied mandrels can be used for a heating time corresponding to the time that 20 tubes are used, *i.e.*, 1.5 minutes × 20 minutes = 30 minutes. This means that if you increase production to 60 tubes per hour, what you have to do is to divide the oven into four and use ten mandrels at a time, so that ten new mandrels are supplied whenever there is a vacancy. This is because mandrels are used now at one-minute intervals, so that while 30 preheated ones are being used, the ten new mandrels are being preheated.

"In any event, your wanting one tube per minute means that you want an interval of one minute to separate the first tube and the second tube. It's a question of *timing*.

How long a mandrel is heated before it reaches a suitable temperature is a question of *time*. Since each mandrel needs to be heated for 30 minutes, reducing the feed units will cut down on the amount of space needed. If the units are lined up and fed successively from one side to the other, the total time it takes them to go through need be only 30 minutes. That would mean you could get by with even less space."

The outcome, then, was that the job could be done with an oven whose capacity was only 40 mandrels. Here, once again, the key to solving the problem lay in distinguishing between timing — or the number of items required, and time — which referred to the question of heating.

Y — MULTIPLE GOALS

Presses Have Only Four Functions

"I'd like to make production more rational," President K of T Ironworks once told me, "but it's awfully hard to do when you're dealing with high diversity and low volume."

"Look," I replied, "your plant does pressing, right? Tell me, just what sort of work is it that presses perform?"

"They do various things."

"What do you mean by that?"

"I mean that we have many types of products, so the presses do various things!"

"That's not what I mean," I said. "No matter how many different products are involved, the work that a press itself carries out is probably restricted to things like punching holes, bending, and squeezing."

"I see," he said. "The press itself does only three things. No, there's one more. It's flattening."

"All right, then. Even with that, you're dealing with only four items. And then after a product has been worked on by a press, it either falls out, stays in the lower die, or remains attached to the upper die. There are only three possibilities, right?"

Then I continued, "You think the job is so awfully hard because you are blinded by the large number of products you work with. But you haven't stopped to think about how many different types of work the presses themselves do."

I had him divide his plants' manufacturing processes into types, and for the main process types, presses were positioned according to process flow. For each of a number of types of processes, an 80 cm-wide conveyor belt was set up down the middle and 12 presses were arranged on either side. A one-piece flow was then established by linking the process via this central conveyor. This easily permitted the reorganization of high-diversity, low-volume production into one-piece flow operations. Half a year later, production had been considerably streamlined:

- Productivity — up 100 percent
- Production period — reduced 90 percent
- Work-in-process — reduced 90 percent
- Defect rate — reduced 87.5 percent

Forming and Achieving Precision Are Different Functions

A form cutter was used to machine mounting blocks for turbine blades. The operation took a long time, and since form cutters are expensive and wear out quickly, repeated grinding was unavoidable.

"Machining a mounting block," I said to the head of the department, "requires the performance of two functions — forming and achieving precision. As far as forming is concerned, why not drill several holes with a boring machine and then *grind* them to the proper shape? Precision can be achieved by using the form cutter only at the last stage of the operation."

Putting this suggestion into effect reduced costs considerably; the operation time was cut by 75 percent and cutter life was extended fivefold (see *Figure 6-3*).

What Do Polishing Machines Do?

Z Machinery is a machine tool manufacturer whose polishing machines were always busy. Six polishing machines running overtime could not get the job done, so the firm was about to buy another machine.

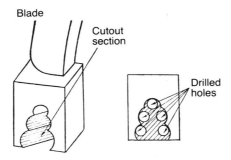

Blade

Cutout section

Drilled holes

FIGURE 6-3. **Turbine Blade Processing**

This was how things stood when I visited the factory to observe operations. The foreman explained that the polishing stone moves across a surface eleven times to polish it. I then asked the head of the shop unit to tell me just what it was that a polishing machine did. He gave me a puzzled look and told me that a polishing machine was for polishing.

"Look," I said, "a polishing machine performs two very different tasks. The first is grinding. In this instance, since an ordinary blade will not stand up to a surface that has been hardened by tempering or by rapid cooling, machining must be done with hard carborundum blades.

"The second task is polishing. This involves giving a mirrorlike finish to surfaces that milling machines or other machines in prior processes have left rough. What you're doing here is cleaning up rough surfaces. That means your goal is polishing. If all you're doing is cleaning up the cuts made by a milling machine, then why do you need eleven passes of the stone?

"Now then," I continued. "I want you to find out for me how much your milling machine is currently leaving to be polished."

The worker checked right away and found that the milling machine was leaving between 0.6 mm and 0.9 mm of material to be polished down.

If the polishing operation really consisted of grinding away the rough surfaces left by a cutter, then the next question was how much leeway the cutter required. I asked the worker to install a gauge that could measure with greater precision the cutting margin remaining after a cut had been made by the milling machine.

By the next time I visited the plant, a 0.09 mm margin had been found to be sufficient, so the gauge was used to ensure that the milling machine cut just that far. Now the job could be done with three passes of the stone, and this reduced the number of polishing machines used from six to two. In addition, it was, of course, no longer necessary to run the machines overtime.

In the final analysis, the milling operation had been on the safe side, cutting conservatively to avoid defects from overcuts. This increased the amount of material that had to be polished. Through the use of a precise measurement device, however, the material to be ground away was minimized, and it became possible to reduce drastically the number of passes made by polishing stones. Certainly, a solution would have been discovered sooner had a sustained effort been made to identify the true purpose of the polishing machines.

Here again, it's safe to say that the problem was insufficient precision in measurement rather than inadequate machining capacity.

Engraving and Oil Removal

In this operation, labels such as "magnification" and "lens performance" were engraved on the hoods of optical machinery. Since cutting oil was used in the course of engraving, subsequent plating could not be carried out unless triclene were used to remove the excess oil.

Manufacturing Department A, on the first floor, had oil-removal apparatus, so it was asked to carry out the job. Because the department had its own tasks to perform, however, oil removal always ended up on the back burner, becoming the source of troublesome delays. This, in turn, caused difficulties for Manufacturing Department D, the site of the operation on the fourth floor.

The people in Manufacturing Department D were in a quandary: When they asked the plant manager for oil-removal apparatus of their own, the request was flatly denied. The low volume of work involved, said the manager, simply did not justify specialized and expensive oil-removal equipment. "Why not have Manufacturing Department A do it for you the way it does now?"

When I decided to visit the engraving workshop, the department head was investigating the possibility of a compact, inexpensive oil-removal device. In the operation, cutting oil was poured on while the magnification, name, and other labels were engraved by a machine equipped with a profiling apparatus. After observing this, I turned to the department head and told him that I had come up with a satisfactory solution to the problem.

"A solution?" he exclaimed. "What is it?"

"All you have to do," I said, "is to eliminate the use of cutting oil."

"No oil? That won't work. You've got to have cutting oil to do machining."

I then asked him why oil was necessary.

"You use cutting oil for cutting. It's just common knowledge, isn't it?"

"And what does that mean," I asked, "that it's common knowledge?"

The department head fell silent.

"There are three reasons for using cutting oil," I explained.

"The first is to cool the blades. Temperatures rise because cutting generates heat, and higher temperatures affect the hardness of cutting tools. The primary effect of using cutting oil is to prevent this. This effect probably accounts for 50 percent of the use of cutting oil.

"The second reason is to remove cuttings. Shavings that adhere to cutting blades reduce sharpness and increase heat buildup, so they must be removed. Especially when you are cutting threads with a tap: the complete removal of cuttings between blades and between grooves in the tap will improve the cut of the thread and can increase tap life by 50 percent or so. This accounts for another 30 percent of the use of cutting oil.

"The third reason lies in the lubricating effect, which reduces friction during cutting. I think we can say that this accounts for the remaining 20 percent of oil use.

"Although it is generally thought that 100 percent of the reason for using cutting oil is lubrication, this is a mistake. The most important use of cutting oil is to cool the blades.

"If cooling is the most important reason for using cutting oil, then one is not obliged to use *oil* at all. For the sort of light cutting involved in engraving, why not come up with some other method of cooling — for example, simply lowering the temperature of the air?"

Rather than using oil, then, I suggested blowing compressed air on the blades. People on the shop floor strongly opposed this idea, saying it would shorten engraving blade life, but they allowed us to go ahead and test the method anyway. When we actually used compressed air, we found that it was sufficient to cool the blades. The principle effect was that all cuttings were blown away so that scrap from the cutting operation did not interfere with the tool. Along with minimizing wear and actually extending blade life by some 30 percent, this made it possible to produce extremely clean engravings.

Naturally, the need for oil removal was also eliminated, and this eliminated the problem of delays.

A majority of technicians at many plants still believe that "common knowledge" dictates the use of cutting oil when machining. It appears that objectives are not being thoroughly examined — that people are not questioning their goals. Why is this?

Steam Is Composed of Moisture and Heat

At a tea processing plant, steam is used to cook tea leaves. The leaves are more or less tough depending on the grade of tea, however, so the quantity of steam needs to be regulated accordingly.

Tea quality is determined by three factors: taste, aroma, and color. The considerable steaming required for tough-leaved Grade 3 teas, though, tends to wash away each of these attributes. There is a subtle knack involved in balancing the demands of tenderness against taste, aroma, and color, and the steaming operation calls for a great deal of skill.

What it came down to was that when high-temperature steaming was attempted, the increased moisture washed out taste, aroma, and color. This was the situation when I addressed myself to Mr. Horiuchi, a master teamaker.

"Let's think about what steaming means. The process is composed, is it not, of two parts: supplying moisture and supplying heat? The temperature has to be raised when the tea leaves are tough, right? But the way you are doing things now, you are adding more moisture than is necessary just so that you can apply large quantities of heat. Why not introduce moisture and heat separately?"

Following this suggestion, the plant adopted a method in which moisture is added in the form of mist, and heat is supplied in the form of hot air. This reduced the level of skill necessary to perform the operation and at the same time made it possible to produce tea of extremely high quality.

There Are Three Methods of Heating

Mr. Horiuchi, an officially designated "intangible cultural trea-sure," is considered a master of "hand-rubbed teamaking." I once vi-sited Mr. Horiuchi to observe his method of tea production. Once there, I noticed that, although charcoal had sufficed in the past for drying the tea, drying had been uneven ever since they had begun using propane gas. I happened to notice that results improved when an iron sheet was positioned between the propane gas and the tea rack.

"Why is the iron there," I asked?

"We don't really know," was the reply, "but when we tried it things improved."

I thought about this for a moment and then turned to Mr. Horiuchi.

"Listen," I said, "heating can take place in three ways: by con-duction, by convection, or by radiation. When you used charcoal, heat radiating from the glowing charcoal created convection currents on top and these dried the tea leaves as they passed through them.

With propane gas, however, the strong flames heat the air in the center and this heat passes first through the middle of the tea racks. Yet this retards drying of the tea at the periphery, doesn't it, so the leaves do not dry uniformly?

"When a sheet of iron is placed in the middle, even when temper-atures in the center are high, the iron conducts heat across its entire surface and radiation from the sheet in turn heats all the upper air by means of convection. This means that the tea is dried uniformly. In the final analysis, local heat from the propane gas burners is spread out across the entire surface by means of the iron sheet."

Here, the knowledge that things improved when an iron sheet was in place amounted to mere know-how. On the other hand, under-standing why this improved things was "know-why": it is know-why that makes it possible to apply the same approach in many other situations.

Danger Interlocks and Safety Interlocks

Interlocking in automation means to assure safety by verifying the completion of one motion before moving on to the next motion.

In a plastic molding operation, interlock functions were provided at each juncture between motions:

- A product removal device was activated and entered the mold after verifying that the mold had opened.
- After removing the product, the device retreated; motions to close the mold began when the removal device completed its motion.

These procedures were improved as follows:

1. Four-tenths of a second are saved by bringing the product removal device to within 50 mm of the mold while the mold is still closed.
2. Rather than starting the product removal device after the mold has completed its opening movement, the device is set in motion as soon as the two halves of the mold have moved apart by about 10 mm more than is necessary to permit entrance of the removal device. The point here is that since the mold is opening, the interlock is for motion in a safe direction. This cut 0.8 seconds off the previous time for the operation.
3. Next, rather than closing the molds after the product removal device had removed the product and completed its motion, 1.2 seconds were saved by beginning the closing motion as soon as the removal device had withdrawn to about 50 mm beyond the range of mold opening and closing movements. Here again, since the product removal device is moving away from the mold, the interlock involves motion in a safe direction.

Thus there are two types of interlocks: interlocks for movement toward danger — *danger interlocks* — and interlocks for movement toward safety — *safety interlocks*. If the product removal device is to enter the mold when the mold is closing, then a danger interlock is called for and safety must be verified before the device is set in motion. If the mold is in the process of opening, however, then the product removal device can be activated as soon as there is enough clearance so that the device will not interfere with the mold.

Thus, it helps to distinguish between danger and safety interlocks.

In this particular example, reducing times for safety interlocks cut a previous cycle time of 25 seconds to 22.6 seconds:

$$25 \text{ sec} - (0.4 \text{ sec} + 0.8 \text{ sec} + 1.2 \text{ sec}) = 22.6 \text{ sec.}$$

In terms of production output, this amounted to a real increase of 10.6 percent.

Z — SYSTEMATIC GOALS

Goals and Means Trade Places

We must learn to think of making progress as moving toward goals, because goals often become means at a higher level. When we think about a goal we are really considering the means toward an even higher-order goal. Thus, it is crucial to understand how goals and means "trade places."

For example, to achieve the goal of filling our bellies when we are hungry, we adopt the means of eating. Filling our bellies, however is only a means for attaining the higher-order goal of taking in nourishment. Similarly, taking in nourishment is actually a means for attaining an even higher-order goal: maintaining life. Furthermore, the maintenance of life is perhaps nothing more than a means to the goal of species survival. At this point, the issue is largely controlled by one's view of life.

As we can see, goals and means trade places with one another in a chain, and the means or measures we choose will vary considerably depending upon what level of goal we recognize.

Similarly, the Toyota production system's focus on the "5 Whys" emphasizes the fact that we can discover the true causes of things by asking why, why, why, why, and why, over and over again. Unless we are aware that goals and means trade places with one another, and unless we persist in tracking each issue to its source, our improvements will remain superficial and inconclusive and we will never be able to improve in essential, fundamental ways.

Consider the following example, which involves assembling a bolt and a nut:

1. Grasp the bolt with the right hand.
2. While adjusting the bolt's orientation, transfer it to the left hand.
3. Hold the bolt with the left hand.
4. Grasp the nut with the right hand.
5. Transfer it while adjusting its orientation with the right hand.
6. Assemble the two.
7. Transfer the assembly with the left hand to the storage bin.
8. Place it in the storage bin.

This sequence of operations is shown in *Figure 6- 4* as a chain of ends and means.

When the purpose of each work element is studied, the following questions can be asked:

1. Concerning the first step, ask:
   • Is there a better way of grasping the bolt?
   • Can the bolts be made easier to grasp?
   • Are the distance and direction of the hand movement optimal?

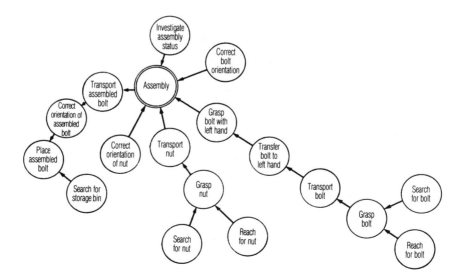

FIGURE 6-4. Series of Ends and Means

2. Concerning the second step, ask:
   - Why is it necessary to adjust the bolt's orientation?
   - Can the bolt be simply tossed to the left hand?
3. Concerning the third step, ask:
   - Can the bolt be held with something other than the hand?
4. Concerning the fourth step, ask:
   - Is there a better way of holding the bolt?
   - Can the bolt be made easier to hold?
   - Can the distance and the direction of the hand movement be improved?
5. Concerning the fifth step, ask:
   - Why does the orientation of the nut have to be adjusted?
6. Concerning the sixth step, ask:
   - Is there a better way of assembling them?
7. Concerning the seventh step, ask:
   - Can the location and orientation of the storage bin be improved?
8. Concerning the eighth step, ask:
   - Can a better storage bin be used to facilitate storage?
   - Should the assembly be placed in a box?

In this way, the means for achieving each objective is studied.

However, when you consider the three therbligs of (1) grasping the bolt with the right hand, (2) transferring the bolt to the left hand while adjusting its orientation, and (3) grasping the bolt with the left hand as a chain of ends and means, a question that arises is why not grasp the bolt with the left hand to begin with. This leads to an improvement, namely, placing the bolts on the left side from the start.

The actions of (7) transferring the assembly to the storage bin with the left hand and (8) placing it in the storage bin may be done in other ways through linkage to the next process.

Thinking of actions as a means to an end provides new ways of looking for possible improvements.

It is important not to limit ourselves to considering only immediate goals but rather to remember that one objective is but a means for achieving higher goals. This attitude, which frequently leads to truly dramatic improvements, should not be forgotten. Moreover, this attitude has something in common with the emphasis placed by the Toyota production system on asking "Why?" five times.

Figure 6-5 shows the results of a motion study for the job just described. By resorting to simultaneous motions consisting of transferring the assembly to the storage bin with the left hand and grasping a bolt with the right hand, the otherwise inevitable delays before the first left-hand movement and at the end of the right-hand movement are eliminated. This reduces the required time by 15 percent and increases production by 117.7 percent.

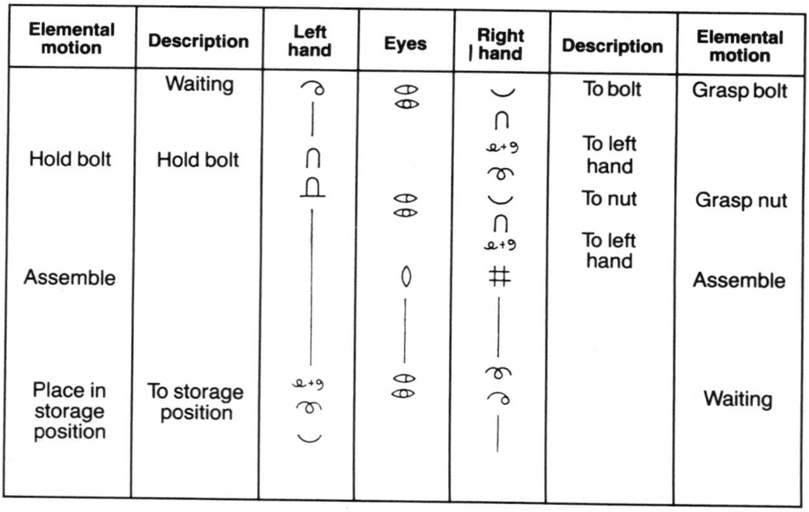

Elemental motion	Description	Left hand	Eyes	Right hand	Description	Elemental motion
	Waiting				To bolt	Grasp bolt
Hold bolt	Hold bolt				To left hand	
					To nut	Grasp nut
					To left hand	
Assemble						Assemble
Place in storage position	To storage position					Waiting

FIGURE 6-5. **Motion Study of Current Method**

When both hand motions are unavoidably delayed, we recognize this as waiting. However, we tend to overlook waiting caused by the left hand's being inactive while the right hand is in motion or by the right hand's being inactive while the left hand is in motion. If the structure of the task is improved as shown in *Figure 6-6*, so that the bolts are placed on the left side and a washboard-shaped rotating jig is used, it becomes possible to (1) grasp a bolt with the left hand and a nut with the right hand simultaneously, (2) screw the bolt into the nut in one or two turns, and (3) slide the assembly along the surface of the rotating jig so as to screw on the nut and leave the screwed-together assembly as is.

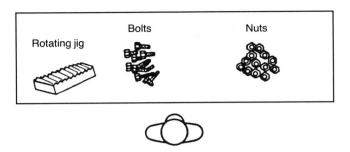

FIGURE 6-6. Improvement Through Conversion of Ends and Means

This improvement reduces the required time by 60 percent and increases production by 250 percent. Obviously, interchanging means and ends and being on the lookout for ever-higher objectives frequently result in significant benefits.

"Know-how" Alone Isn't Enough; You Need "Know-why"

Akira Shibata, executive director of Daihō Industries, once gave me a good piece of advice. Although it is considered important to have a firm grasp of "know-how"; know-how is not enough by itself. He explained that "if know-how is all that's passed along, you may be able to perform a task the way it was taught, but you won't know what to do when conditions change or the least bit of trouble crops up. If, on the other hand, you also understand why things are the way they are — the "know-why" of the task — then you will be able both to cope with changes, and apply your knowledge to other tasks."

This impressed me as being right on the mark. All too often, people visit other plants only to copy their methods. Or, they are satisfied to learn know-how, but too lazy to raise know-how to know-why and find out *why* things are done the way they are. We must make the effort to grasp what lies behind even the most superficial method.

Does Heating Cause Distortion?

The myth that heating and cooling necessarily induce distortion is widely believed by plant technicians. Are they right? Absolutely not!

Heating does cause materials to expand, and cooling causes them to contract, but that does not necessarily mean heating or cooling will cause distortion. The problem is that the various parts of a product are not heated or cooled uniformly. Thus, the true cause of distortion is that temperatures are not raised or lowered uniformly or at a uniform speed.

At S Electric, in an operation for solenoid parts, two cylindrical parts were fit together. A ring of solder was placed between the two parts and then the parts were joined by melting the solder with a gas burner. In the method used, the product was held in a lathe chuck and the gas burner flame melted the solder and formed the joint as the product was slowly turned at a rate of about five revolutions per minute. Distortion seemed inevitable. The cylindrical joints became elongated and it took considerable effort to make them round again. There seemed to be no way to make the parts stay perfectly round.

When I suggested that the distortions should not be introduced in the first place, the plant manager maintained that heating inevitably generated distortions.

"Not at all," I replied. "What you have to do is heat and cool the material uniformly."

This having been said, the following procedures were adopted for the operation:

- The rate of lathe rotation was increased to 300 revolutions per minute. With the burner flame blown against the workpiece, this high-speed rotation meant that the entire circumference was heated uniformly. The slow rotation used in the previous method had allowed only part of the circumference to be heated at a time which generated distortions.
- The burner flame — used to melt the solder — was reduced and then gradually enlarged. This allowed heat to be conducted adequately from the joint to the main body of the workpiece and therefore did away with abrupt temperature transitions near the joint.
- Similarly, when heating was completed, the burner flame was gradually reduced to avoid causing any extreme temperature changes.

These new procedures completely eliminated welding distortions and operations to correct distortion.

This experience dealt a mortal blow to the myth that heating necessarily induces distortion.

Change Adjustments to Settings

At U Television, adjustment was the final stage of the television assembly process. Skilled workers looked at waves on an oscilloscope and tightened an adjustment screw accordingly. The process took a long time and demanded a high level of skill. After watching the task for a while, I turned to the head of the Manufacturing Division and asked him whether the actual purpose of the task was to adjust the television sets. "It seems to me," I said, "that the real job is to find the right settings."

"What do you mean?"

"When I watch the task as it's being performed now, the worker turns the adjustment screw first to the right and then to the left. This is clearly adjusting. Even so, the real task is surely to set the screw at the proper place."

"If that's true, then all the worker should have to do is turn the screw to the left or right and stop at the proper place."

We then made the following changes:

- Oscilloscope waveforms were converted into numerical voltage readings.
- Because it was difficult to make small turns of 3 mm adjustment screws with a small screwdriver, a 60 mm diameter circular plate was mounted on the driver. With a graduated scale at the circumference of this plate, screws could be turned by as little as one-twentieth of a revolution, making it possible to stop turning precisely when the numerical readout reached zero.

These improvements permitted ordinary workers to perform the task and cut the time required for the job in half. In the final analysis, improving the precision of settings enabled the plant to eliminate adjustments.

Removing Paint from Masks Does Not Necessarily Mean Dissolving the Paint

Painting often involves the use of masks to ensure that only certain areas are painted. Paint adheres to the masks, however, and removing the paint often turns into a major problem. Typically, the mask is soaked in thinner to dissolve paint adhering to the surface. Since this is not done until after the mask has been used many times, removing the paint from the mask takes quite a long time.

Yet removing paint from a mask does not necessarily mean dissolving the paint. It simply means taking paint off the surface of the mask. Thus, it is more effective to strip paint off with a blade or a brush. The entire procedure can be completed in a very short time if only the remaining paint is dissolved with thinner.

In any event, it is crucial to recognize that the goal is to *remove* paint, not *dissolve* it.

Furthermore, while it may be effective to dissolve paint with thinner where the paint buildup is slight, other successful techniques include agitating the mask, spraying on thinner, or soaking the mask in a moving stream of thinner.

Use Washing to Prevent Buildups Rather Than to Remove Buildups

Machine tools generate cuttings and sometimes these cuttings are removed by a worker with a brush. Because this is inefficient, oil or some other fluid can be used to wash away shavings. Cuttings are not always easily washed away, however. The job is much simpler if cuttings are washed away continuously rather than after large clumps have accumulated. An important trick, then, is to use washing to prevent buildups rather than to remove buildups.

7

Basic Approaches
to Improvement

(III) Better Means

No improvement could take place in this world if there were only a single means to each end. Indeed, it is only when one believes in the existence of multiple means that the possibility of improvement first appears.

Progress will never pay a visit to those who stubbornly insist that their way is right and no other means are possible. Yet if we keep an open mind and believe that there are several possible means to each end, improvement ideas will emerge through the process of selecting the best method.

Thus, the single most important prerequisite for improvement is an open mind.

MULTIPLE MEANS TO A SINGLE END

If we believed there were only one means to each end, any sort of improvement would be impossible.

Yet, all too often we imagine that only our current methods will bring about the ends we are aiming for. Even if we don't make that assumption, we frequently persuade ourselves that current methods are the best. These attitudes will ensure that improvement never takes place. Indeed, we may even end up believing that current methods are goals in themselves.

Our current approach is never more than a means. Beyond it lies another goal, which is itself only a means toward a higher goal. If we understand this and pursue our goal vigorously, we can expect to discover even better methods. At the same time, even more means will present themselves if we consider our goals or ends from a variety of perspectives.

If today is going to be any different from yesterday, we must blaze new trails every day.

Smoothing Rough Surfaces with Unhulled Rice

At one company, sandpaper was used to smooth the rough surfaces inevitably remaining on pressure-formed ebonite switch holders. Ebonite is hard and brittle, so that while rubbing it too hard could damage the material, rubbing it lightly took a great deal of time. The task was made all the more frustrating because the sandpaper wore out quickly.

At this point a decision was made to place the product in a drum with an abrasive and rotate the drum to remove the rough surfaces. No suitable abrasive could be found, however. Steel pellets were tried first, but they produced defects in the form of rounded edges. Plastic beads were tried next, but this time the abrasive material wore down too quickly. Moreover, efficiency was poor because it took such a long time to smooth the rough surfaces. A variety of tests were conducted to find an abrasive that could satisfy the contradictory demands of softness and sharp cutting ability, but no suitable substance turned up.

Eventually, Mr. A, the second son of a farmer, recalled that his family used to remove the dirty skins of potatoes by rotating them in unhulled rice. When he suggested using unhulled rice in the plant, everyone laughed at the idea and said it was silly, but the plant manager was willing to give the idea a try.

Excellent results were obtained from a test using the rice. The folds in each rice grain are knife-sharp, but the air inside the grain makes it soft overall. The rice did not damage the product or take a long time to smooth the rough surfaces.

Too often we reject ideas we have tested only in our heads. Even approaches that seem ridiculous, however, cannot be evaluated unless we give them a try. I have had numerous experiences in which — despite advice to the contrary — actually testing an idea yielded first-rate results. If someone suggested to you that unhulled rice would make an excellent abrasive for smoothing rough surfaces, would you immediately agree to give the idea a try? When we have the courage to try them, such unexpected methods often lead to success.

Attaching Fiberglass

This example involves the construction of boats used to collect edible seaweed in the Ariake Sea off the island of Kyūshū.

The outer hull of each boat was made of a plastic material, and several layers of fiberglass attached with adhesives to the interior made the boats both strong and light. The boats were popular, because they lasted a long time; unlike wooden boats they were not subject to rotting.

Y Industries had learned how to manufacture these boats from a high-tech plant in Osaka, but it could not manage to produce a high-quality product. Labor costs were unexpectedly high, and the business was not profitable. For these reasons, I was called in to observe the operation.

- First, fiberglass was attached and then painted with adhesive.
- This inevitably trapped air inside, so holes were bored to remove air bubbles.
- The surface was rubbed with a roller to distribute the remaining air bubbles uniformly.

When these air removal and air bubble dispersion operations were not carried out carefully, the hulls could break. These operations became the crucial factors determining quality.

The plant manager hoped there might be some quick, easy method for removing air and dispersing bubbles by machine rather than by hand. He lamented that things were not going smoothly even though his plant adhered faithfully to the know-how it had learned from the plant in Osaka.

After observing the operation for a while, I suggested to the plant manager that a better method existed.

"A better method?" he exclaimed, "what method is that?"

"All you have to do," I said, "is to attach the fiberglass so that air can't get into it in the first place."

"That won't work. Air gets in even at the plant in Osaka."

"What you must do is simply dip the fiberglass into the adhesive," I said.

In the new procedure, then, the adhesive is kept in a container, and sheets of fiberglass are dipped into the liquid adhesive. Since the liquid adhesive seeps into the fiberglass from below, any air inside the fiberglass is pushed out the top. This method completely eliminated air bubbles in the glass wool.

Now the whole operation is conducted as follows:

- Adhesive is first spread generously on the inside of the hull.
- Fiberglass is spread on top.
- When the adhesive has soaked through and risen to the top, a roller is applied to the entire surface and all air is removed.
- Another generous layer of adhesive is applied on top.
- Fiberglass is spread on top.

Thus, the operation has essentially been reversed. Before, adhesive was spread over the fiberglass; now, the fiberglass is laid over a coating of adhesive. This improvement resulted in extremely high quality and reduced labor costs to one-fifth of what they were.

In the final analysis, it would have been better if more rigorous thought had been given to the essential nature of the task.

Coating Washers with Rustproofing Oil

In this operation the surfaces of spring washers are coated with rustproofing oil. Originally, this was carried out as follows:

- Place a number of washers in a cage and dip into liquid rustproofing oil.
- Place cage in a holding area to allow excess oil to drain off.
- After washers have dried to a certain degree, collect washers, count out specified number, and place in packing crates.

Even though workers carried out this task wearing rubber gloves, the rustproofing oil inevitably harmed their hands. There were complaints from the shop floor, furthermore, that it was difficult to carry out the operation with gloves on. This was a job no one enjoyed — especially because the workers were female part-timers who very much disliked the fact that it was rough on their hands.

I suggested the following improvements:

- Specified numbers of dried spring washers are placed in packing crates.
- Rustproofing oil is sprayed onto the tops of the washers.

The group leader opposed this idea, saying that the oil would not coat the entire surfaces of washers that were close together. We made a trial run anyway, and obtained magnificent results. Although only the tops of the washers were sprayed, the rustproofing oil spread to the entire surface of each washer through osmosis. An appropriate amount of oil adhered to each washer, so that quality actually improved. Unlike before, there was no excess. No oil at all adhered to workers' hands and complaints of rough hands ended. Moreover, the amount of rustproofing oil used dropped to one-tenth of what it had been.

We should never assume that an idea for improvement will not work. Only by giving it a try can we know for certain whether it will work.

Peeling the Protective Film Off Double-Stick Tape

Quite a few jobs these days involve sticking double-sided adhesive material to the backs of nameplates or labels and then attaching these items to fenders or other parts. To prevent these adhesives from sticking to other items during handling, the adhesive surfaces are protected by thin vinyl films. Peeling off this protective film, however, can be a considerable chore.

In many cases, a worker inserts a fingernail between the adhesive and the film and then peels off the entire film. Workers dislike this operation, though, because after peeling off a number of films, fingernails break and fingertips show signs of wear and tear.

At Y Synthetics, workers were unhappy about this peeling operation and would not do it for long. At this point the following suggestion was made: "Why not use a nozzle to blow compressed air under the corner of the protective film? Since very different effects will be obtained depending on the angle of the nozzle, test a number of angles to find the best one."

Tests were begun immediately. They showed that this technique not only lifted the corner of the film — it blew the entire film off. At this point, a special mechanism was constructed:

- The compressed air nozzle was secured at a suitable angle.
- The nozzle was flattened and squared off so that it emitted a knife-shaped jet of air.
- When a nameplate is pressed into a certain position, the compressed air is blown out.
- The protective film that has been peeled off is held by a vacuum suction device and placed in a trash bin.
- Although the 4 kg/mm² air pressure ordinarily used in the plant was sufficient to do the job, using 6 kg/mm² in cases of powerful adhesion nearly always allowed the protective film to come off by itself.

This completely eliminated complaints about painful fingernails.

Small Minds Want More Space

"The plant is too small."

"This operation needs more room."

Such complaints are heard quite often in production plants. When you look a little further into the matter, however, these pleas for more space are frequently the products of small minds. For example, take the complaint that "the plant is too small." Again and again, when we actually examine the plant in question, we find that the space occupied by idle work-in-process takes up 70 percent of the total area. As often as not, this idle space can be reduced by diminishing processing lot sizes and it can be obviated entirely by instituting one-piece flow operations in earlier and subsequent processes.

As for the lament that "this operation needs more room," space requirements can be dramatically cut by increasing the frequency of parts supply or by setting up parts storage areas in three dimensions so as to cut down on the floor space such storage occupies.

Surprisingly, the opportunity to use space above and below conveyors is often missed. Rotating parts bins also make it possible to cut back tremendously on the "domain of operations."

To summarize:

- Use vertical space.
- Since available room is determined by the interaction of space and time, cutting idle time in half means to cut room needed for storage in half.

In any case, it is essential to realize that it is a small mind that wants more space.

Not Enough Resourcefulness

Sometimes when I go into a production plant and try to do something new, I am told that it will not work because "there aren't enough people" or "there aren't enough machines." Quite often, though, the real problem is not enough resourcefulness. Often when we look closely at the problem and observe the work area, possibilities for creating extra workers present themselves because, for example:

- No more than 30 percent of the people are doing useful work.
- Simple devices will allow some procedures to be mechanized.
- Machine operators can run other machines while their own machines are engaged in automatic processing.

Moreover, when we take the time to really look at the operation of machines, we find a surprising number of instances in which main processing operation times are short and much of the work is taken up by auxiliary operations, such as mounting and removing items.

"Because" Never Solves Anything

The "National Because League" is one of the most powerful groups in Japan. How often we say, "It won't work because of this" or, "It's impossible because of that." The arguments we come up with are cogent and plentiful.

But no matter how many persuasive reasons we cite, no problem was ever solved by arguing in terms of "because."

The biggest problems, however, are the words that come after the "because." The final answer to the problem will depend on whether we say, "It won't work because of this, so let's give up" or, "It won't work because of this, but how could we do it so that it will work?"

Since we are discussing real problems, it is inevitable that the first thing we think of when a problem is raised is *why* something will not work. Whether many plans for improvement will see the light of day, however, depends on the next thing we think. Will we say, "It won't work because of such and such" or "How can we make it work?"

This is the difference between "assuming" and "thinking."

Mean Values Are Maximally Undependable Values

The concept of mean values is often considered important in our understanding of phenomena. In fact, however, a mean value is nothing more than the average of actual values and is not in any way an expression of fact.

Although mean values may be convenient for grasping overall tendencies, maximum values or minimum values are frequently more significant when we actually want to improve a task. Asking what generates the differential between maximum values and minimum values often gives us information that can help us identify areas needing improvement.

In brief, as we try to understand phenomena, we must decide whether we want merely to perceive the outline of a problem, or whether we want to comprehend it so that we can find a solution and make improvements.

8

Stage Three:
Making Plans for Improvement

This chapter discusses the steps involved in actually putting together plans for improvement.

LOCKING IN ON THE PROBLEM

We lock in on a problem when we're not satisfied with the way a job is performed and ask why a particular method is used. At this stage there is doubt and dissatisfaction with the status quo — doubt and dissatisfaction that arose in response to a thorough pursuit of goals, when we asked, "What are the real objectives of this job?" As we saw in Chapter Five, the problem should be considered from all angles:

- X: focus
- Y: identify multiple goals
- Z: systematically pursue higher-order goals

At this stage, no thought whatsoever should be given to specific ideas. If an idea comes up, we may make a note of it, but we must not be imprisoned by it. This weakens the spirit of criticism and hinders locking in on subsequent problems. In this sense, it is extremely important that *locking in on the problem* be separated from *brainstorming*.

Keep Locking in on Problems Separate from Brainstorming

Locking in on a problem occurs when we entertain doubts about the status quo and formulate specific criticisms. Brainstorming, on the other hand, is our response to having locked in on a problem; essentially it involves coming to terms with reality. In this sense, just as there are positive and negative mental activities, the functioning of the mind is said to involve the interplay of both locking in and brainstorming.

It follows that brainstorming immediately after locking in on a problem will neutralize and weaken the critical mind and, in the end, few plans for improvement will be forthcoming. Thus, it is crucial to keep the process of locking in on a problem separate. In other words, we concentrate on that task alone and avoid thinking of specific ideas for change. If an idea comes up, we may make a note of it *and then forget it*. A desirable approach is to begin thinking of ideas that correspond to various observations we've made only *after* the last observation about the status quo has been made.

The observations that we make in locking in on problems *do not* foreshadow specific ideas; they are purely an intensive search for goals, the focusing of our attention — through exhaustive criticism — on why certain things are done. It is perfectly acceptable if:

- Two ideas are forthcoming for observation no. 1
- There are no ideas for observation no. 2
- No ideas at all come to mind for observation no. 3
- There are five ideas for observation no. 4

Someone else may come along and say "Hey! I've got an idea for that." Or we may hit on more ideas later on.

In any event, observing or locking in on problems is the key that opens a rich treasure house of improvement ideas, and this is why it is important to record observed problems separately even if no ideas for dealing with them immediately present themselves. The treasure house may look empty in the morning, but the afternoon sunshine can illuminate new discoveries. How we look at things changes over time and new ideas for dealing with problems show up suddenly where none were visible before.

The act of locking in on problems sows the seeds for improvement; strict separation of observing and brainstorming is an invariable condition for generating many improvements.

BRAINSTORMING

During the brainstorming stage, we come up with the means of responding to goals.

Since a single goal or end can have a number of means associated with it, numerous ideas can undoubtedly address a single observed problem. Moreover, if there are what we may term parallel ideas for approaching a given problem — for example, securing objects with bolts or with cams — there are also completely different alternatives conceivable (such as securing objects via interlocking).

Just as there are highly suitable ideas, there will also be ideas to be discarded. It does not matter, in short, if ideas overlap or contradict one another; every effort should be made to come up with large numbers of them. Group brainstorming can be extremely effective for this.

At this stage, judgment is inappropriate. Making judgments about tentative ideas will end up nipping them in the bud. In other words, brainstorming must focus solely on generating ideas without any type of criticism.

Keep Brainstorming Separate from Judgment

Brainstorming, in which various ideas for improvement are proposed, is a creative process, while judgment, in which specific aspects of ideas are rejected, is a critical process. Quite often, we may withhold ideas if we were worried that someone might criticize them. Since this is undesirable, it is important, in formulating plans for improvement, to have any and all ideas put forward at the brainstorming stage without any criticism whatsoever, and to have judgment begin only *after* all ideas have been presented.

Not only is criticism (judgment) by others inadvisable, it is undesirable for an individual to criticize his or her own ideas immediately after having aired them. When someone is coming up with ideas, it is important for him or her to bear in mind that *judgment comes later*. This is an absolute precondition for generating improvement plans in large numbers. According to a psychologist's report, over 60 percent more ideas are generated in an atmosphere where there is no criticism whatsoever.

We have already said that locking in on problems should be kept separate from brainstorming, but it is 100 times more vital to keep brainstorming absolutely separate from judgment. This, indeed, is the essence of brainstorming.

Shin-Tō Plastics set up what it calls a brainstorming room and displayed on its walls both set procedures for coming up with ideas and the Four Rules of Brainstorming. "No criticism may take place in this room," it is stipulated. "A fine of ¥ 100 will be levied for each criticism." This has reportedly put an end to the custom of criticism.

Resourcefulness and Money Offset One Another

How often we hear that someone would like to make improvements but is hampered by the cost! Actually, since resourcefulness and money offset one another, someone with little resourcefulness must use a great deal of money, while someone with a great deal of resourcefulness can get by with very little money. The superior improvement scheme uses little money and a great deal of resourcefulness.

FIGURE 8-1.

We need to realize that complaints about inadequate this or that really boil down to inadequate resourcefulness. This brings to mind the following story.

H Industries manufactures metal parts for automobiles, and numerous magnetic conveyors are used on its processing lines. These conveyors grip pieces of metal and transport them vertically by running conveyors along magnetic surfaces. The devices provide quite a convenient means of transportation because metal pieces of any size or shape can be moved securely either up or down.

One day, the purchasing manager for a customer came to visit the plant. After seeing a conveyor, he took off a piece of metal that was being transported and brought it near some iron filings. When he did, the residual magnetism in the metal picked up all the filings. "We can't have residual magnetism in the metal," he said. "I want you to get rid of all your magnetic conveyors."

The plant used so many magnetic conveyors that getting rid of them would have posed a considerable problem, so at this point I was consulted about what might be done. I immediately went to the plant and observed the situation there. Then I addressed myself to the head of the production department:

"There's no reason to get rid of your magnetic conveyors," I said. "Since all you have to do is keep residual magnetism out of metal pieces delivered to D Technical Research Industries, why not look into a demagnetizer?"

When I visited the same plant the following month, I asked what had happened about the demagnetizer.

"Demagnetizers are available," I was told, "but they run as much as ¥ 1.5 million ($5,000) — so expensive that we've held back on using them." In response to this, I made another suggestion to the production department head: "Why don't you study a demagnetizer and find out exactly what the central mechanism is that actually demagnetizes?"

A month later I went to the plant again and the department head reported that they had made a demagnetizer. Right away, I went to the shop floor where metal pieces were being completely demagnetized as they passed beneath two simple magnetos mounted above the conveyor line at the final inspection process.

In the final analysis, the commercial demagnetizers turned out to be expensive because of various accessory devices, and the real demagnetization function merely involved passing objects through the magnetos' magnetic field. Thus, an investment of around ¥ 100,000 ($300) made it possible to demagnetize the metal pieces, and this eliminated subsequent claims from the customer.

Often, improvement can be had at a surprisingly modest price by thoroughly hunting down the real issues involved. Indeed, perhaps this is an example of improvement through resourcefulness rather than money.

Twelve Rules for Idea Formulation

Idea formulation for improvement can be broadly categorized into the following two groups: elimination and optimization.

Elimination means that the purpose of the job can be accomplished even if the job is eliminated. This is the best remedy. The next approach is to think of a better way of doing a job that cannot be eliminated. This is *optimization*. It will be necessary to consider many different approaches.

1. Elimination (Can It Be Eliminated?)

Example: Cutting and burrs. One operation at plant S consisted of cutting oval valves used in carburetors. About 20 sheets were laid on top of one another and cut at the same time. Burrs were always present on the last sheet, and these required manual elimination. However, because of the need for a high degree of precision, nearly all the manually reworked sheets had to be discarded owing to their poor finish. Because the sheets were made of expensive phosphor bronze, this became a problem.

I said to the workers, "When you place five wooden boards on top of one another and cut them with a saw, the top four boards will be cut without burrs but not the fifth and final board. Why?"

No answer.

I continued, "Because the top four boards are each supported by the board below, which resists the cutting force of the saw blade. Because the fifth board does not have a supporting board below it, the saw tends to tear the material and leave burrs."

"We know that scissors don't leave behind burrs as they shear, because the top and the bottom blades meet together in a line. We also know that scissors don't cut well if the two blades aren't properly aligned."

"Because the present cutting job is similar to shearing, burrs won't be produced if you provide a support that is aligned with the cutting blade. Also, if you dramatically increase the rotational speed of the cutter when finishing the cut and, at the same time, dramatically reduce the grain depth of the cut, the number of burrs will be reduced. Moreover, if, instead of feeding the saw blade vertically, it is fed in a horizontal direction with the blade upright, the resistance that this generates to the cutting blade will minimize the number of burrs produced in the last sheet."

An aluminum plate with the same shape as the phosphor bronze stock from which oval valves were cut was placed in the position of the last phosphor bronze plate. When the sheets were cut, burrs were seen in the aluminum plate but not in the phosphor bronze products. The aluminum plate had served as a "decoy." After several dozen cuts, the aluminum plate was replaced with new aluminum plate. This procedure totally kept burrs from forming on the phosphor bronze valves. The aluminum plates that were thus sacrificed were melted down and reused.

When grinding the cutter blades for juicers, burrs formed when cutter blades were ground one at a time. The burrs had to be removed by being ground off the rear surface, a process that reduced the sharpness of the cutter blade. Even here it was found that cutting many blades at a time using a "decoy" plate significantly improved productivity.

While the problem of burrs can be solved by eliminating the burrs after they occur, a better way is to prevent their formation. The use of decoys is an efficient way to do this.

2. Forwards and Backwards: Reversal

Example: Weighing a casting. When I visited the casting plant at a railroad works, I saw a cylinder liner weighing more than 50 kilograms being weighed on a scale. Two workers passed a pipe through the liner, hoisted it onto the scale, weighed it, and then lifted it off and lowered it to the ground using the pipe. Other items were lifted and lowered repeatedly to be weighed. After an hour, the two workers were sweating. I looked for ways to make their job easier. After thinking for some time, I realized that burying the scale in the ground would eliminate the need to lift the items up to be weighed (*Figure 8-2*). A single worker can roll cylindrical items like cylinder liners onto the scale. Other items also can be weighed with greater ease. The objective of weighing the item is accomplished with less effort.

Example: Replacing a fuel pipe. I was asked to attend a meeting where the results of improvements implemented at the Smelting Division of company M, a mining company, were to be announced.

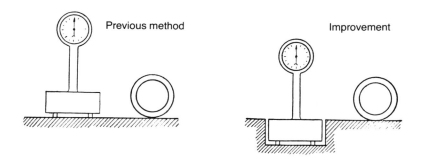

FIGURE 8-2. Measuring the Weight of Castings

About a dozen good examples of improvements were presented. The example that impressed me most was one entitled "shortening fuel-pipe replacement time."

The original procedure consisted of the following. To melt copper, a stainless steel fuel pipe was shoved into the middle of a melting furnace and fuel was blown in through it. As the tip of the fuel pipe burned away, the pipe was shoved farther and farther into the furnace to inject the fuel. Once the melting was completed and the molten material was discharged, the fuel pipe was removed. However, because of pipe deformation caused by heat and by the slag adhering to it, a strong force, frequently applied with a winch, was required to remove the pipe. The tuyere of the furnace would be severely damaged during pipe removal. Repairing the tuyere with refractory material and drying the refractory material required about one hour for setup.

Improvement was as follows. A pipe made of mild steel was connected to the stainless steel fuel pipe with a joint. As the stainless fuel pipe burned away, it was shoved farther and farther in, to inject the fuel. When melting was completed and the molten material discharged, the joint and the mild steel pipe were removed. The shortened stainless steel fuel pipe was hammered into the furnace. Even if the portion of the fuel pipe inside the furnace was deformed or had slag adhering to it, the outer pipe was not deformed and was easily removed without damaging the tuyere. Because the setup consisted only of replacing the seal, the setup time was only about five minutes. The force required for pipe replacement was also minimal.

I was asked the next day to evaluate all the various improvement plans. I replied: "There were many good examples, and each of them impressed me. I was most impressed, however, with the fuel-pipe replacement plan. Improvement of that procedure traditionally focused on the removal of the fuel pipe. I rate highly the different approach that was taken — namely, that the only requirement was to eliminate the fuel pipe from the tuyere, and that one way of doing this was to drop the pipe way into the furnace."

"The improvement is very simple once you are shown how it is done. It must be remembered, however, that this improvement represents a breakthrough from the conventional approach and focuses on a higher objective, namely, to eliminate the fuel pipe from the tuyere."

"You have all probably heard of a natural spring in Suizenji Park located in Kumamoto City. You probably know of a singer named Kiyoko Suizenji, who was born and raised near the park and who bears the same name as the park. In one of her songs, she sings, 'If pushing doesn't work, trying pulling.' The essence of that improvement lay in reversing the conventional approach: 'If pulling doesn't work, trying pushing.'"

In any case, there are numerous examples in which pulling works where pushing fails or pushing works where pulling fails.

3. Normality and Exceptions

An exception is something that occurs only rarely, maybe two or three times in a hundred. Therefore, if various operations can be treated as exceptions, the management process is greatly simplified.

Example: What is absence from work? Company R decided to improve its payroll processing. I was told that the attendance clerk's job took too much time. So I checked out what the clerk did.

Each worker would deposit his or her attendance card, taken home the day before, in card boxes according to work station, located by the gate. At a designated time, the attendance clerk would sort the attendance cards by job number, stamping "present" on them. Using the attendance cards as a guide, the clerk would then stamp "present" on the attendance chart. Next, the clerk would check the attendance charts maintained at each work station. Absences for paid vacations or illness and other previously reported absences were duly marked on the attendance chart. Unauthorized absences were recorded as "absent without notice."

The above procedure could be grouped into three tasks:

- Sorting the attendance cards by job number.
- Sorting the "absents" and the "presents."
- Checking the attendance charts maintained at each work station.

I started by improving the task of sorting the attendance cards by job number. To do that, I had two card bins installed, the right one being the departure card bin and the left one being the arrival card bin (*Figure 8-3*).

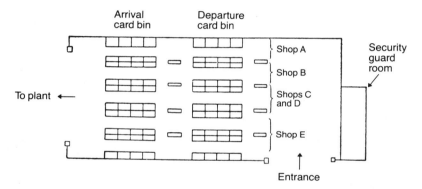

FIGURE 8-3. Gate Layout

Now, when workers arrived at the plant, they would remove their cards from the right bin and drop them into the left bin. This automatically sorted the cards by job number without involving the attendance clerk.

One problem arose. The attendance cards that had previously been taken home had to be left behind at the plant. Company R was located at Nobeoka City, whose citizens, for the most part, were employed by company R or one of its affiliates. Various benefits such as reduced-price movie tickets and credit at retail stores were provided to company R employees, using their attendance cards as ID cards. So the workers objected to leaving their attendance cards at the plant.

At first we were disturbed by the opposition, but we realized that the essential problem was not that the workers wanted the attendance cards themselves, but that they wanted some way of identifying themselves as company R employees.

Someone suggested issuing a new set of ID cards. Finally, however, we settled on using the previous month's attendance cards as ID cards for the ensuing month.

By keeping the attendance cards at the plant, problems caused when workers forgot to bring their cards or lost them were eliminated.

After the task of sorting the cards was improved as just described, we set about to improve the sorting of absent workers from present workers. We got together and started discussing what attendance meant. Various ideas were put forward, for instance, attendance means that a worker is present at the plant, or attendance means working at the plant. Finally, we agreed that "attendance is not being absent," a great answer.

Because attendance is not being absent and absence is not being present, we decided to collect the cards remaining in the right-hand card bins as evidence of an absent worker, study the reasons (paid vacation, illness, etc.) for the absence, stamp the cards accordingly, and stamp the remaining cards as "absent without explanation," and check the attendance chart prepared at each work station. This eliminated the need to touch the attendance cards. As a result, it was possible to manage the attendance status simply by managing the exception phenomenon, in this case, absence from work. This greatly simplified the clerical task.

Because the average attendance rate at company R was 97 percent and the number of employees was 6,000, the earlier procedure of processing 5,820 cards for those present and 180 cards for those absent was reduced simply to processing the 180 cards of those who were absent. Obviously, the effort involved was significantly reduced.

Another problem also arose. Some workers did not like the idea that nothing was done with the cards of those who were present. I asked why. The answer was that if someone erased the absent mark, that would mean that the worker was present. I said that this would not be a problem because any discrepancy would be noted when the attendance chart was compared with the attendance charts kept at each work station. Moreover, the absence record is compared with paid vacation reports and illness reports.

I also pointed out that wages were paid on the basis of the attendance chart and that even if the absent mark on the attendance card were erased, other records were available (attendance charts, etc.) for easily correcting any error.

I also asked whether such an erasure of an absent mark would actually occur, and if so, how often. Finally, we concluded that the complaint had arisen because some workers wanted some positive action to be taken when they were at work, not only when they were absent. I told the workers that they would get used to the new procedure and that seemed to solve this problem. When I visited the plant three years later, I was told that the new procedure was working flawlessly.

As for the third task, that of checking the attendance charts kept at each work station, we simplified the procedure by making sure that the master attendance chart and the attendance charts kept at each work station had the same format (column size, job name, sequence, etc.). This is an example of managing the exceptions.

4. *Constants and Variables*

These are things that change and things that don't.

Example: Automation of stringing. One of the jobs performed at company T was to use string to tie the boxes containing the products. Some boxes were large, containing, for example, an electric iron for pressing trousers. Others were small, containing, for example, an electric pot. Management wanted to use one automatic stringing machine to tie up boxes of all sizes. But this was impossible and a worker had to perform the job.

I asked a worker to bring out eight boxes, each different in size and color. The distance between the two spots at which the strings were to be hooked also differed. With the boxes used for irons, the distance between the two spots was about 500 millimeters; with the smaller boxes used for pots, it was about 300 millimeters. It seemed difficult to detect their sizes and to tie them automatically.

After looking at the boxes for some time, I had an idea. I asked that the boxes be placed against a wall. I had noticed that the distances from the hooking spot to the box edges were quite similar. After determining the average distance from the box edge to the hooking spot, we decided that (1) a string could be hooked automatically by leaving a constant forward distance from the front edge of the box out to the string-hooking location, and (2) a string could be hooked automatically by leaving a constant rear distance from the back edge of the box out to the string-hooking position.

In this way, it was possible to automate the tying-up of boxes of eight different sizes by using the same "constant distance from the edge."

Frequently we see only the *variables* and claim that something cannot be done. However, this is only one way of looking at a situation. More often than we realize, a *constant* can be found when the same situation is viewed from different angles (from the top, bottom, left, right, or obliquely).

5. Enlargement and Reduction

Example: Draft adjustment. Company M rolls steel plates. The draft must be adjusted so that the plates are rolled with a precision of within about 0.01 millimeter. To do this, screw-down axes must be moved using a mechanism consisting of several sets of gears or a worm gear and a worm wheel. A disk about 2 meters in diameter is attached to the first screw-down axis. Scales are marked along the outer perimeter of the disk.

The mechanism is adjusted so that each turn of the disk by one graduation on the scale causes a known corresponding movement of, say, 0.001 millimeter. The minute adjustments of the rolling dimensions are magnified on the disk scale to help achieve the required precision.

6. Concentration and Dispersion

Example: Oil-Shale furnace. Some time back, there was a project to recover oil from shale. After much effort, researchers succeeded in recovering some oil using an experimental 1-ton furnace. Their success led to the fabrication of a 100-ton furnace that was to be used for large-scale oil recovery. Because of the difficulty in creating the proper conditions, this project failed and no oil was recovered. After those in charge had resigned, Mr. Godō was appointed to head the project. He went to the oil-shale site, where an engineer briefed him in detail on all that had happened from the time of fabrication of the experimental furnace to when the commercial furnace was produced.

Mr. Godō was told that the 1-ton furnace had succeeded but that the much larger 100-ton furnace had failed.

"The solution is obvious," Mr. Godō said.

"What is it?" asked the engineer.

"Just build a hundred of the 1-ton furnaces!" said Mr. Godō.

They did just that and, lo and behold, succeeded in recovering the oil.

Here, because a 100-ton furnace was built simply by enlarging a 1-ton furnace 100 times, with no thought given to the reaction conditions, the commercial operation had failed. In this way, when you enlarge or reduce, it is important not just to enlarge or reduce the physical dimensions. Careful attention must be paid to the similarity of conditions and functions.

Example: Building a "Panama Canal" in a factory. The Panama Canal located in Central America allows ships to cross over a high isthmus and travel from the Pacific to the Atlantic. It works as follows: The ship is steered into the first lock. The gates are closed; water is introduced, and when the water level rises to the height of that in the next lock, the gates are opened and the ship moves into that next lock. This procedure is repeated until the highest level is reached. The whole sequence is reversed when a ship descends to the Atlantic.

A similar approach also can be used in a factory. For example, when you have to slide a long rod sideways through a chute, the rod can tilt and fall out of the chute, depending on the shape of the rod and any bends or differences in the friction coefficient. Yet there is a safety margin within which a long rod can slide sideways without excessive tilting. The safety margin varies with the properties of the rod but is usually around 300 millimeters.

Hence by putting stoppers at every safety-margin interval along the chute, one can control the rod's orientation and slide it along the chute without fear of its falling off. When a rod that is sliding along a chute starts tilting, the tilting is corrected when the rod strikes the first stopper. The stopper is lowered, and the rod slides further. When the rod again starts to tilt, it strikes the second stopper, which corrects its orientation.

Very frequently an item can be transported quite efficiently by using a canal approach, that is, by moving it along by means of a sequential, divided control.

7. Linking and Separating

Example: Pressing a rice-cooker body. In an operation that involved pressing the body of a rice cooker, a circular hole was made in the bottom surface to accommodate the heating element, and a square hole was made in the left and right sides for installing handles. I noticed on the workshop floor that two presses using similar dies and with the same performance rating were being used to perform this task in a two-step process.

"Why don't you do this job using just one press and one process?" I asked.

I was told that it was impossible. I asked why.

"Because the press's performance rating is not high enough," was the answer.

I was told that the existing 60-ton press could not simultaneously make a circular hole in the bottom plate and two square holes in the side walls.

I thereupon suggested the following, "In volleyball there is an attack technique called the off-timing play. You have to use the same approach. What you do is first make a circular hole in the bottom plate, wait one second, and then make the two square holes. One 60-ton press should suffice."

We tried it, and it worked. Here the single process did not mean making the holes all at the same time. What it did mean was that the workpiece could be inserted in a die and removed only once in order to shorten the operation time. Generally speaking, the time that it takes to make a hole with a press is about 0.7 second. Much more time is required for inserting and removing it from the dies. Any lack of press capacity can be overcome easily by using a time differential. As this example shows, a very effective improvement can be made by combining two processes into one.

8. Adding and Deleting

Example: Piston assembly. At company Y, an automobile manufacturer, piston assembly involved fitting piston rings and installing a gudgeon pin. One operation consisted of applying grease to a shaft and installing the shaft in the subsequent operation.

A partitioned pallet contained a dozen or so different parts required for the assembly. Each part was stored in its designated place on the pallet. The parts were taken from the pallet and assembled, and the assembled piston was then returned to a designated spot on the same pallet. Although very rarely, sometimes the workers forgot to grease the shaft. When this was discovered, the assembly line had to be stopped to return the defective part to the previous process and apply grease. The workers were instructed to be careful, but the problem did recur, albeit infrequently.

To overcome this, an additional empty pallet was provided. A piston and some piston rings were removed from pallet B and placed at a designated spot on pallet A. A shaft taken from pallet B was greased and placed at a designated spot on pallet A. Because this procedure required parts first to be taken from pallet B, there were no further instances of workers forgetting to grease a shaft. In the previous procedure, when workers returned the greased shafts to the same pallet, they sometimes became confused as to whether a shaft had been greased or not. Even though 2,000 automobiles were produced per day, by using one empty pallet (pallet B served as a spare for pallet C and so on), the problem of forgetting to grease the shafts was completely eliminated. This is a good example of how a key spare item can greatly simplify a job.

9. Parallel and Sequential

Example: Cylinder boring. One operation consisted of boring the cylinders of an automobile engine. The job was performed in accordance with the layout shown in *Figure 8-4a*. Management wanted to reduce the cycle time by about 10 percent. When I went to the production floor, I noticed that cylinders that had been bored were transported on roller conveyor B to roller conveyor C, and cylinders to be bored were transported on roller conveyor A to roller conveyor B and from there to the boring machine.

In other words, the cylinders already machined and those still to be machined were traveling sequentially. I then suggested adopting one-way, parallel directions of travel (see *Figure 8-4b*). Roller conveyor B was extended so that a machined cylinder could be transported to the next machine by detouring around the boring machine. Machined cylinders were removed from the boring machine and

Cylinder movement

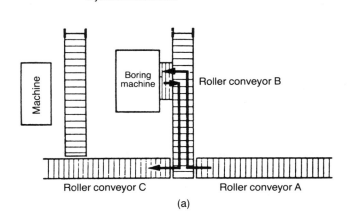

Roller conveyor C

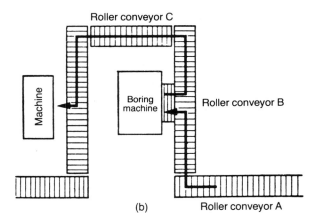

FIGURE 8-4. Cylinder Movement

pushed down on roller conveyor B. Unmachined cylinders were sent from roller conveyor A to roller conveyer B in advance. When a machined cylinder was removed from the boring machine, an unmachined cylinder was immediately inserted and the machining began. A machined cylinder traveled along roller conveyor B, detoured around the boring machine, and was sent to the next machine.

This "one-way travel" reduced the cycle time by 15 percent.

In other words, the previous procedure involving sequential insertion and removal was replaced with parallel operations, which significantly improved the efficiency.

With most machine tools and presses, dies and workpieces are usually inserted and removed sequentially. Using parallel operations can provide significant benefits.

10. Changing a Sequence

Example: Spot-welding a guard. Hirose Spring is a company that manufactures protective gratings used on kerosene heaters. The protective grating (*Figure 8-5*), curved to conform to the shape of the front of the kerosene heater, is composed of three parts: (*a*) an outer frame, (*b*) vertical runners, and (*c*) horizontal runners. The outer frame and vertical runners are bent in advance to conform to the shape of the protective grating. The horizontal runners are straight. The three parts are placed in a jig and spot-welded into an integral whole. However, this process always distorts the shape of the finished product, which has to be corrected with a special tool.

The correction requires skill and is time-consuming, constituting a bottleneck. Too much force caused the spot welds to separate; too little force would not correct the distortion.

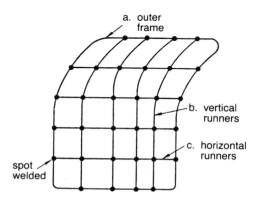

FIGURE 8-5. **Kerosene Heater Protective Grating**

However, Mr. M improved the operation in the following manner:

- Instead of bending the outer frame (*a*), it was formed as a flat piece.
- The vertical runners (*b*) were formed straight just like the horizontal runners (*c*).
- The flat frame, vertical runners, and horizontal runners were placed in a jig and spot-welded.
- The flat integral whole was bent into the required shape with a press.

Initially, the workers opposed the idea, claiming that bending the spot-welded piece would separate the spot welds. Tests proved them wrong. The improvement eliminated the distortion-correcting operation plus the need for skilled labor. Productivity increased and the bottleneck vanished.

The previous sequence of (1) cutting the parts, (2) bending, (3) assembling, (4) spot welding and (5) distortion correction was changed to (1) parts cutting, (2) assembling, (3) spot welding and (4) bending. Changing the sequence resulted in dramatic improvements.

Example: Piping work on a ship. Oil tankers are fitted with a complicated network of pipes. After the hull is built, the ship is moored and the piping work is performed inside it. Scaffolding measuring some 50 centimeters wide is erected along the perimeter of the engine room. Stairways are erected at four locations inside the engine room.

Once one level of piping work is completed, the workers walk down a stairway to a lower-level scaffolding and connect the pipes. Because the job is performed high above ground level, the workers are tethered to a safety line. The height and poor illumination inside the hull make the job dangerous and inefficient.

Modern shipbuilders use a technique called *block construction*, whereby 30- to 50-ton modular blocks are constructed inside a large indoor work area and then, at a berth, are welded together to build a ship.

It was suggested that the piping work also be done during the welding and assembly of the blocks. Despite objections that the pipes could then not be connected correctly, the plan succeeded with only minor adjustments.

The improvement meant:

- No danger of workers falling to the ground
- Easier worker movement
- Better illumination
- Welding with the welder facing down instead of sideways improved welding speed and quality.

Productivity increased fivefold when the job sequence was changed from first building the hull and then the piping work to first doing the piping work and then building the hull.

11. Differences and Common Features

Example: Managing the flow of boxes. An operation at company H consisted of boxing sausages. Boxes of sausages arriving from several production lines were merged into a single line and then placed in a big cardboard carton at the end of the line. When merging into the single line, unless the timing was perfect, those arriving from the different lines collided and blocked the flow of boxes behind them.

I observed the situation and implemented the following improvements (*Figure 8-6*):

- The height of the last conveyor was lowered so that boxes arriving from the tributary lines slid down a chute.
- A hinged chute was installed so that a box traveling on the line below was pushed up onto it where a stopper prevented the box from sliding down the chute.
- Once the box traveling on the lower line passed the chute, the gap between the stopper and the hinged chute increased so that the box being held back by the stopper would then slide down the chute.

This arrangement completely eliminated colliding boxes.

Example: Fronts and backs of washers. Company T manufactures washers. During the fabrication process, the washers had to be inserted into a machine with the burr side down. Distinguishing the burr side from the smooth side was not easy.

I went to the shop floor and attached a piece of rough sandpaper to a board. I placed two washers on the board, one with the burr side

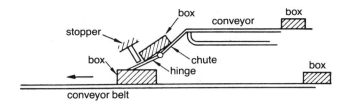

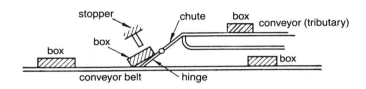

FIGURE 8-6. Controlling the Flow of Boxes

down and the other with the burr side up. As I gradually increased the angle of tilt of the board, I noticed that the washer with the burr side up started sliding at a smaller angle (angle [alpha]) while the washer with the burr side down started sliding at a larger angle (angle [beta]).

We placed a belt sander at an angle [theta] larger than angle alpha but smaller than angle beta (*Figure 8-7*). One by one, washers were placed on the belt sander.

The washers with the burr side up slid down the belt sander. As this occurred, the washers were flipped over. The washers with the burr side down were carried up by the belt sander, and as they reached the top of the belt sander, they slid down a chute.

This made possible a simple automatic sorting of the washers. As this example shows, automatic sorting can frequently be accomplished by taking advantage of differences in shape, movement, surface roughness, etc.

12. Adding and Alternating

Example: Pressing a side plate. I observed a press punching out side plates at company Z, a manufacturer of agricultural machinery. The job sequence was as follows:

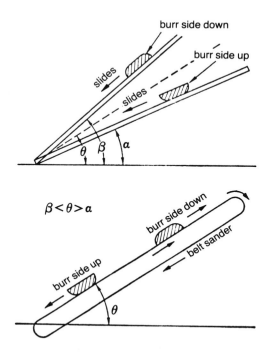

Figure 8-7. Automatic Sorting of Burrs

- A workpiece situated to the left of a worker is picked up with both hands.
- The workpiece is punched out with a press.
- The finished piece is placed with both hands in a storage bin situated to the right of the worker.
- Both hands are moved to the left to pick up the next workpiece.

This sequence reveals one empty motion, namely, moving both hands to the left to pick up the next workpiece. To eliminate this empty motion, I suggested placing the finished-product storage bin to the left of the worker. Now, the finished piece is placed with both hands in a storage bin situated to the left of the worker and the worker then picks up a new workpiece positioned nearby, minimizing the amount of empty motion.

Some workers objected, claiming that there was not enough room to the left of the worker for placing both the workpieces and the finished products. They said placing the finished products to the left of the worker but significantly farther away was no different from placing them to the right of the worker.

This made sense. However, what was in short supply was storage area, and the improvement's purpose was to release the hands from the finished piece at a place close to the workpiece storage area.

To accomplish this, a guide for sliding the finished products to their storage area was erected close to the workpiece storage area. This allowed workers to place the finished pieces on the guide and immediately pick up the next workpiece. Empty motion was minimized, and productivity increased by 70 percent (*Figure 8-8*).

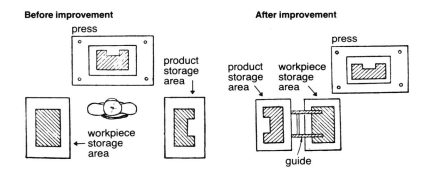

FIGURE 8-8. **Side-Plate Pressing Operation**

Example: Placing instruction sheets. An operation at a food-processing plant consisted of placing instruction sheets on cans moving along a conveyor belt. I noticed one worker working at a frantic pace. I asked myself why. I also noticed that the worker was not using both hands and looked to see how the other workers were doing. Typically, they grabbed about three sheets and applied one after another to cans. A pretty good idea, but I asked myself whether both hands might be used.

I noticed that the instruction sheets were placed on a workbench situated in front of the conveyor belt. I also noticed that the conveyor belt was so far away from the workers that they had to reach out with one hand to reach it.

We made the following improvements:

- A portion of the workbench was cut away so that workers were closer to the conveyor belt.
- A rack was suspended above the conveyor belt to hold the instruction sheets.
- Workers were permitted to sit while working.
- Then two instruction sheets, one held in each hand, were applied to cans simultaneously.

This ended the need for workers to do their work at excessive speed (*Figure 8-9*).

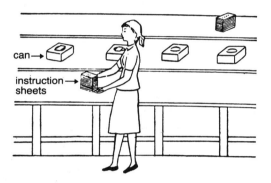

FIGURE 8-9. Placing Instruction Sheets

Idea formulation ultimately depends on creativity. There are many ways of honing one's creativity, but one of the most basic is the association method. It is difficult for one to come up with an idea that is totally new. The easiest way to form new ideas is via associations based on past experience. It is particularly helpful to remember the rules of association.

With improvements, it is frequently more helpful not to ask "What ideas can I come up with?" but "What rules of idea formulation can I use?"

JUDGMENT

Ideas generated by brainstorming are the product of momentary mental flashes. The function of *judgment* is to choose from among them and criticize them in order to develop plans that can actually be used. It is important at this stage to adopt an approach in which, rather than merely shooting down ideas, one tries more positively to find ways to put them into action.

Stepping Stones for Rapid Progress:
Thesis, Antithesis, and Synthesis

The dialectic is a procedure for thinking.

First, a *thesis* is put forward. Then a contradictory opinion, an *antithesis*, is espoused. As long as the thesis and antithesis are advocated at the same plane of understanding, no amount of time will be sufficient to lead to a conclusion.

In general, a compromise is reached by combining the two views and splitting the difference. This is the wrong way to go about things. Rather, one should discard the defects of the two arguments, adopt their good points, and develop an improvement strategy from a higher perspective. This is known as *synthesis*. For example, suppose it is proposed that to reduce inventories, deliveries should be made to the parent plant four times per day. Opposing this, an affiliated plant asserts that the plan will not work because truck-loading operations are inefficient. Continuing to express only these views (thesis and antithesis) will lead nowhere. In many cases, a compromise position would be reached in which the parties agree to deliveries twice a day. A compromise, however, is not an improvement plan.

Suppose, on the other hand, that a method of combined loading were adopted in which trucks went around to four different companies and took on one quarter of their loads at each before making a delivery:

- Stock could be reduced
- Truck-loading efficiency would not be lowered

This method would be a *synthesis*, in which undesirable features of both arguments are discarded and only the good points are adopted.

In this example, assuming that a company's goods had to be transported by company trucks constituted an invisible obstacle to resolution of the problem. All that was needed was to discard that assumption and consider the issues from a higher perspective.

Thus, theses and antitheses are always in opposition when we engage in discussions, and rather than continuing those discussions on the same plane and ending up with a compromise, we can ask everyone to take off their shoes, stand on the table, and from that higher perspective consider once more the possibility that some obstacle is holding things up. This will make it possible for us to think up better plans for improvement.

Nyet Engineers Who Oppose Improvements

I have had many occasions to visit foreign plants for consultation or to give seminars. Whenever I do, I make the following statement: "In Japan, there are three types of engineer who stand in the way of improvements: table engineers, catalog engineers, and *nyet* engineers."

1. *Table engineers*. Table engineers like to voice their opinions around the conference table. They object to proposed improvements on the basis of theoretical logic and reasoning, but they do not actually go to the shop floor. Their arguments are based on theory. When one visits the shop floor and observes the actual facts, one sees that such engineers are full of misunderstanding and wrong assumptions.

    Frequently they are quite intelligent and like to argue. They dominate a meeting and allow others little opportunity to speak. Because they use up all the time, meaningful discussions cannot take place. Their views tend not to be constructive, but because they sound logical, they easily persuade other participants that such and such a proposed improvement is unworkable.

2. *Catalog engineers*. These engineers like to collect catalogs for new equipment. When they see something appealing, they tell the company president, "We need this equipment." They are proud when the new equipment is purchased and put into use. They have no compunction about buying more equipment than is really needed.

    There are alternatives to buying ready-made equipment. We can study what equipment is needed for the job, prepare drawings, and design and assemble it in-house, using machine tools available at the plant. Shortcomings can be gradually eliminated through trial runs and in-house modifications. Catalog engineers, however, make no such efforts. They do not mind spending ten times the cost of making the item themselves to buy one ready-made. Their only ability lies in collecting catalogs.

I once visited company Y, an automobile manufacturer. There I met some engineers who told me that they knew the most in the world about making cars and that they designed and built their own production equipment at one-tenth the cost of buying it ready-made. They were confident and enthusiastic. Just the opposite of catalog engineers.

3. *Nyet* engineers. *Nyet* is the Russian word for "no." A Soviet ambassador to the United Nations was once nicknamed "Mr. *Nyet*" because he invariably said *nyet* to proposals put forward by Western nations. There are many people like that ambassador who say, "No, that's impossible," "No, that's too difficult," or "No, that won't work" to almost all proposed improvements without giving them any real thought.

In any plant there are usually several of these *nyet*-sayers who always have their reasons for claiming that things will not work. *Nyet* engineers tend to be well educated and to hold relatively high positions, which makes the problem all the thornier. Any proposed improvement is bound to entail problems, some minor, some major. But saying "this won't work" all the time will never lead to progress.

FIGURE 8-10.

At company B, it used to take 42 days to fabricate dies for a vul-canizing press. I suggested shortening the time to four days. Supervisor A immediately said that this was impossible and started itemizing what he considered the "unsolvable" problems involved. I listened for a time and said, "You have used the word *unsolvable* 15 times in the last five minutes. Would you mind explaining what you just told me without using the word *unsolvable*."

Surprised, he finally replied: "Let me use the word today. Otherwise, I won't be able to explain my views. I promise not to use it the next time."

He kept on saying things like, "That's impossible, no matter what you do" or "That's very difficult, no matter how you do it."

After he finished his explanation, I said, "Mr. A, I don't mind your itemizing all the problems. But please don't keep saying that everything is impossible. Concentrate instead on what can be done to solve the problems." I then proposed possible solutions to each of the problems he had cited.

After listening to my suggestions for a while, he started proposing solutions of his own. We actually conducted experiments. From then on he stopped using the word *unsolvable* and became more con-structive. After six months, we were able to reduce die-production time to four days. Our success lay in the fact that supervisor A had stopped being a *nyet* engineer.

Do you know people who belong in any of the preceding three categories? Are you sure you aren't among them?

The Most Correct Reasoning Comes After Repeated Trials and Ultimate Success

The world is full of negative reasoning — reasoning that ignores actual trials and arrives at the conclusion that things "aren't possible" or "won't work." Yet, in many cases, surprising success is achieved by trying out things thought to be impossible. The most powerful weapon for bringing about improvement is a willingness to try. Even with the most splendid logical reasoning behind it, impossibility arguments never lead to progress. In a correctly reasoned approach, a solution is discovered in the course of trying out various possibilities.

Count Your Difficulties

Often when I visit a plant where there is some problem, I make a suggestion or two as to how things might be done. The response? "Well, that's a little difficult."

"What do you mean by 'difficult'?" I reply. "Name six problems that are making things difficult."

Oddly enough, the person I am speaking to often reels off six problems. We then discuss them one by one and nearly always come up with solutions. The point is that, rather than saying somewhat vaguely that things are "difficult," it is better to clarify difficult elements using concrete terms. Improvements can be made with unexpected ease when these difficult points are demolished one by one.

In short, avoiding vague talk about "difficulties" and expressing problems in a concrete and clear way makes an effective shortcut to discovering solutions.

If the Results Are No Good, Doubt the Premises

In visiting production plants where defects are occurring, I am given many reasons why those defects should not exist:

- "Our materials are all up to specifications."
- "We maintain our machines well."
- "Our workers adhere to standard operations."

Yet if defects are actually occurring, then the facts are indisputable. Since the claim is that defects "should" not occur, we are compelled to suspect that something is amiss with that word, *should*. In other words, we have to go back to our premises and thoroughly examine them with the suspicion that something is wrong. When we do, we are liable to discover unexpected problems:

- Materials have the same labels, but they come from different manufacturers.
- Machines have been switched.
- Switching workers has meant that certain standard operations have not been adhered to.

Too often we grasp facts by guessing. In a case like this one, it is surprising how easily we can uncover the causes of problems starting with a clean slate and rethinking each premise that we used to accept unconsciously.

"Thoroughbred Experiments"

Sometimes, even though we know defects are occurring, we don't know which process is generating them or what is causing them. In this type of situation, not knowing what we don't know means the problem will never be cleared up.

An effective approach for dealing with a situation like this is to carry out a "thoroughbred experiment." For example,

1. Carefully inspect every one of 100 items being supplied as raw materials to process no. 1.
2. Carry out processing at process no. 1 using this material and then carefully inspect every one of the finished products. From these, select only acceptable items.
3. Supply only these acceptable items to process no. 2 and carry out processing.

Each of the resulting products is carefully inspected and only acceptable items are sent on to process no. 3. This procedure of carefully inspecting all products at the end of each process and then sending only acceptable items to the next process is repeated down the line. This will make clear the extent to which each process is generating defects, and the specific causes of these defects can be traced through detailed investigations of the principal processes.

Causes will never be revealed and defects will never be reduced, however, if all one does is to say vaguely that defects are causing problems. It is in such situations that I recommend that this sort of thoroughbred experiment be carried out.

If You Don't Know Why Defects Are Occurring, Make Some Defects

Sometimes in plants there are situations in which defects are occurring but their cause is unknown. In such cases, make a guess as to the most likely cause and then try to generate some defects intentionally. A comparison of the intentional defects and the previous defects will, with surprising frequency, make it possible to identify the real cause of the problem.

Rather than assuming that you must at all costs make acceptable products, experimenting on the basis of hypothetically plausible ways in which defects might occur can make it possible to trace the causes of the problem.

In any event, simple repeating that you don't know what is causing the problem will only ensure that you will never know. Thinking imaginatively about problem areas, actually performing the procedure and tracking the results, and comparing the outcome with the real phenomenon are enormously effective means for getting a grip on "unknown causes."

PROPOSAL

Improvement proposals are of no use unless they can actually be put into effect and unless they promise significant results with only modest investments. Considerable attention must always be given to so-called investment efficiency. In the next chapter, we will consider ways to implement improvement plans.

9

Stage Four:
Translating Improvement Plans
into Reality

The most stupendous improvement plans in the world will be ineffective unless they are translated into practice. Often at this stage the resistance of habit will prevent shop workers from implementing improvement plans. Indeed, such plans cannot be fully realized unless consent is obtained along with understanding, and unless tenacious efforts are sustained.

BEFORE ANYTHING ELSE, GIVE IT A TRY

An Engineer's Instincts and a Manager's Instincts

This example involves a moisture-proofing operation in which stabilizers used in fluorescent lights were dipped in varnish, dried, and then removed. Fifty stabilizers were hung from hooks on plates and dipped into liquid varnish. Since at this stage varnish would inevitably adhere to the holes on the stabilizers from which they were hung and to the hooks, the stabilizers would stick quite firmly to the plates as they passed through the drying oven. After a worker shook the stabilizers to undo the adhesion, the stabilizers were peeled off the hooks and sent down a conveyor.

There were four sets of conveyors, and four workers were kept busy as they desperately carried out the operation of removing stabilizers one by one. When I asked the plant manager, Mr. K, why the stabilizers couldn't be removed by machine, he told me the idea wouldn't work. "The units wouldn't come off because of all the varnish stuck to them. We tried that once and the experiment failed. You've just got to have people shake the plates and then peel the stabilizers off."

"You may be right," I said, "but let's try it just once more." I used a suitably sized veneer board to push up and down against the stabilizers from below. Of 50 stabilizers, only 35 came off. "You see," said the plant manager, "it just doesn't work."

"Look," I replied, "didn't 35 of the units come off? You seem to be concerned that not all 50 came off, that 15 were left on. But if you can remove 35 stabilizers automatically by using air cylinders and the installing of a vibrating pusher, then only 15 stabilizers are left to be removed manually. At that rate, you could have a single worker handle two lines and cut down on labor costs.

"The point here is that when you say the idea won't work, you're talking about an all-or-nothing proposition. But isn't it all right to remove 35 of the stabilizers even if you can't take them all off? Rather than using your engineer's instincts and assuming that every last item has to be removed, why not use your manager's instincts and recognize the advantages of being able to remove at least some of the items?"

After I had my say, a mechanical removal device was installed that saved the work of two people. Later on, improvements stemming from an investigation into the shape of the hooks eliminated human labor entirely and achieved a considerable cost reduction.

Thus, surprising as it may seem, a manager with the temperament of an engineer may be spellbound by technical perfection and neglect to use his instincts as a manager when thinking about improvement.

Do Humans Work Faster?

In my visits to production plants I often hear workers grumbling that management prefers mechanization even though humans work faster.

A production engineer once told me his firm had mechanized a hole-drilling operation, but the people in the plant wouldn't use the machine. They said that, although a human worker could do the job in 20 seconds per item, the automatic machine took 30 seconds. This meant that the human could process 180 items per hour, whereas the machine could handle only 120 items. "So," they concluded, "we ought to have humans do it."

I visited the plant and observed that, indeed, a human worker could process one item in 20 seconds and at 30 seconds per item, an automatic machine took longer because of the interlock time between each operation.

This was precisely why the shop foreman wouldn't use the machine — he maintained that it was useless because humans worked faster.

At this point, I asked the production engineer how much machines like this cost to make. He told me that they were extremely inexpensive — only ¥ 300,000 ($1,000) each — because they were assembled in-house, and only the parts were purchased from the outside. They were, moreover, of relatively simple construction:

1. Parts are lined up in a magazine.
2. A pusher pushes them out, where they are secured in a jig and drilled.
3. Parts that have been drilled are then automatically expelled.

"All right," I said to the foreman, "when I look at the job being done, there seems to be no question that a human worker is faster than the machine. But look, the only thing a human has to do for the machine is to load parts into the magazine, right? If that's the case, then even if there's another ($1,000) machine involved, the human worker's only job would be to load magazines and take away boxes of finished products. Doesn't that mean that one worker could be in charge of two machines?"

"Sure, we could do that," he replied. "And all the worker would have to do is load the magazines and then replace the boxes of finished products, right? There would be plenty of time for that — so much that we could even have the worker take care of deburring the holes as well."

"With another machine," I continued, "a single worker's output — given, say, 30 seconds per item for each machine — would be 240 items. That means that with another ¥ 600,000 ($2,000) invested in two machines you will have upped productivity by 33 percent. In the end, you'll have cut costs!"

The foreman agreed that was a more profitable approach. He arranged for another machine to be made and for a single worker to operate the two machines at the same time.

People on the shop floor often tend to look at the job in front of them and conclude that a machine is useless because humans are faster. In fact, however, even if a machine takes a bit more time, as long as the investment is modest, ultimate costs can be reduced by building another machine and thereby increasing human productivity.

Per-item processing speed is not all there is to the problem here. The important lesson is that we consider issues like this from a higher vantage point by asking which alternative would more effectively cut costs.

THE POSITIVE POWER OF EXECUTION

IE (industrial engineering) generates improvement plans based on waste found in an investigation of the status quo. By contrast, the work-design approach starts from zero in dealing with materials costs and labor costs. It allows two kinds of expenditures in the course of developing improvement plans: unavoidable materials costs and minimal labor costs. The proponents of work design claim that their approach is by far less costly than IE, since, without exception, work-design improvement plans are less expensive than IE improvement plans.

To be sure, this claim tends to be borne out: only lukewarm improvement plans can be developed when — while identifying areas for improvement — we make compromises with the status quo.

Fighting with Your "Backs to the Water"

When I visited the Y Automobile Company in 1969, the head of the auto body division told me that setups on a Schiller 1,000-ton press were taking four hours. At Volkswagen in West Germany, however, setups on the same machine only took two hours. "Mr. N, our managing director," he said, "has demanded that we find some way to do better than Volkswagen, so somehow I'd like some improvements to be made."

We first separated internal and external setup operations, and them streamlined procedures in both areas. Six months later, this had made it possible to performs setups in one hour and a half, and everyone was happy.

A month after this success had been achieved, I visited Y Automobile again. This time, the auto body division head told me that Mr. N's new instructions were to cut setup time on the same 1,000-ton press down to three minutes! For a moment I was speechless. It took six months of hard work, I thought, to reduce setup times from four hours to an hour and a half. To cut them now to three minutes is impossible! But then inspiration began working.

Recently we had improved setup times for engine beds on an open-sided planer at the shipyard in Hiroshima. The point there was that we shifted what had been done during internal setup to external setup. I suddenly comprehended the most significant conceptual revolution involved in the SMED idea: take procedures that everyone assumes have to be performed during internal setup and shift them to external setup.

With the cooperation of engineers from Y Automobile, we succeed within three months in attaining setup times of three minutes.

It is all very well to demand that four-hour setups be cut in half, but what on earth did Mr. N have in mind when he demanded that setups already cut to an hour and a half be further shortened to three minutes — one-thirtieth of the previous time? Unable to fathom his real intentions, I had Mr. Akiyama, a close friend of Mr. N's and the president of S Automobile, ask Mr. N what he had been thinking. Mr. Akiyama reported to me that in response to my question, Mr. N had said: "My friend, in three minutes a man can walk 200 meters."

The response left me unsatisfied. This time, learning that a delegation from the French automobile maker Citroen was to meet with Mr. N, I had them ask him why he thought to have the setups cut to three minutes. This time he answered in the following way: "I always like to cut things in half. For instance, I give instructions for production time to be cut in half. People are always surprised at first, but even so they come up with various ideas and work hard at them. In the meantime, I constantly visit the shop and ask how things are going. "Progress is slow at first, but sooner or later someone comes up with a really superb idea and the pace begins to pick up. Eventually production time is cut in half.

"At that point, I thank everyone for their efforts, but in three months or so I give instructions for the new production period to be cut in half. This proves to be more difficult than the last time, but eventually we succeed in cutting the time in half.

"It's funny. People don't think of cutting an hour and a half to an hour as much of a goal, but if you tell them to cut the time to three minutes, then you put them in a desperate state and they come out with real resourcefulness."

What Mr. N seemed to want to say was that if you provide people with timid goals, all they will come up with are run-of-the-mill ideas — for instance, to tighten bolts with a nut runner rather than by hand. But if you give them overwhelming goals — for example, to secure objects without using threaded fastenings at all — they will think of completely new methods, such as using an interlocking system.

Later, I spoke to the delegation from Citroen.

"I gather that you have just visited the Y Automobile company. It won't mean very much, though, if all you have done is to observe improvements superficially. Those improvements spring from the extraordinary faith and zeal of leaders, but more than that, the success you see today was only brought about through the tireless efforts of workers in the plant.

"Let me tell you a story. In the Sengoku period in Japanese history, there was a battle between the forces of the Tokugawa and the Takeda clans. The Tokugawa forces numbered only 3,000, as opposed to 10,000 Takeda soldiers, and some of the outnumbered Tokugawa troops retreated, frightened by the size of the enemy force.

"This move induced other troops to do likewise, and the entire army crumbled and pulled back. At this point, the great general Tokugawa Ieyasu skillfully guided his troops toward the banks of a wide river. If they retreated further, they would drown. With the enemy's massive army attacking from the front, death in battle was inevitable. The Tokugawa soldiers knew they were going to die and they reasoned that it was better to die fighting the enemy. So they battled like madmen, heedless of death, and contrary to all expectation, they routed the great Takeda army of 10,000.

"In Japan the Tokugawa army's predicament is referred to as *haisui no jin*, which means troops arrayed with their backs to the water.

"In a similar position, people will fight like madmen and accomplish what is generally thought to be impossible. The striking success attained at Y Automobile came because people strove hard when their backs were to the water.

"None of us can bring about a revolution with ordinary efforts. First-rate results can not be achieved unless people are given the sort of goals that put their backs to the water and unless extraordinary efforts are put forth. I want you all to plant this idea firmly in your minds before you return to France."

As a sequel to this story, I am told that the untranslated Japanese phrase *haisui no jin* is still often heard at Citroen.

How About Doing It Tomorrow?

This is a story from my childhood.

A man wanting a haircut goes to a barbershop and sees a sign posted outside that reads "Free Haircuts Tomorrow."

"Free haircuts tomorrow?" the man thinks. "I'd miss out if I got one today."

The next day he returns to the barbershop and the sign is still there: "Free Haircuts Tomorrow." Once again, he decides to wait. The following day the same sign is up and in the end, of course, the man lives the rest of his life without getting his hair cut.

The point is that human beings rely on tomorrow even more than on God or other people. Yet for people who believe in tomorrow, tomorrow never comes. People who always intend to get things done tomorrow end up never being able to do anything as long as they live.

In another well-known fable, a baby skylark says to its mother, "We have to move our nest because the farmer who owns this field of wheat has asked his neighbors to reap the wheat tomorrow."

"Don't worry," the mother replies, and they do not move.

The next day, the baby skylark tells its mother that the farmer has come and said that the neighbors would not come because they were all busy. "The farmer said he had no choice but to have his relatives help reap the wheat tomorrow," says the baby skylark. "We have to move!"

"Don't worry," his mother says, and shows not the slightest sign of moving.

The following day, the baby skylark says, "Mother, today the farmer came and said that his relatives had found some reason or other not to help him. He said he had no choice but to ask his children."

"There's nothing to worry about," the mother says, and still they do not move.

The day after that, the baby skylark says, "Today the farmer came again and he said that his children were all heartless. 'They come out with some excuse or other and won't lend me a hand. At this rate, I'll miss the season for reaping. I guess *tomorrow I'll have to do it myself.*'"

When the mother hears this news, she declares that they must move the nest right away.

Everyone tends to want to rely on others, but things don't get moving that way. The job cannot be done unless you lead the way and do it yourself.

At Y Automobile, Mr. N tells me:

"Whenever I ask the fellows in purchasing why some item we ordered is late, they say that they've reminded the supplier. Then I ask whether they've checked to see how much headway has been made on the problem. Whoever is in charge of the order at the supplier's has told them over the telephone that he'll take care of it, they say. They have confidence in him.

"But this is all wrong. I'm always nagging my people, telling them that the items they've ordered will never be delivered on time unless they're ready to go in person to the supplier and check out the facts for themselves — to plant themselves on the supplier's doorstep if need be. The problem is that they don't do what I tell them to."

Somehow, when I hear Mr. N's story, I can't help but wonder if those suppliers of his might be the kind who would believe they can get a free haircut tomorrow.

The Same as Yesterday Isn't Good Enough

Sometimes when I visit companies, I find people who say "no" to improvement plans from the start. "After all," they say, "we've been doing things this way for ten years and never had any problems. Everything's fine."

"I see," I say for the sake of politeness, but underneath I want to ask them if they really have made no progress in ten years.

Human beings cannot progress unless somehow they do things differently today from the way they did them yesterday.

To be sure, there is a sort of peace of mind that comes of doing things the traditional way if that way has led to a certain degree of success. It is perfectly natural that doing new things is accompanied by certain risks.

But there will never be any progress made if yesterday's methods are used forever. You have to try out new ways of doing things. If you do, perhaps half of what you try will end in failure, but the other half will be linked to progress.

Before World War II, Japan had an enormously accomplished finance minister named Hijikata. Hijikata had graduated with a first-rate record from a teacher-training school in Kōchi Prefecture. On the occasion of his graduation, he went to pay his respects to a teacher he greatly admired. "I hope to be as great as you are," he told the teacher.

"Hijikata," the teacher admonished him, "there would never be any progress at all in the world if students were satisfied to attain the same level as their teachers. You've got to set your sights on surpassing me."

Spurred on by these words, Hijikata worked hard and went on to a higher teacher-training school. Afterward he studied economics on his own, became a politician, and achieved the distinction of becoming Minister of Finance. In his autobiography, Hijikata tells how that single counsel from his teacher changed the course of his life.

Indeed, there would be no progress in the world if students did not surpass their teachers.

Plant "Trees" Throughout the Factory

In recent years I have frequently travelled to Europe and the United States. Every time I go, I am impressed by how clean European and American factories are.

The cleanliness of the insides of buildings is part of the reason for this impression, of course. In addition, lawns and courtyards are planted with trees and are full of greenery and blooming flowers, all to please the sensibilities of the observer. Indeed, many factories give the impression of being located in the midst of a park.

Lately, perhaps as a result of foreign influence, there has been a most felicitous trend toward environmental beautification in Japan, and there is a greater number of graceful and neat industrial plants here than ever before.

For example, the president of K Metals recently participated in a number of study trips to other countries and, perhaps because of having seen attractive factories there, he has worked hard within the last two or three years to beautify his company's facilities. Visitors to K Metals are said to spare no praise in complimenting him on the firm's neat and pleasant plant.

In this same plant, however, many argumentative people have been slow to make progress on recommended improvements such as SMED or poka-yoke. In fact, there is a tendency to ignore such ideas altogether.

I once commented on this situation to the company's president. "You have," I said, "recently made your facilities quite attractive by planting trees and flowers. But there are more important trees that you seem to have forgotten to plant."

"More important trees?" he replied. "What do you mean?"

"I'm talking about planting trees inside the factory," I said.

"Inside the factory? What trees would I plant inside the factory?"

"Trees of will — the will to do things right."

He seemed to understand what I meant, because later, under his leadership, rapid improvements were made and considerable success was achieved.

There is no question that a beautiful exterior environment is important for an industrial plant, but even more crucial is increased efficiency inside. To achieve this, there is nothing more important than planting "trees of will."

Don't Use the Same Slogan for the Foreman and the Company President

Whenever a new policy for improving efficiency comes out, some Japanese companies make up a slogan to announce the president's plans. If the company president's slogan is "Reduce Inventory!" then division heads and department chiefs will take up the same cry and group leaders and foremen will similarly issue calls for inventory reduction.

But this isn't the way things should work. If a company's president makes an appeal to "Reduce Inventory!" the division heads and department heads should adopt a more concrete policy, like "Shorten setup times throughout, in order to carry out small-lot production!" Next, the group leaders and foremen need to translate this into an even more specific slogan that shop workers will immediately understand: "Standardize all die heights and clamping surface thicknesses!"

If this isn't done, the same slogan will be chanted like a meaningless litany all the way down the chain of command and solid results will be few and far between.

Fair Weather Always Follows the Rain

I joined the First Kurume Tank Corps in 1931, a time when we might have been sent into battle at any moment. Our training instructor, a Lieutenant Harada, made a profound impression on me that has lasted to this day.

"From this instant on," he told us, "you may be sent into battle at any moment. When you do move onto the battlefield, sometimes things will go well for our side and you will be on the offensive. At other times you will be surrounded by powerful enemy forces and will be obliged to take defensive measures and persevere until reinforcements arrive.

"Everything will go fairly smoothly for you when you are battling from a position of strength. The problem will come when you are holding out patiently in a defensive position. In such a situation, those of you who are weak of spirit may be seized by fear and rush wildly out of the trenches. The enemy will be waiting for you and you will be shot dead on the spot. Not only that, the enemy will learn our location and the entire squad may be wiped out.

"If you find yourselves in this situation, you must be calm and never give up the hope that reinforcements will arrive. It is supremely important, moreover, that you rest and save your energies for the next offensive.

"Once a good opportunity springs out in front of you, you should run the 100 meters to the next trench and jump in. Those who hesitate and are slow to come out of the trenches will be spotted and will end up being targets for enemy rifles.

"As you all know, fair weather always follows rain and rain always follows fair weather. Neither rain nor fair weather ever lasts uninterrupted for a year.

"I believe that life moves sort of like a wave motion and just as wave crests do not continue forever, neither do wave troughs. This is true both in battle and in life, and the attitude with which you face the troughs is extremely important."

These words have had a significant impact on my entire life ever since. When my improvement work has not gone as well as I expected, when relations with other people have turned sour, and, in particular, when I have fallen ill, I think, "Aha! This is the trough of a wave; this is life's rainy season. Fair weather will come along soon." Time and time again, this thought has dispelled my impatience and restored my sense of equilibrium.

On a visit to Y Automobile, I met someone who had attended my IE course five years earlier, Mr. Sametani of the Production Engineering Department. He seemed a little depressed and I asked him if he was feeling well.

"It's not that," he replied. "I just don't get along with the new department head. All he does is find fault with what I do and I'm sick of it. I just can't get excited about my job — even you noticed it."

I tried to comfort him before I left. "Listen, Mr. Sametani," I said. "Life moves in a sort of wave motion. Right now you're in a rainy season. Rather than brooding about it, you've got to recharge your batteries for the future. In other words, do some studying or make what improvements you can and get to know the people on the shop floor. Believe me, if you take an interest in something and turn yourself around, fair weather will show up before long.

When I went back to Y Automobile after about a year I sought out Mr. Sametani. This time he was full of energy and in high spirits. When I asked him how things were going, he thanked me vigorously. "What you told me really snapped me out of it," he said. "Fortunately the new department head really dotes on me and I'm working in top form. It's just like you said. Fair weather always follows the rain."

To digress a bit, I have always felt that, rather than berating our spouses for dawdling when they are struggling with a job and stuck in the trough of one of life's waves, we should provide the protective psychological support needed to tide them over to the next wave crest so that together we can look forward to sunnier days. Indeed, I find it profoundly telling that the Japanese written character for "person" depicts two individuals helping one another.

Defensive Territories

One of the directors of Y Automobile told me the following story:

"Universities nowadays are teaching nothing but theories — theories of organization, and ideas about responsibility and authority, and so on. Managers end up thinking of these as sacred principles. They seem to forget that organization means an arrangement for running a business efficiently.

"Their organization theories say that if a baseball game were to begin right now, the infielders would get together and confer. They might agree on various things: the defensive boundary between first base and second base, the defensive boundary between second base and the shortstop, the defensive boundary between the shortstop and third base. If a grounder came rolling out, each infielder would ascertain which side of the boundary the ball was on and stand by and watch if it wasn't on his side. Many theories of organization are like this.

"In a game, the significant thing is winning, not deciding whose territory the ball is going to roll into. When it's hard to tell which side of the line the ball is going to end up on, or when one player is in a better position, even though the ball is not in his territory, it seems to me that the most important thing is to go for the ball — even if you bump into your teammate — and to throw it to first base to get the hitter out.

"Of course, not having any standards at all would result in confusion, so defensive territories should be staked out in a general way. The problem is that since the crucial thing is winning, it's clearly wrong to give precedence to the mechanical guarding of defensive territories.

"I find it annoying that so many managers claim I am 'overstepping my authority' or 'exceeding my responsibilities' if I call attention to issues concerning work in departments other than my own. Of course, when I do, I still have to get in touch afterward with whomever is nominally in charge.

"At any rate, even outside the realm of general organization theory, urging people to come up with ideas to benefit the company is not particularly well thought of."

Fortunately, the atmosphere at Y Automobile was such that opinions poured forth without regard to the company's organization. Indeed, it was impressive to see how truly lively the environment inside the company was.

It may be important to adhere to formal organizational charts, yet there are many issues to consider. For example, would it be better to deviate from the organization a bit and let everyone show what he or she can do?

As I go around from one company to another, how often I hear managers respond to problems that have been raised with, "That's not in my jurisdiction!"

10

Understanding and Conviction

Understanding Alone Isn't Enough to Get People Moving

People will understand something if the reasoning is explained to them. But understanding by itself will never get things put into practical operation. People will not swing into action until they are convinced by the arguments.

Understanding is a function of reason, whereas *conviction* is an emotion. We may very well deal with someone's new idea by saying, "What that guy says is correct, but I'm not going to do it because I don't like him." We may believe that demolishing someone with logic will get him to do what we want, but in fact, using arguments to overwhelm people often has the opposite effect.

People will not be set in motion until they are convinced on an emotional level based on trust — until they can say, "That's right! I know that'll make the job easier and improve quality at the same time!" or "It looks kind of hard, but I believe the guy who's telling me this, so it's got to work!"

For example, in an effort to improve a setup operation at T Auto Body, the head of the Production Engineering section made measurements of the operation and indicated various areas for improvement, but these suggestions never seemed to be put into practice. At this point, the department head, Mr. Yamaguchi, suggested that the setup operation be videotaped and then that the videotape be shown to the workers when the setup was completed. When the workers saw the tape, they came out with all sorts of observations ("You mean I do *that*?" "We sure spend a lot of time looking for tools." "Why the delays?"), and improvements made right away cut setup time in half.

In the end, then, the workers didn't really believe the Production Engineering representative when he told them what he had observed. They insisted that delays were not much of a problem or that they didn't behave as the production engineer claimed they did. Actually seeing themselves and watching their own movements on the videotape convinced them, however, and they quickly took action to remedy the situation.

I still remember what Mr. Yamaguchi told me about the experience at the time. "People can't see themselves from the back," he said, "so even if someone tells them that there is a dirty spot there, they tend not to believe it. But if they see the spot themselves on videotape, they will be convinced and will move quickly to deal with the problem."

Thus, people tend not to swing into action on the strength of the logic of some new idea. Putting new ideas into effect demands, above all else, that the people involved be *convinced*.

It is crucial, also, to understand that being convinced of something is a function of emotion rather than of reason. The observation that "people cannot see themselves from the back" is an apt one, indeed.

A Two-Step Method of Persuasion

S Manufacturing Company makes plastic home electronics products. On a visit to the parent company in Osaka, the president of S Manufacturing was asked to increase output by 30 percent within three months.

As soon as he got back to Tokyo, the president called a meeting of division and department heads. "Yesterday," he told them, "our parent company, A Television, asked us to raise production output by 30 percent within the next three months. I'd like us all to talk about what steps we should take to achieve this."

He had no sooner made this announcement than the head of the plant's Manufacturing Department volunteered the opinion that he would need three more machines installed.

"All right," the president replied.

Then the head of the Management Department spoke up: "We'll have to have three shifts, so with three people each shift, that will mean getting nine people.

"I see," said the president.

The head of the Inspection Department added that he would need more inspectors and the head of the Finishing Department said, "We'll need more workers for finishing and also, we're short on space even now, so we'll have to have a new operations area built."

One after another, people from each department asked for more equipment, more people, or more space.

To everyone, the president nodded and said, "I see" or "Uh-hm." About an hour later, when everyone's opinions had been thoroughly aired, he suggested that they take a short break. For the next ten minutes, they all drank coffee and made small talk.

When the meeting started up again the president addressed the group: "I listened to what you all had to say earlier, and I must say, I sympathize with your requests — they all seem quite reasonable to me. As you know, though, this plant is located in the middle of a residential area and people's houses come right up to our wall. We might be able to buy more equipment or add workers, but I regret to point out that there's simply no more space available on our plot of land. I realize this is probably asking the impossible, but I wonder if there isn't some way to increase output with the space and the machines we have currently available to us."

Everyone fell glumly silent at this and not a word was spoken for two or three minutes. Suddenly, the head of the Engineering Department asked, "What's the work rate for our current machines, anyway?"

"About 65 percent," the Manufacturing Department head replied.

"And what accounts for the largest portion of the remaining 35 percent?"

"Well, that would have to be setup time. We've been getting a lot of small-lot orders from our parent company recently, and the number of setups we have to perform has risen about 30 percent."

"About how long does a setup take now?"

"I'd say about one hour."

"Look, our parent company has been recommending for about six months now that we implement single-minute exchange of die. How about giving it some thought? The word is that one of our sister firms, the M Company, reduced its setups to around eight minutes."

"That's true," said the Manufacturing Department chief. "We should definitely give it a try."

At that point, the head of the Engineering Department spoke up and suggested looking into applying SMED to vacuum forming right away. He had heard, he said, that it might eliminate deburring completely and cut the defect rate by four-fifths. The company president added, "If we can directly link the forming process and the finishing process, we can cut down on inventory and free up some space."

"How about hooking up finishing with the packaging process as well?" someone suggested.

"And we could use ultrasonic waves to disconnect the gates." said someone else.

The atmosphere had changed completely. Innovative ideas came pouring forth. A number of these ideas were in fact put into effect, with the result that three months later, a 27 percent increase in real output was achieved without the addition of either machines or workers.

There can be no doubt that the environment from which these changes sprang could never have taken hold if the company president had immediately countered everyone's views with, "No, we can't do that. We can't make the plant any bigger so it won't work. You ought to know that." It seems to me that the president's success lay in a two-step method of persuasion. At first he nodded and let people with opposing views express them fully; then, when they had emptied their brains, he took a new tack and had everyone think of more innovative ideas.

It is an impressive approach, one that makes it possible to grasp the oblique strands of people's thoughts.

The Magic Words, "I See What You Mean"

At a tobacco processing plant, I once suggested that each package of cut tobacco be sent down a chute and onto a conveyor as soon as it was glued and sealed. The proposal was immediately rejected: "It won't work because the glue won't hold."

What had to be decided at this point was whether the objection was frontal or whether it was essentially cautionary. Resolving such questions demands winning time, and in situations like this, time can be won by using the magic words, "I see what you mean."

The phrase indicates neither agreement nor disagreement; it is neutral and says only, "Yes, that's true." While you are saying, "I see what you mean," you should be scrutinizing your listener's counter-argument and if, in spite of its negative tone, you find it to be essentially cautionary, then you should accept it.

Your "I see what you mean" may give a hostile listener the impression that he has gotten you to accept his assertions and in that sense it acts as a psychological neutralizing agent, for the atmosphere surrounding the subsequent exchange will have been changed from one of debate to one of discussion.

If you challenge people with the accusation that they do nothing but object, exchanges will flare into emotional debates, and in the end, satisfactory conclusions will be unattainable. With "I see what you mean," you can take in what your interlocutor says and, if his objection is essentially cautionary, you can agree that you have overlooked something and then address the issue. This non-confrontational, affirmative approach is an effective way to develop better improvement plans. The fact is that most people on the shop floor tend to oppose improvement schemes. The liberal use of neutralizing phrases such as "I see what you mean" and "that's true" will change the atmosphere from one of debate to one of discussion, and this is extremely effective in implementing improvements.

99 Percent of Objections Are Cautionary

The cut-tobacco packaging operation mentioned above consisted of several repeated motions:

- Apply glue to the right edge of the packaging paper and glue the package shut.
- Line up five sealed packages of tobacco on the left.
- Take up groups of five packages and, reaching out, place them on the conveyor.

When I suggested to the plant manager that a chute could be used to send each package to the conveyor as soon as it is sealed, he rejected the proposal outright: "It won't work because the glue won't hold. Amateurish ideas like that don't work out."

I thought about this for a bit. The point of my improvement was that:

- Fully extending the arm to reach out to the conveyor is wasteful.
- It is annoying to have to think about how many packages have been completed.
- The rhythm of movement in the task is interrupted by the intrusion of a different movement every five items. Yet there was really no objection to these issues. The objection was simply that the idea was no good because the glue would not hold.

In effect, I felt, the objection was unjustified, because it was an objection to a *means*, and not to the *goals* of the improvement. Since all that was needed was to make sure the glue held, I experimented to see how much drying was required. Differences in chutes were negligible and I knew that the glue would dry in the time it took to prepare five packages, so I made a suggestion:

- When gluing and sealing on the first package is complete, set that package to the left.
- When the second package is complete, place it to the left, pushing the first package over.
- Continue pushing the row of packages over as each new one is completed and the sixth package will fall into the chute and onto the conveyor.

This worked beautifully.

The manager had protested that the idea would not work because the glue would not hold. Yet suppose he had said, "That's a good idea, but you'll have to give some thought to whether the glue will hold"? If he had, his view would clearly have been cautionary. Thus, by changing the way the view is expressed, pointing out that the glue will not hold becomes either an objection or a piece of cautionary advice.

Even if the tone of voice is confrontational, the content of an objection is often cautionary, so we must entertain that possibility. There is no doubt that the whole idea would have fallen on its face if I had responded to the manager's objection by ignoring what he had to say.

I suggest to you that 99 percent of all objections are cautionary. The words used tend to determine whether the response is a warning or an objection, but the basic content is nearly always cautionary. The remaining one percent of cases most likely involve some sort of mis-apprehension or hostility.

No matter what the tone of an objection, seize the essence of what is being said, use it to offset the weakness in your suggestion, and develop a better proposal.

The 90 Percent Strategy

I had not seen Mr. Tsuji of F Electronics for a long while when he told me this story.

"I was so impressed after taking your Production Technology Seminar that I have devoted myself to plant improvement ever since. When my department head gave me a topic, I carried out on-site surveys and considered the problem from all angles. I'd put together a report outlining what I thought was a perfect improvement plan and take it to the department head's office. He'd glanced through the report and say, 'Tsuji, this won't do. Think it over again and come up with something else.'

"'But what's wrong with it?' I'd ask.

"'The whole thing is wrong,' he'd reply. 'Just give it some more thought, all right?'

"I would rethink my proposal and submit it again, but once more I would be sent back to do more work on it. Finally, the third time he would give the plan his approval.

"This sort of thing happened two or three times and I was on the verge of a nervous breakdown. I couldn't get any work done because all I could think about was how incompetent I was and how I wasn't qualified to be a production engineer.

"Around this time, one of the old hands, a section chief named Ueno, noticed that I seemed to be having a hard time of it. 'How about coming over to my place tonight?' he suggested.

"That night, although I wasn't too enthusiastic, I visited Mr. Ueno at home. He gave me a serious talking to and let me in on some secrets. When I went back home I still wasn't sure whether I should believe what he told me or not.

"The next time I got a new topic from my department head, I kept in mind what Mr. Ueno had told me as I drew up and submitted my report. The department head looked at the report and pointed out some things I had left out. And he was right — I had skipped a few things. I apologized and promised to make corrections immediately.

"When I had made the necessary additions and resubmitted the report, the department head chided me for leaving out such elementary things. 'Be more careful from now on,' he said, and then he approved the report by affixing his personal stamp.

"Mr. Ueno told me I'd been unwise to provide my superiors with 100 percent of the answers to the problem. 'Give them 90 percent of the answers and let them hold on to some dignity.' Perhaps I had doubted Mr. Ueno, but when I put his plan into effect I did things a little better than I had been told to.

"The big lesson I learned in all this is that obstinately sticking to your arguments doesn't get you anywhere. You've got to pay attention to human psychology."

Of course not all department heads are like Mr. Tsuji's, but his story reminded me that on occasion one has to think about satisfying the boss's pride.

Improvement Assassins

Nowadays, nearly all Japanese companies have adopted suggestion systems, and many suggestions for improvements are being generated.

Proposals for improvement that come out of the shop must be evaluated. Some evaluators, however, spend most of their time pointing out shortcomings in the proposals they see. They go over one proposal after another and reject them, saying "No good....No good....We've seen this before." I call committee members of this sort *improvement assassins*. People in the shop will rapidly lose interest in making suggestions if their proposals are killed off so readily. They will either start to think all their suggestions are bad ones or question their own abilities, and eventually they will stop making any suggestions at all.

Generally speaking, although the impact of actual proposals received is important, even more crucial is a sense of participation in the company — a sense that everyone wants to work to make his or her own company better. Shop workers' desire to make suggestions will cool in companies with negative-thinking improvement assassins, and only a few diehard "suggestion freaks" will continue to make proposals.

When a proposal is rejected at A Electric, the person who made the suggestion is summoned and the evaluation committee explains to him or her what aspect of the suggestion was unacceptable and why it was not adopted. Then the person who made the proposal is urged to rethink the suggestion. Alternatively, the committee might explain that the suggestion was a good one, but that it could not be adopted because similar proposals had already been submitted. "Keep the good suggestions coming!" the committee urges.

In the past, people in the shop had no way of knowing that similar proposals had already been made and therefore felt dissatisfied because they did not understand why their good ideas had not been adopted. This problem reportedly has disappeared now that the evaluation committee explains the reasons for rejected proposals.

Often, companies kill suggestion activities entirely by presenting awards for prizewinning suggestions but ignoring rejected proposals. We look forward to seeing this issue addressed by the adoption of a system of explaining rejections such as the one used by A Electric.

IE, You E, Everybody E

I first instituted a five day IE improvement course at A Electric in 1962. I made the following remarks at a discussion session on the evening before the final day of the course:

"During the last four days, you have been studying basic IE concepts and techniques, but when you go back to your plants to make improvements, you've got to take back more than just IE. There's one other important thing I want you to remember to take back with you — You E.

"No matter how good you may think your plans are, you must see to it that the people involved understand and are convinced by those plans so they will go out of their way to implement them; they must believe your methods are good ones — that they will generate good products easily.

"So, I want you to remember to take You E back with you along with IE."

At that point, the Manufacturing Department head, Mr. Horii, suggested the problem be tackled in a spirit of "IE, You E, Everybody E." That phrase later became a watchword at A Electric, and improvements progressed smoothly and with lively acceptance in the shop.

Division of Labor Is Not Necessarily a Good Thing

This example involves an operation in which ink is applied over the stamped portion of a golf ball and then, after drying, the surface is wiped off to bring out the imprinted characters.

Workers A and B:

- Take roughly 50 balls apiece and paint ink onto their surfaces with brushes
- Arrange the balls in no particular order on a workbench
- After a specified period of time elapses, reveal inked-in characters by wiping with a rag the surfaces of balls that were judged to have dried

These procedures had shortcomings, however:

- Workers had to determine which balls had dried
- When workers picked up inadequately dried balls they often smeared the ink

These shortcomings were overcome in improved procedures that involved a division of labor:

- Worker A painted ink onto the surface of the balls and placed them one by one into a chute provided between worker A and worker B.
- B took the balls in the order they came down the chute and wiped them off.

This method included several innovations:

- There was no need to pick out balls on which ink had dried because adequately dried balls were fed to worker B in order.
- No balls were smeared because none were picked up until fully dry.
- A division of labor eliminated the wasteful operations of picking up and putting down brushes and rags.

The results, however, were mixed:

- The output of imprinted balls rose by roughly 15 percent.
- At the same time, the inking operation was often done crudely, so that inadequately inked characters showed up more frequently. This in turn necessitated increased re-inking operations.

- This lowered the efficiency of imprinting operations by 5 percent.

Overall, then, the operation ended up being cruder because it did not give workers ultimate responsibility for quality.

In the end, the operation was improved as follows:

- Workers A and N each perform the same operations.
- They paint ink onto the surfaces of golf balls.
- Each worker places balls in order onto a turntable that holds fifty balls. A place is provided for a fifty-first ball, and when only this last space remains, the inking operation is halted.
- Workers use rags to wipe balls on which ink has dried. This change led to an eventual 10 percent increase in efficiency.

This example underscores the fact that beyond the simplistic view that division of labor increases efficiency, a crucial factor must be considered: People need to take responsibility for their own work.

11

The Force of Habit

ENOUGH IMPROVEMENT PLANS, ALREADY!

According to the physical law of inertia, a body in motion tends to remain in motion and a body at rest tends to remain at rest. In the same way, when human beings perform a given task, they tend to resist any change in the procedures they use.

In this connection, a scientist once performed an experiment to see whether goldfish could remember things. First he built a glass tank with a glass barrier in the middle; in the center of the barrier he made a hole large enough to for a goldfish to swim through (See *Figure 11-1*).

When he placed a goldfish on one side of the barrier and food on the other side, the goldfish headed straight for the food and ran into the transparent pane of glass. After repeating this action a number of times, the goldfish managed to pass through the central hole to the food.

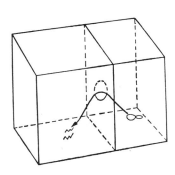

FIGURE 11-1. Glass Tank

After numerous repetitions, the goldfish would head straight through the hole and eat the food. Apparently, repetition taught the goldfish to remember that all it had to do was swim through the central passage.

Next, the researcher removed the glass barrier and placed the trained goldfish on one side of the tank and food on the other side. In spite of the fact that the barrier was gone, the goldfish still swam to the food via the place where the hole had been. In other words, *force of habit* led the goldfish to persist in its old behavior despite a change in the situation.

Surely, humans too, are affected by the force of habit.

ARE OLD WAYS BETTER?

It is clearly true that the easiest methods are those we are familiar with. When a method is familiar, we move naturally, without having to think about what should be done next or how each task should be done. Consequently, the job can be carried out without burdening the brain.

This means that there is no psychological burden involved, and a worker can hum as he works. Workers end up believing that familiar operations are the easiest and therefore the best way of doing things.

But is this in fact so?

Lillian M. Gilbreth devised some "tabletop improvement experiments" that help clarify this point.

Experiment 1: Habit

- Write *production engineering* on 15 3 × 5 cards.
- Measure how much time it takes to write each card and graph the values onto a curve, as shown in *Figure 11-2*.
- In the language of psychology, your unburdened brain "anticipates" as you write. When you are writing the *p*, your mind is already telling you to write *r* next and how to write it. This allows your hand to move fluidly.
- As a result, the task requires very little time and there is minimal deviation among the values obtained. The effect of practice makes itself felt, as well, so times are slightly shorter at the end.

- This familiar method involves only a slight mental burden and little time. The output of letters — *i.e.*, quality — is stable.

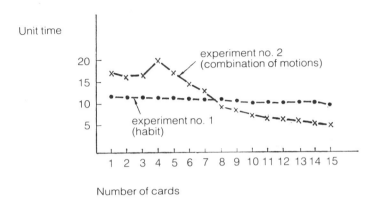

Unit time

experiment no. 2
(combination of motions)

experiment no. 1
(habit)

Number of cards

FIGURE 11-2. **Time per Card in Seconds**

Experiment 2: Combined Motions

- Write the first letter of *production engineering* but not the second letter. Then write the third letter but not the fourth. Continue writing every other letter. Repeat this process fifteen times.
- The correct outcome will be *p o u t o e g n e i g*.

Figure 11-2 gives the results of this experiment. Even though you wrote only half as many letters as in Experiment 1, writing the letters the first four times took far more than half the time needed for the first four repetitions in the first experiment. The fourth and fifth repetitions took a particularly long time. Increasingly less time was needed after that, so that the fifteenth writing took far less time than in Experiment 1.

Discussion

Why did writing letters in Experiment 2 take more time at first than writing the letters in Experiment 1 even though only half as many letters were involved?

The answer is that, in Experiment 2, after writing *p* you had to think about what letter to write next. You had to determine that the next letter was *o* and the one after that was *t*, etc. Thinking as you wrote each letter entailed hesitation and the process took more time because the next letter was not automatically anticipated.

As you wrote out the letters in Experiment 2 several times, however, an image of the sequence, *p o u t o*, etc. began to form and writing grew more fluid as mental anticipation began to occur. At this point, the fact that you were writing fewer letters began to take effect and total time diminished.

The fourth and fifth repetitions took so much time because time was taken up verifying that the letters were indeed the correct ones. This is a normal response that ordinarily occurs when people are faced with a new task.

Thus, even though there is no question that dealing with half the number of letters is an improvement, initial decisions and hesitations will keep mental anticipation from taking over and will entail considerable difficulty and time. In addition, quality may occasionally suffer as you write the wrong letters.

As you write the sequence over and over again, however, you will gradually memorize the new task and mental anticipation will occur. You will end up learning *p o u t o e g n e i g* as a single phrase and decision and hesitation will vanish, allowing the effect of fewer letters to take over. In the end, then, it will take less time than Experiment 1. Since improvements to a greater or lesser extent demand new procedures, a certain amount of difficulty will be encountered and a certain amount of time will be needed to decide how to carry out those new procedures and then to memorize them. Initially, then, new methods will be difficult. Old procedures, however, are easy just because they are familiar; just as mental anticipation made it easy to write the larger number of letters smoothly.

This explanation is no doubt accurate, but is it really reasonable to go on to claim that old ways are easier *and therefore better*?

For instance, as long as it is unfamiliar, even an improved procedure will be more difficult and will take more time than the old procedure because decisions and hesitations will occur and because mental anticipation is absent. Thus, no improvement shows its true worth right away. Its real efficacy will become apparent only after a certain period of practice.

This means that 99 percent of all improvement plans would vanish without a trace if they were to be abandoned after only a brief trial. People in charge of plant improvement must grasp this fact, so that they can provide necessary encouragement when people on the shop floor complain during trial implementation that the improved procedures are too hard or take too long. "Keep at it a little bit longer," they have to say. "Improvements are nearly always more difficult at first."

If shop workers say that the supposedly improved procedures take just as much time as the old methods, the response must be, "That's only true because you aren't accustomed to them yet. Once you get used to the new procedures, they will definitely take less time." Once again, people must be given strong encouragement and urged to continue with the improved procedures.

In a surprising number of cases, however, supervisors will agree with workers that new methods take too long or are too difficult, and will abandon them right away. It is crucial to recognize that this attitude is entirely wrong.

In any event, while it is absolutely true that old ways are easier, it is a mistake to conclude that they are therefore better. It is important to understand that even the finest improvements will not demonstrate their true worth until they have become familiar.

CAN YOU EVER BE TOO BUSY FOR IMPROVEMENT?

Frequently, when I go to production plants and promote improvement, I am rebuffed by people who say they are too busy and have no time for such activities. If business has slowed down a bit the next time I visit and I suggest that perhaps now there is time for improvement, I am often turned down outright. "We've got no work to do," people will say. "We're busy looking for work and haven't got any time. Anyway, it's hard to get fired up about improvement when there's no work — no need to, either."

At this rate, there's no telling when improvements can be made. I make it a point to respond by telling people, "Look, you'll stop being busy either when you die or when the company goes bankrupt. Think about it. It's precisely because you are busy that you've got to analyze the factors that keep you busy. Revitalize the company by changing those factors for the better."

No salaried worker will ever save money if he or she decides to put away only what's left over at the end of the month. If you want to save, you've got to decide to have a fixed payroll deduction and then live on the rest. You'll never be able to own your own home unless you use that accumulated savings as a down payment and then pay monthly installments.

The same thing holds for improvement. No company can develop unless efforts at improvement are sustained with the regularity of payroll deductions — through good times and bad, whether busy or not. It seems to me that a company that refuses to sustain improvement work is past the stage of needing a doctor. It's going to have to be taken to a priest and then to the cemetery.

I visited Yoshioka Plating when the worldwide economy was in such bad shape during the oil crisis. Construction work was under way there on new automated plating equipment. I asked the company's president why they had begun such costly construction when business was so bad.

"Actually," he replied. "It was my father's last wish."

"What do you mean by that?"

"My father," the president said, "always told me that I would make a lot of money if I kept plant facilities running hard when I was busy. He taught me that I should use slack periods to rebuild and augment equipment. For one thing, if you invest in facilities during slumps, big equipment makers who wouldn't even look at you when they're busy will figure that you're running a solid operation. They'll be receptive to unusual specifications and other requests, and you can have things done at relatively low cost. What's more, there will be no negative impact if you have to halt plant operations for a while."

I marveled at the wisdom of the father who had left such a legacy and at the son who had the courage to put it into effect.

THE "DYNAMITE HOLE" APPROACH TO IMPROVEMENT

It goes without saying that to improve work in production plants requires that everyone in the workplace understand the improvements, be persuaded by them, and actively work to put them into effect. In the early stages of improvement, however, it can be effective to use a "dynamite hole" approach.

When cutting a tunnel for extracting ore from a mine, rather than working the entire tunnel face with a mandrel, it is more efficient to drill holes with a small bit, pack the holes with dynamite, attach a fuse, and throw a switch — the electric current will blast open the tunnel.

Given the difficulty of getting everybody to think the same way, you should choose active people — vigorous department or section heads and, in particular, shop floor foremen and group leaders — and persuade them first. By way of experiment, have them first focus on a single topic and demonstrate their success to everyone else. This initial topic need not involve the most crucial task in the plant, but making it visible is the quickest route to persuading everyone that improvement really is possible.

People in the shop simply will not be convinced if all you do is give them logical arguments.

If you have as many as 100 people in a group, it is difficult to get them all headed in the same direction. Generally, one third of the people in a given group will be in favor of a new proposal, one third will be against it, and the remaining third will be neutral. By bringing even one person from among the neutral third over to your way of thinking, you can bring the neutral faction surging over to the "yea" side to form an absolute majority. When this happens, the remaining "nays" will naturally come around as well.

Look at it another way. If you start by aiming for 70 percent success rather than 100 percent, successful implementation of a new scheme will get everyone to believe in it and the climate in the entire workplace can be shifted in the direction of improvement.

When I want to implement SMED, I have workers bring out two dies for machines of approximately 100 tons or less. In the course of about an hour, I carry out a demonstration:

- Use blocks to make die heights uniform.
- Secure blocks at clamping sites with gummed tape and use clamps.
- Place blocks on the far sides of dies so that the dies are centered when they strike the stoppers.
- Bring a new die near the machine during external setup.
- If possible, have two workers carry out parallel operations.
- Keep all needed tools within reach.

Without exception, these procedures make it possible right away to reduce setups of an hour and a half to seven or eight minutes.

Seeing a demonstration like this helps people see that SMED is possible, and improvement is frequently speeded up because categorical opposition to SMED vanishes.

The first time I visited the French auto maker Citroen,, in 1981, I spent the first morning talking about production control to about 50 management people and engineers. I had a hard time getting on with my speech, because objections kept popping up while I was lecturing. In particular, a welter of objections came up when I talked about SMED. "It can't be done," said some. Others said, "It'll be too expensive," or, "You'll need incredibly expensive equipment."

When operations began that afternoon, I went to the plant and had two dies brought out. I checked their dimensions myself and then asked to have some needed work done. I said that I wanted blocks of such and such size in certain places and 50 mm² blocks in other places to make clamping surfaces uniform.

In my lecture that afternoon, continual questions and objections arose, just as they had in the morning.

When we went to observe the SMED demonstration the following morning, what had been a one hour and 40-minute setup had been shortened to a mere 12 minutes. The engineers and the management people looking on were stunned.

We returned to the conference room afterwards and I gave everyone a little talk.

"Before I left Japan, I was told that the French were very argumentative and my experience yesterday confirms that appraisal. It seems to me, however, that all your arguments were negative ones, such as 'This won't work' or 'That's impossible.'

"As I see it, no matter how informed your opinions are, you'll never make any progress if you insist that things are impossible. In Japan, when arguments are deadlocked, we still believe new methods to be possible. We give them a try and look at actual results to find ways of overcoming problems. I am persuaded that this is the most important reason for Japan's having raised the level of her industry and succeeded in producing high-quality, inexpensive products.

"Instead of sitting around conference tables and trading arguments whenever doubts arise, how about actually giving new ideas a try and seeing what happens?"

This time no one objected, because they had all seen the success of SMED in action.

From that point on, not only did the people at Citroen listen to what I had to say, but their positive efforts brought significant success. SMED was achieved on most machines and inventories were slashed by more than half.

Indeed, we might draw an analogy between this simple two-die SMED demonstration and drilling holes for dynamite.

NEVER SAY "IMPOSSIBLE"

One day I had lunch with Mr. Kōno, a director of Z Machinery. What he told me that day was of some interest:

"Mr. M, the president of our parent company, M Diesel, succeeded in producing the first Japanese diesel engines. He's a dedicated entrepreneur who tenaciously devotes himself to getting the job done.

"One morning he showed up at the Engineering Department and said he had thought up a new design for an engine. 'I want a prototype built and tested before the end of tomorrow,' he said. 'Who will do it for me?' The engineers all hung their heads in silence, each fearing that he might be chosen. 'Do a four-week job in two days,' they asked themselves, 'Impossible!'

"Seeing their reaction, the president continued calmly: "Well, it seems there are no volunteers. I suppose I'll just have to do it myself.'

"Mr. M then flopped down in a chair next to a young engineer and began giving him instructions on how to draw up plans for the engine. He telephoned an old fellow who had long done work for him and, as soon as the first page of plans was completed, he had the old man take it by bicycle over to a wooden pattern workshop. One by one, he gave directions for the building of wooden mock-up parts for the engine. When complete plans had been drawn up, Mr. M went to the workshop himself, sat next to a woodworker, and had the mock-up finished according to his instructions. As soon as each piece of the wooden mock-up was finished, Mr. M had it taken back to his own company's casting shop and had a casting die made. Soon it began to look as though the casting dies would be finished that night, so he had the foreman in charge of melting show up early the following morning and had each piece cast. As each piece was completed, it was taken to the machine shop and finished. Here, too, Mr. M sat next to the machine and gave step-by-step instructions. By the end of the following day, the engine had taken shape and trials could be run in overtime."

Mr. Kōno had said that building the engine in two days was impossible and he had bet a cake that it couldn't be done. When the testing was completed, the president turned to Mr. Kōno and said, "Well, how about it?" So Mr. Kōno had a cake purchased and served it to everyone involved.

Mr. Kōno had watched the company president in action throughout the task and he was powerfully impressed. "If you are really dedicated and determined to accomplish something," he told me, "it doesn't matter if others think it's impossible — you can do it. All right, then, I vowed to myself: As long as I live, I swear I will never again say anything is impossible."

Two months afterward, the president of the company again came to work early. "This time," he said, "I've thought of a new transmission. Who will make one for me before the end of the day tomorrow?" The other engineers said nothing, but Mr. Kōno courageously offered to get the job done somehow. Working in much the same way the president had, Mr. Kōno completed the task by the close of the following day. Under normal circumstances, the work would have taken three weeks to carry out.

This success increased Mr. Kōno's confidence and he vowed again that he would never use the word "impossible" as long as he lived. Mr. Kōno concluded his story by telling me that, since then, he has not once said that anything was "impossible."

As I listened to Mr. Kōno's story, I felt deep admiration for the dedication and tenacity of the founder of Z Machinery.

A PROBLEM WITH THE MIRACLE DRUG?

When I began visiting companies and production plants, there was one thing I almost always used to tell company presidents: "The medicine I am prescribing for you is a miracle drug and very powerful, but there is one problem with it."

"What problem?" they would say.

"The problem," I would explain, "is that the medicine won't work unless you take it. I may tell you wonderful things, but you're not going to be successful unless you actually do what I'm telling you.

There are a lot of people in this world who worry that medicine might be bitter or might have side effects, and who find excuses to avoid swallowing it. Behavior like that will never lead to success. Are you ready to take your medicine?"

"Sure," the executives always tell me. "We'll make it a point to take it."

SECTION TWO

Zero Quality Control:
Source Inspection
and the Poka-Yoke System*

* Readings in this section are excerpted entirely from
Zero Quality Control: Source Inspection and the Poka-yoke System
(Cambridge: Productivity Press, 1986)

INTRODUCTION

In a 1983 study of all but one of the manufacturers of room air conditioners in Japan and the United States, Professor David A. Garvin of the Harvard Business School documented some facts which surprised him, and no doubt shocked many people who read them at the time.[1]

This particular industry was chosen for study because of the desire to avoid an "apples vs. oranges" comparison: Each company used a simple assembly line, similar equipment, and made a standardized product. It turned out that products from the lowest quality manufacturers had failure rates between 500 and 1000 times greater than those from the highest quality manufacturers. The American companies had assembly line defect rates which averaged seventy times higher than their Japanese counterparts; service calls under the first year of warranty averaged seventeen times higher. The Japanese companies had average warranty servicing costs three times lower than the best American manufacturer, and nine times better than the worst.

A consumer who buys an air conditioner that constantly breaks down during a shortened life will naturally look around for a more reliable one the next time. The extent to which consumers avoid the poor products the next time is, as W. Edwards Deming wrote, one of the most important facts a company needs to know, yet is unknown and unknowable. The magazine *Consumer Reports* has a circulation of over five-million at the time of this writing, and is no doubt consulted by many times that number before decisions about major purchases like air conditioners are made. The combination of available product-quality information and worldwide improvement in quality means that life will continue to get harder at an accelerating pace for companies whose quality is not in step with that of the best-practice firms in their industry.

Much of the last two decades of progress in raising standards of quality is due to the ascendancy of Statistical Quality Control (SQC). When first introduced into a production process, it adds teeth to the quality control function by forcing the meticulous record-keeping of inspection data (which helps to track down defects) and

---

[1] David Garvin, "Quality on the Line," *Harvard Business Review*, 5, September-October 1983, pp. 64-75

using the well-developed science of statistics to allow the maximum amount of information to be drawn from a series of small samples. In fact, it often detects more defects (and is certainly cheaper) than one-hundred percent inspection, because inspectors, who can be hypnotized by monotony like any other human being, will certainly miss a trick or two as they become increasingly jaded.

And yet, as you will read in this section, SQC may not be the best answer to a production manager's prayers, if he or she cannot afford any defects whatsoever. Because it is based on probabilities and only samples from the product flow, SQC necessarily tolerates some defects. In the following section, you will read of Dr. Shingo's visceral hatred of any defects whatsoever and his consequent rejection of statistical methods. You will discover what procedures he advocates to assure quality. He does not mince his words. The first step, he writes, is to distinguish between quality control and statistics:

> True quality control supposedly requires the use of statistics. Although statistics is only a means, it is sometimes considered so important that the goal of quality control is forgotten.[2]

If the error causing a defect is known, a poka-yoke device (Japanese for "mistake-proof") will permanently prevent the recurrence of the error, and therefore the defect resulting from it. As was mentioned in the introduction, poka-yoke devices are often very simple and inexpensive. Self-checking and successive-checking are techniques designed to shorten the time that it takes to act when a defect is found. Source inspection is another useful tool; it eliminates errors before they cause defects, and frequently makes use of poka-yoke devices to do so. Enough prevention of this kind can bring a process to a state where no defects occur. Such a state was reached, as you will read, almost thirteen years ago at a plant in Matsushita Electric's Washing Machine division.

It is well to remember that the prevention of a defect is usually much cheaper than the correction of it once it has occurred. I was recently in a plant observing an operation where vegetables were being packed into glass jars. The vegetables and the jars met in a machine designed to rain the food down onto a moving conveyor belt which carried the empty (and open) jars below. Any food which missed a jar

---

[2] Non-Stock Production, p. 318.

was retrieved below the conveyor belt and recirculated into the rainstorm to be packed into a later jar. The problem was that the glass jars, which were hit on all sides by hammers in an effort to shake them and settle the food, often shattered. When they did so, the broken glass fell into the retrieval system below the conveyor belt, and was faithfully recirculated and packed into subsequent jars. If the problem was noticed by workers further down the production pipeline, the entire assembly line was shut down. All the tainted jars had then to be emptied, and the packing equipment had to be purged and restarted. Although no one could tell me exactly how often a jar broke, it was clear that it happened at least a few times a week. The company was incurring considerable loss with every such incident: lost materials, machine downtime, and the idling of a good number of workers for an hour or two until the line could be restarted.

Dr. Shingo would have something to say about how to avoid such a mess, and so will you, after you have read the next section.

12

Inspections

THE SIGNIFICANCE OF INSPECTIONS

We have explained that production activities form a network of processes and operations. What, then, is the significance of inspections?

Inspections Supplement Processes

As we have seen, production is constructed of a network of processes and operations. Processes, we said, can be further broken down into four categories: work, inspection, transportation, and delay. We also said that inspections consist of comparisons with standards, but this is merely a description of the act of inspection. Within a process, inspections are characterized by the following functions:

- Inspections reveal and prevent defects in the course of work.
- Inspections reveal and prevent defects in the course of transportation.
- Inspections reveal and prevent defects in the course of delays.

In this way, inspections may be said to supplement work, transportation, and delays. Strictly speaking, the inspection function can be thought of as secondary to production, with inspections themselves playing only a passive, wasteful role.

Although from an operations point of view it is necessary to conduct maximally efficient inspection operations, the fact that inspections are of little value on the process side means that even the most efficient inspection operations are nothing more than efficiently wasteful. It follows that we need, first of all, to examine why we are conducting inspections at all. Even more, we need to carry out higher-order investigations aimed at finding methods of work, transportation, and delays that obviate the need for inspections.

Although inspections are supplementary to work, transport, and delays, from this point I am going to focus on the functions of inspections with respect to work, or processing.

On Defects and Inspections

Isolated Defects and Serial Defects

Isolated defects are essentially those that occur only once. An example would be a single part that is defective because one particular unit of raw material was flawed.

Serial defects, in contrast, occur repeatedly. For example, many pieces might lack holes because a broken punch was not detected right away.

Sensory Inspections and Physical Inspections

Sensory inspections are inspections performed by means of the human senses, for example, judgments of plating adequacy or inspections of paint saturation. It tends to be difficult to set criteria for inspections of this kind, because different people will make different judgments and even the same person might make different judgments on different days.

Physical inspections involve the use of measuring devices, such as calipers or micrometers.

Subjective Inspections and Objective Inspections

Subjective inspections are made by the same person who performed the work. This method always suffers from the dangers of compromise and inattention.

Objective inspections, on the other hand, are made by someone other than the operator who performed the work. This method provides for more rigorous inspections — with fewer lapses of attention — than does the subjective method.

Process-Internal Inspections and Process-External Inspections

Inspections carried out at the same process where the work was performed are process-internal inspections, and inspections carried out at a different process are process-external inspections. Because process-internal inspections permit rapid transmission of information, or feedback, in the event a defect occurs, they are more efficient in reducing defects.

Statistical Inspections and Nonstatistical Inspections

In carrying out inspections — especially sampling inspections — the number of samples may be chosen either in accordance with statistical theory or not. Obviously, it is more rational to determine the number of samples on the basis of statistical theory.

100 Percent Inspections and Sampling Inspections

An inspection of every processed item is a 100 percent inspection, and the method of extrapolating from an appropriate number of samples constitutes sampling. Inspection labor costs can be considerably reduced where it is permissible to conduct sampling inspections. It is sometimes claimed that 100 percent inspections generally take a great deal of trouble and increase the risk of oversights.

Feedback and Action

When a defect occurs, information to that effect sent back to the work process is known as inspection feedback. Such feedback is most effective when it is given promptly, for it permits counter-measures to be devised and methods altered at the work process where the defect occurred. This devising of countermeasures is known as action.

Measurement and Judgment

Measurement refers to the determination of numerical values through the use of measuring devices such as calipers or micrometers after work has been completed. A decision to accept or reject the item is then made on the basis of these numerical results.

Since inspections essentially involve distinguishing acceptable from unacceptable goods, however, it is not always necessary to make numerical measurements. Sometimes a simple gauge-like judgment tool is adequate for determining whether an item is acceptable. When inspections focus on judgments rather than measurements, automated inspections can make use of extremely simple and inexpensive devices.

Quantity Inspections and Quality Inspections

Checks to ascertain that needed quantities suffer from neither excesses nor shortages are quantity inspections, while quality inspections include checks such as the following:

- Is the part machined to within permissible limits?
- Has the surface been ground to within permissible limits?
- Is the degree of hardness obtained in heat treatment suitable?
- Are any parts missing from the assembly? Are all parts present the right ones?
- Are there any scratches? Is the part clean?

Quality inspections may even involve judgments made with the aid of numerical measuring devices as long as what is being checked is product quality.

INSPECTIONS DON'T REDUCE DEFECTS

A plant manager at A Industries complained during one of my visits that he simply could not find any way to reduce defects.

"What have you tried?" I asked.

He told me that an inspector at the very end of the process in question separated the good products from the defective ones, but that about 100 units out of every 1,000 were defective. At that point, the plant manager ordered an increase in the number of inspectors. The next day, the number of defective units dropped to 80 and the second day it fell to 60. He felt somewhat relieved to be on the right track, but on the fourth day the number of defective items rose again, this time to 120 (*Figure 12-1*). "What on earth am I supposed to do to cut defects?" he asked.

This is what I told the plant manager:

"Two inspectors may be able to catch defects that might slip by one inspector, and using the two inspectors may, indeed, eliminate

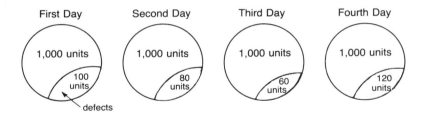

FIGURE 12-1. Inspections and Defects

such oversights and keep you from mixing defective items in with the good ones you send to customers.

"That issue, however, is unrelated to the question of reducing defects.

"In any event, there isn't much point in inspecting goods at the end of the process. Since defects are generated during the process, all you are doing is discovering those defects. Adding inspection workers is pointless, because there's no way you're going to reduce defects without using processing methods that prevent defects from occurring in the first place.

"It follows, then, that when a defect shows up, you've got to send information to that effect back to the work stage so that processing can be corrected. At any rate, it's an unalterable fact that processing produces defects and all that inspections can do is find those defects. That's why approaching the problem only at the inspection stage is meaningless."

13

Approaching the Zero QC Method

PRELIMINARY STAGE: THE OLD METHOD (JUDGMENT INSPECTIONS)

I was taught that an inspection within a process is the act of comparison with a standard, principally to eliminate defective goods. When 100 percent inspections took too much trouble, I used appropriate sampling inspections. I imagined that the occurrence of a certain level of defects was inevitable in any work done by humans, and thought that we should pay attention so as to not produce defective items as we work. At the same time, I vaguely assumed that we could reduce defects by making inspections more and more rigorous. In short, I thought that judgment inspections were the only kind of inspections there were.

STAGE 1: ENCOUNTER WITH THE STATISTICAL QUALITY CONTROL (SQC) METHOD

In 1951, when I was in charge of education for the Japan Management Association, Mr. A from Nippon Electric Company came to my office and asked me if I had heard about quality control. I replied that I understood the term to mean efforts to inspect products, make high-quality goods, and eliminate defects.

"That's not good enough," he told me. "It's not quality control unless you use statistics." He then proceeded to explain the American-style statistical quality control (SQC) method to me. He told me about experimental planning methods, determination of significant differences, factor charts, histograms, and control charts for informative inspections. For the next several hours, I listened to him explain such things as standard limits and control limits, control charts and 3 SD limits, X.R control charts, P control charts, and sampling inspections based on statistical science.

What particularly impressed me was the revolutionary idea of informative inspections that could reduce defects in the future. With this approach, control charts would be drawn up and, whenever values appeared outside of the control limits, information to that effect would be fed back to the process involved and work methods would be improved. I was further struck by the truly revolutionary technique of determining whether a situation was normal or not through classification according to 3 SD control limits. At the most basic level, I was enormously impressed by the theoretical backing provided by the science of inductive statistics. It seemed to me, too, that the theory-based techniques of experimental planning methods and the determination of significant differences were extremely effective.

Mr. A told me he had total confidence in this theoretical sampling inspection system, in which sampling inspections that used to depend solely on intuition were put on a scientific, statistical footing.

His final words left a powerful and lasting impression. "From now on," he stressed, "if it doesn't use statistics, it's not quality control." For a long time afterwards, I believed that quality control systems that used the science of statistics were the ultimate in quality control methods. I believed, furthermore, that informative inspections constituted a revolutionary control system for raising quality, and inductive statistics provided the most rational technique available. I invited Dr. Eisaburo Nishibori to the Japan Management Association and devoted myself to studying the statistical quality control (SQC) method.

STAGE 2: ENCOUNTER WITH POKA-YOKE METHODS

In 1961, I visited Yamada Electric in Nagoya. There, the plant manager told me the following story.

"One of the operations we do involves the assembly of an extremely simple push-button device that we deliver to our parent company, Matsushita Electric, in Kyushu. The device is composed of two buttons, an *on* button and an *off* button, under each of which we have to enclose a small spring. Sometimes, though, one of our workers forgets to put in a spring. When Matsushita Electric discovers a switch without a spring, we have to send an inspector all the way to Kyushu to check every switch that was delivered.

"This is a real pain in the neck, so whenever it happens, we tell workers to be particularly careful and for a while things improve a bit. The same thing happens again before long, though, and these chronic defects are getting to be a real nuisance. Matsushita bawls us out every time for making mistakes in such a simple operation, and recently I had to go to Kyushu myself to apologize. Is there anything we can do to keep these defects from occurring?"

I immediately went into the plant to observe the assembly of the switches.

The operation was an extremely simple one. A worker would insert two small springs and then install the buttons. As I watched, however, a worker neglected to put in a spring before installing the button. The head of the manufacturing department saw this, too. In a panic, he scolded the worker for forgetting the spring and then had the switch reassembled.

I thought about what I had seen for a moment and then turned to Mr. Y, the manufacturing department chief.

"What," I asked him, "does it mean for a human being to 'forget' something?"

Mr. Y looked puzzled and replied, "To 'forget' means . . . well . . . it just means to forget, doesn't it?"

When I asked him to explain, he was unable to answer and finally fell silent. After a brief pause, I suggested to him that there were really two kinds of forgetting. The first involves simply forgetting something. Since people are not perfect, they will, on rare occasions, inadvertently forget things. It is not that they forget things intentionally; they just happen, inadvertently, to forget now and then.

"Haven't you ever, in your whole life, forgotten anything?" I asked Mr. Y.

"Sure I have," he replied. "I forget things now and then. My wife always chews me out about it."

I observed that, that being the case, he was probably in a poor position to complain to his wife that his workers were forgetting things.

The other type of forgetting, I told him, involves forgetting that one has forgotten. We are all familiar with this kind of forgetting. It is the reason, for example, that we make checklists for ourselves. If people had the omnipotence of gods, they would be able to re-member everything and they would not need checklists.

"When I go to play golf," I said, "I carry a checklist with me in a notebook. When I am about to leave, I mostly depend on my memory when I'm getting together the equipment I need. Afterwards, though, I look at my checklist and when I notice, for example, that I have forgotten my gloves, I immediately get my gloves and put them in my bag. That way, I have all my equipment with me when I get to the golf course.

"The same thing applies to this operation. Rather than thinking that workers ought to assemble the switches perfectly every time, you should recognize that, being human, they will, on rare occasions, forget things. To guard against that," I suggested, "Why not take the idea of a checklist and incorporate it into the operation?"

The next question was how this could be done, so I had them put the following suggestions into effect (*Figure 13-1*):

- A small dish was brought and, at the very beginning of the op-eration, two springs were taken out of a parts box containing hundreds of springs and placed on the dish.
- Switch assembly took place next; then springs were inserted and buttons installed.
- If any spring remained on the dish after assembly, the worker realized that spring had been left out, and the assembly was then corrected.

This change in the operation completely eliminated the problem of missing springs and the parent company made no more claims on the subject.

Since springs in the earlier operation had been taken out of a parts box containing hundreds of other springs, there had been no way of knowing whether a spring had been removed or not. The new operation made it possible to know that a part had been forgotten and so eliminated the problem of missing springs.

Whenever I hear supervisors warning workers to pay more atten-tion or to be sure not to forget anything, I cannot help thinking that the workers are being asked to carry out operations as if they possessed

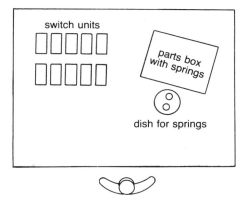

FIGURE 13-1. Ensuring Spring Insertion

divine infallibility. Rather than that approach, we should recognize that people are, after all, only human and as such, they will, on rare occasions, inadvertently forget things. It is more effective to incorporate a checklist — that is, a poka-yoke — into the operation so that if a worker forgets something, the device will signal that fact, thereby preventing defects from occurring. This, I think, is the quickest road leading to attainment of zero defects.

This poka-yoke concept is actually based on the same idea as "foolproofing," an approach devised mainly for preserving the safety of operations. In the early days, I used the term "foolproofing" (in Japanese, *bakayoke*), but around 1963, when Arakawa Auto Body adopted a "foolproofing" device to prevent seat parts from being spot-welded backwards, one of the company's part-time employees burst into tears when her department head explained that a "foolproofing" mechanism had been installed because workers sometimes mixed up left- and right-hand parts. "Have I really been such a fool?" she sobbed. She ended up staying home the following day and the department head went to see her there.

He tried all sorts of explanations. "It's not that you're a fool," he told her. "We put the device in because anybody can make inadvertent mistakes." Finally, he managed to persuade her.

When the department head told me this story, it was clear to me that "foolproofing" was a poorly chosen term. But what name would be suitable? After some thought, I gave the name poka-yoke (mistake-proofing) to these devices because they serve to prevent (or "proof"; in Japanese, *yoke*) the sort of inadvertent mistakes (*poka* in Japanese) that anyone can make.

Since the word poka-yoke (pronounced POH-kah YOH-kay) has been used untranslated in the English version of my book, *A Study of the Toyota Production System**, and appears in the French, Swedish, and Italian-language editions, it is now current throughout the world.

In the years following the development of the idea, poka-yoke devices were used widely. Because the adoption of appropriate poka-yoke devices results in the total elimination of defects, I began to have some doubts about the conventional view of exclusive reliance on SQC methods.

I think the source of this doubt lay in the fact that the poka-yoke approach uses 100 percent inspections to guard against inadvertent mistakes. I had come to assume that if we admit the existence of inadvertent mistakes, then 100 percent inspections are superior to sampling inspections based on statistical theory. Nevertheless, my belief that SQC provided the best quality control methods available remained largely unshaken. At the time, I thought that the total elimination of defects had been an effect of 100 percent inspections. If, instead, I had noted the significance of checking actual working conditions, the concept of "source inspections" would surely have been developed sooner.

It is clear to me now that my belief that SQC methods were unsurpassed impeded development in the direction of source inspections.

STAGE 3: ENCOUNTERS WITH SUCCESSIVE AND SELF-CHECKS

Application of the poka-yoke concept in numerous plants brought success that exceeded my expectations. Unfortunately, however, although poka-yoke devices were fine in situations permitting the use of physical detection methods, there are a surprising number

---

* This book, one of the first available in this country on Just-In-Time, has been re-translated and is available from Productivity Press (Cambridge, MA).

of things that can only be checked by means of sensory detection methods. The poka-yoke approach cannot be applied in such cases.

Despite the fact that SQC methods had achieved markedly better results than conventional judgment inspection methods, I still felt there was something missing. In particular, I wondered why it was that, appropriately applied, the poka-yoke method was capable of eliminating defects entirely while SQC methods could only lower defect rates. I concluded that, although the SQC system was characterized by informative inspections, the answer to the question lay in the fact that the detection of abnormalities was performed selectively and corrective action took place slowly. If that was the case, I thought, then more rapid action would be provided by *self-checks*. It seemed to me that the answer lay in having the processing operation worker carry out both checks and action.

Given the long-standing emphasis on the objectivity of inspections, however, this concept was flawed by the idea that if the worker involved carried out his or her own inspections, he or she might be apt to compromise on quality, or might inadvertently let defects slip by. This is why stress had always been laid on the need to guarantee the independence of inspections — on the idea that inspections had to be performed by disinterested inspectors.

Since this inevitably slowed down corrective action, it occurred to me that the need for objective inspections did not require that inspections be carried out — as is common — at the end of the work process. Why not have the closest person perform inspections? The "closest person," that is, the operator at the next process, could just as well take on the job of inspector. This would have the benefit that information about any abnormality discovered could be relayed immediately to the worker at the previous process. This is how the *successive check system* was devised. This method garnered considerable success in subsequent experimental applications at a number of plants (*Figure 13-2*).

Emboldened by the success of the successive check system, I realized that a *self-check system* would allow even faster corrective action to take place. Self-checking, though, was said to be flawed by workers' tendencies to make compromises and inadvertently overlook problems.

Those issues related to sensory inspections, however, and it dawned on me that, in cases where poka-yoke devices could be used, a self-check system was even better than a successive check system.

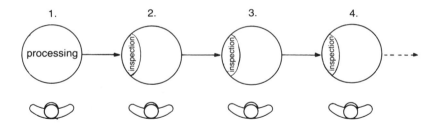

FIGURE 13-2. Successive Checks

With this in mind, I actively developed poka-yoke devices and worked to expand the use of successive check systems. In instances where it was technically or economically unfeasible to apply poka-yoke methods to self-check systems, we tried hard to incorporate poka-yoke functions into successive check systems.

This way of using self-check systems and successive check systems proved to be markedly more successful than SQC systems using control charts.

Yet these self-check systems and successive check systems remained approaches based on the idea of informative inspections, and in that sense were founded on the same concepts as were SQC-based control chart systems. The reason that they were far more successful in reducing defects resided in large part, I think, in the fact that the detection of abnormalities was carried out by means of 100 percent inspections rather than sampling inspections, and when abnormalities occurred, corrective action was taken extremely rapidly. Considerations such as these were already outside the scope of inductive statistics, and I felt my confidence in statistically based SQC systems collapsing rapidly. Yet I was still spellbound by my preconceived notion that quality control methods backed by scientific statistical theory were superior. I still could not completely escape this idea.

STAGE 4: SAMPLING INSPECTIONS DO NOTHING BUT MAKE INSPECTION PROCEDURES MORE RATIONAL

In 1964, Mr. Tokizane, managing director at the headquarters of Matsushita Electric's Television Division, told me that he didn't want a single television made by his company to be defective.

"I feel that way," he said, "because an individual customer generally buys only one television set. If that one set is defective, then that customer may assume that all Matsushita television sets are lemons. I won't allow defects in even one set, and so I'm in the plant nearly every day keeping an eye on workers."

I replied that I thought his attitude seemed reasonable, but then something about the use of statistically based sampling inspections had suddenly occurred to me: No matter how scientific a basis sampling inspections may have, the entire method rests on the notion that a certain level of defects is inevitable, whether it be one television set in 10,000 or one in 100,000.

Yet here was Mr. Tokizane, saying that he could not allow even one defective television set — even if it were one in 10,000 or one in 100,000. The idea that sampling inspections were extremely rational measures backed by the science of inductive statistics contradicted Mr. Tokizane's perfectly justifiable assertion that he would not allow a single defective television set in his company.

Unable to resolve this conflict, I fell to thinking as I headed home from Osaka by train. My confusion continued until we reached the outskirts of Tokyo, when suddenly it hit me: The statistical basis of sampling inspections meant only that such inspections made inspection techniques more rational; it did *not* make quality assurance more rational. Sampling inspections, in other words, may represent a rationalization of methods, but in no way do they represent a rationalization of goals.

The superiority of 100 percent inspections clearly dawned on me as I realized that they, and not sampling inspections, had to be used if one wished to put quality assurance on a more rational basis.

The justification for using sampling inspections was that 100 percent inspections would take too much trouble and cost too much. Why not, then, use 100 percent inspection techniques like poka-yoke ones — techniques that require little in the way of trouble or expense? This realization for the first time released me from the spell of sampling inspections and the inductive statistics behind them.

STAGE 5: ENCOUNTER WITH SOURCE INSPECTIONS

As explained above, I had been concentrating on the use of 100 percent inspections and on speeding up feedback and action. My thinking had never gone beyond the concept of informative inspections, and although I had given considerable thought to reducing defects, I had not adopted the more radical position of wanting to eliminate defects entirely.

As I went about applying poka-yoke methods, however, I noticed that the installation of suitable poka-yoke devices had the effect of reducing defects to zero. Was there some approach, I wondered, in which carrying out suitable inspections would make it possible to eliminate defects altogether?

Then it hit me. Why not just perform inspections at the sources of defects? Thus, around 1967, I arrived at the concept of *source inspections*. It had dawned on me that the occurrence of a defect was the *result* of some condition or action, and that it would be possible to eliminate defects entirely by pursuing the cause. The causes of defects lie in worker errors, and defects are the results of neglecting those errors. It follows that mistakes will not turn into defects if worker errors are discovered and eliminated beforehand.

I began advocating source inspections based on this fundamental notion and, in terms of actual techniques, installed a variety of poka-yoke systems that proved to be enormously successful.

In 1971, I joined the Japan Management Association's first overseas study group in visits to various plants in Europe. During that trip, we toured the facilities of Wotan, a molding machine manufacturer in Dusseldorf, West Germany.

During a question-and-answer period following the tour, Mr. K of the M Spring Company — one of our group who always asked lively questions — stood up and asked the people at Wotan if they carried out quality control.

"Of course we do," the manufacturing division chief representing the company replied.

"But," continued Mr. K, "in touring your plant I didn't see a single control chart."

"Control chart? What on earth is that?"

Mr. K then triumphantly proceeded to explain control charts while the Wotan representative listened in silence. When Mr. K had finished, the Wotan executive responded:

"That's a very interesting idea, but don't you think it's fundamentally wrong-headed?"

Mr. K bristled. "Fundamentally wrong-headed?! What are you talking about?"

"The idea you just described deals with defects after they occur," the Wotan representative explained. "The basic idea behind our approach to quality control is to prevent defects from occurring in the first place."

"How in the world do you do that?" Mr. K asked.

Our host said that, rather than checking quality after a task had been completed, they checked whether operating methods were suitable before the job started.

As I listened to the Wotan representative, I recalled a scene I had just witnessed in the machine shop. When the operator in charge of a radial boring machine had put drills in place and was ready to begin, he motioned to a roving quality control officer, who came over to the machine and, using a chart as a guide, checked both drill positions and the positions of stoppers used to determine hole depths. Only when he gave the OK sign did the operator start the machine. As I listened to the division chiefs words, I realized that it was this type of operation he was talking about.

The Wotan representative then asked Mr. K what the process defect rate at his company was.

"Only about 2.5 percent," said Mr. K proudly.

"I see," our host replied. "but the process defect rate at my company isn't any higher than 0.3 percent."

That took the wind out of Mr. K's sails and he was silent for the rest of the question-and-answer period.

I realized that the idea of checking operating conditions before the operations rather than after them was precisely the same as my concept of source inspections. I remember taking courage from this realization and thinking that this attested to the superiority of the source inspection concept. It was at that point, in fact, that my philosophy with regard to source inspections took definite shape.

At the same time, I repeatedly heard people say that the SQC system "builds quality into the process." But where was the evidence?

My claim was that a process is a flow in which raw materials are converted into finished products, and that any errors in process standards would naturally generate defects.

It is in this way that we finally arrive at a Zero QC system aimed at zero defects.

STAGE 6: THE ACHIEVEMENT OF A MONTH WITH ZERO DEFECTS

In 1977, I hurried to the Shizuoka plant of Matsushita Electric's Washing Machine Division when I heard that the facility had achieved a continuous record of one month with zero defects in a drainpipe assembly line operation involving 23 workers.

When I got there, I found that this significant goal had been attained by the use of source inspections, self-checks, and successive checks, and by the installation of effective poka-yoke devices — ingenious and relatively inexpensive mechanisms that everyone had cooperated in developing. These devices were installed according to the characteristics of the processes involved. This success resulted from the extraordinary efforts of supervisors working under Mr. Izumi, the department head, as well, of course, as those of the foreman, Mr. Muneo Iwabori, who directed actual work on the shop floor.

Before Matsushita's accomplishment, I had secretly been afraid that it might be impossible for a drainpipe assembly line employing so many workers and handling 30,000 units each month to actually go through an entire month with zero defects. Seeing this achievement gave me an unprecedented jolt, therefore, and I drew boundless confidence and courage from the realization that, given the proper conceptual approach and appropriate techniques, and given suitable leadership and general enthusiasm and cooperation, people can in fact achieve things that have been thought to be impossible.

The Matsushita Washing Division's Shizuoka plant continued zero defect production for over six months, and I confidently appealed to a number of other plants with the assertion that they, too, could achieve zero defects for the space of one month. Lo and behold, these plants began to achieve zero defect production for one month, and even for several months running. To myself, I thought how difficult such success would be to achieve with SQC methods based on inductive statistics.

STAGE 7: BASIC CONCEPTS FOR A ZERO QC SYSTEM

A Zero Quality Control system is built on the following basic ideas:

1. Use source inspections, that is, inspections for preventing defects, to eliminate defects entirely. This does not mean dealing with the results of defect generation, it means applying control functions at the stage where defects originate.
2. Always use 100 percent inspections rather than sampling inspections.
3. Minimize the time it takes to carry out corrective action when abnormalities appear.
4. Human workers are not infallible. Recognize that people are human and set up effective poka-yoke devices accordingly.

A RESPONSE TO INDUCTIVE STATISTICS

When I first heard about inductive statistics in 1951, I firmly believed it to be the best technique around, and it took me 26 years to break completely free of its spell.

Considered from an independent vantage point, several observations can be made with respect to inductive statistics:

- Inductive statistics remains an excellent technique.
- Active use should be made of statistics in the sense that the technique is extremely effective in the planning phase of management.
- Nevertheless, statistics is not always effective in control and execution phases. In fact, it can surely be said that an infatuation with statistics has impeded the progress of the management function itself.
- A major feature of SQC systems is the capacity for information inspections, and it is extremely important to pursue this function to the limit.
- In any case, inductive statistics is an excellent technique for making methods more rational; it does not necessarily have anything to do with rationalizing the attainment of goals.

14

More on Inspection Systems

We will now discuss three inspection methods:

- Inspections that discover defects: *judgment inspections*
- Inspections that reduce defects: *informative inspections*
- Inspections that eliminate defects: *source inspections*

INSPECTIONS THAT DISCOVER DEFECTS: JUDGMENT INSPECTIONS

Even today, many plants conduct judgment inspections, that is, inspections whose sole purpose is to categorize finished products as defective or acceptable after processing has been completed. The point of this method is to keep defective goods from moving on to customers or subsequent processes, and in this sense it is an effective tool. It remains inherently a kind of postmortem inspection, however, for no matter how accurately and thoroughly it is performed, it can in no way contribute to lowering the defect rate in the plant itself. This inspection method is consequently of no value whatsoever if one wants to bring down defect rates within plants.

Furthermore, the question of whether one chooses to perform judgment inspections by sampling or by the 100 percent technique is totally unrelated to the essential nature of the inspection method. The question involves only a choice of methods that bear on the issue of whether inspection labor costs can be reduced.

Even though the true purpose of judgment inspections is simply to find defective goods, many plants set up independent inspection processes that also inspect items that are not defective. Surely this is tremendously wasteful.

What is wrong, I often wonder, with the idea of getting rid of all inspections performed at special processes that have to check all items either between work processes or at the end of the final work process? We have long assumed that "inspection" is synonymous with judgment inspection. Yet, in fact, the judgment inspection is the lowest order of inspection and we have to escape from its clutches as soon as we can. All we need to do to accomplish this is to realize that the effective use of informative and source inspections will itself keep defective goods from moving on either to customers or to subsequent processes.

There are some cases in which it is thought that judgment inspections have been made considerably more rational by having been automated. In the manufacture of the H automobile, M Industries in Japan maintains a technical cooperation arrangement with the L Company in the United States, to which it furnishes door lock technology. The head of manufacturing of the L Company came to Japan at one point and boasted that his firm had streamlined operations by automatically inspecting all assemblies in a final inspection process, thereby preventing even a single defective item from being delivered to the parent company's plant. He was somewhat taken aback when Mr. Kurozu, plant manager at K Industries, explained that at his company, poka-yoke devices had been provided at every process so that defects did not occur in the first place. Since absolutely no defect could move to the next process, he explained, the shipping of defective items to the parent company was prevented by a simple function inspection at the final process. When the two men then compared defect rates at their companies, it turned out that the L Company's defect rate was far higher.

In the final analysis, the fact that the L Company's inspections had been automated meant only the automation of judgment inspections. This may have reduced inspection labor costs, but it was of no use whatsoever in reducing the defect rate in the plant.

INSPECTIONS THAT REDUCE DEFECTS: INFORMATIVE INSPECTIONS

An informative inspection is an inspection in which, when a defect occurs, information to that effect is fed back to the work process involved, which then takes action to correct the method of operation. One can expect, consequently, that the adoption of this system of inspections will have the effect of gradually reducing production defect rates.

Informative inspections can be divided into three categories:

- Statistical Quality Control Systems (SQCS)
- Successive Check Systems (SuCS)
- Self-Check Systems (SeCS)

What follows is a detailed description of each, complete with examples.

Statistical Quality Control Systems (SQCS)

The characteristics of so-called SQC systems include, first of all, the notion of informative inspections, which use statistically based control charts to reduce future defects by feeding back information about defects to the offending processes; work methods are then corrected accordingly. Also characteristic of SQC systems is the use of statistics to set control limits that distinguish between normal and abnormal situations. The number of samples taken to detect abnormal values is similarly determined according to statistical principles. Thus, the use of statistical principles may be considered to be the essential condition identifying a method of inspection as an SQC method.

Specification Limits and Control Limits

In using a control chart system, two limits have to be established:

- *Specification limits*: tolerance limits demanded by product functions
- *Control limits*: limits within which normal operations will fall; for example, the outside diameters of all processed rods might fall within the range of 30mm ± 0.06mm

In this case, if specification limits are greater than control limits, all items processed under usual work conditions may be satisfactory. If, on the other hand, specification limits are narrower than control limits, it is possible that, under usual processing conditions, portions of production outside the specification limits will show defects. In any event, operating conditions should be examined and improvements made at the planning stage, so that control limits fall within specification limits.

Establishing Control Limits

Generally used 3 SD control limits are established in the following manner (*Figure 14-1*):

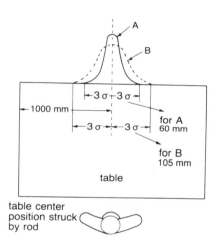

FIGURE 14-1. Strike Distribution Curve

1. One thousand attempts are made to strike the table's center point with a shaft.
2. The center is set at 1,000mm from the edge and values for each strike point are recorded.
3. These observed values are summed and the mean value is found to be 1,000mm.
4. The differences between the observed values and the mean value are found. Their sum is 0.
5. These deviations, or differences between the mean value and observed values, are squared.
6. These 1,000 squared deviations are added and then divided by 1,000. From the square root of this can be found the standard deviation (SD), which shows the degree to which the observed values are scattered. In this case, the SD for worker A is 20mm. (*Figure 14-2*).

	A			B	
observed value	deviation	deviation squared	observed value	deviation	deviation squared
x (mm)	x − m (mm)	(x − m)²	x (mm)	x − m (mm)	(x − m)²
990	− 10	100	985	− 15	225
995	− 5	25	1020	20	400
1012	12	144	1100	100	10000
1000	0	0	905	− 95	9025
1001	1	1	910	− 90	8100
1007	7	49	1050	50	2500
......	......	......	......	......	......
......	......	......	......	......	......

| 1000)1000000 | 0 | 1000)400000 | 1000)1000000 | 0 | 1000)1225000 |
| 1000 | | 400 | 100 | | 1225 |

mean value (m)

deviation squared per strike

$\sqrt{400} = 20$

standard deviation (σA)

mean value (m)

deviation squared per strike

$\sqrt{1225} = 35$

standard deviation (σA)

FIGURE 14-2. Calculation of Standard Deviation (SD)

7. If a similar experiment carried out by worker B yields a standard deviation of 35mm, then we can say that A's strikes are less scattered than B's.

8. If we draw lines three standard deviations apart on either side of the center line, both A's SD (60mm) and B's SD (105mm) are found to fall within the range 3 SD = 99.73 percent.

9. Thus, a mere 0.27 percent of strikes — or about three strikes in 1,000 — fell outside the 3 SD limit.

10. Since we are dealing with a phenomenon that under ordinary conditions shows up only 3 times out of 1,000, it seems highly probable that it is an abnormal situation. Therefore we may think of this 3 SD limit as marking the boundary between normal and abnormal.

In reality, the use of statistics allows us to find control limits more simply than this, but in any case the basic approach is the same: control limits are established, and the results of actual operations are measured and their values recorded. If an abnormality is observed in those values, the information is fed back to the process where the abnormality occurred. A check of actual results is then carried out by means of sampling techniques based on statistical theory.

Thus, the compilation of control charts is a necessary condition in SQC methods.

$\bar{X}.R$ Control Charts, and P Control Charts

As seen above, under ordinary operating conditions, the mean of measured values X falls within the specification limits. If the spread of measurements also falls within three SDs, then defective items will not be produced under ordinary operating conditions.

The appearance of a value outside the control limits is taken as an abnormality, and feedback is accordingly sent to the process where the value appeared. This allows defects to be reduced by means of improvements made when abnormal conditions are discovered in the course of checking operating methods.

In such cases, defective items will show up as a matter of course either when the control limit $\bar{X}$ is considerably more distorted than the specification limit $\bar{X}$, or when the $\bar{X}$ is fine, but the scatter, that is, the 3 SD range, is so large that it extends beyond specification limits. The reason for using a control chart system, therefore, is that it permits quality improvements and the vigorous promotion of defect reduction by a reconsideration both of conditions making up $\bar{X}$ values and of conditions accounting for large SDs.

In Japan, the adoption of this sort of control chart method has improved the level of quality control considerably.

Like these $\bar{X}.R$ charts is a defect rate control chart used in the workplace called a *P control chart*. In this approach, abnormal values are eliminated from defect rates and control limits are established by taking statistically based samples of these defect rate values for ordinary conditions. Then defect rates in actual shop operations are observed and no action is taken if values are within control limits. When abnormal values show up outside control limits, that information is fed back to the process where defects occurred. The process is examined and improved so that no more abnormal values occur.

This strategy has several advantages. It makes it possible to keep defect rates from rising, and, because action is taken when abnormal values show up, the causes of defects can be corrected. This makes possible a decrease in the overall defect level.

The other side of the coin is that, while it is understandable to want to prevent defect rates from rising, a somewhat more cynical view of the matter makes it look as though the point of this approach is to preserve past defect rates. Why not take a more aggressive stance and ask why defects cannot be cut further and further — even eliminated? The sin involved in getting caught up by this passive approach, surely, lies in a false sense of security stemming from reliance on the high-powered scientific techniques of statistics. This false sense of security causes one to misunderstand the true nature of what is going on.

In Toronto in 1982, I gave a two-day series of talks to a group of senior executives from large American firms. A number of questions concerning Japanese total quality control (TQC) methods came up in those two days, and at one point I asked an executive of the D Aircraft Company who was sitting in the front row whether his firm engaged in quality control.

"Of course we do," he replied.

"In that case," I continued, "do you use control charts?"

"Yes."

"How about P control charts?"

"Yes, we draw up P control charts, too, depending on the process."

"I see," I said. "Tell me, why do you draw up P control charts? After all, P control charts are designed to maintain previous defect rates. They certainly won't actively lower defect rates, will they?"

For a moment, he looked as though he did not understand what I was saying. I remember being struck by the forced smile that came over his face when he said, "OK. Well, maybe you've got a point there...."

Control Charts Serve Only as Mirrors

In 1955, I had some business to attend to at Nippon Steel's Kamaishi refinery and happened to run into Dr. Eisaburo Nishibori at the inn I was staying at in Sendai. At the time, Dr. Nishibori was in charge of quality control at the Japan Management Association.

In talking with Dr. Nishibori, I learned that he was going to the Kamaishi refinery that day, and the next day he was traveling to Hirosaki, in Aomori Prefecture, to consult at F Chemical Industries, where enthusiastic QC activities were under way. That night he was scheduled to be in Sapporo, in Hokkaido.

I told him that I, too, would be at the Kamaishi plant and then stay in Sapporo the following night, because I was going to visit the Toyobane mines in the Jozan Valley.

The next evening, I chanced to run into Dr. Nishibori again, just as I arrived at my hotel. I asked him how the quality control situation was progressing at F Chemical Industries.

"Well," he replied, "they've got a young quality control department head who's pursuing QC really enthusiastically. I asked if I could take a look at the plant and he showed me around right away. The thing was, that in a plant of about 150 people, there were control charts posted everywhere. When I asked him how many control charts they drew up, he told me they used about 200.

"When we got back to the conference room, the department head asked for my impressions. I told him I thought he was putting a lot of effort into the job, but there was one important control chart he wasn't making.

"Missing an important control chart?" he said. "What chart is that?"

"What I mean is that you don't have a control chart for your control charts."

"He stared back at me with a blank look on his face, so I explained that he wasn't distinguishing between necessary control charts and unnecessary control charts.

"'Oh, that! . . . ,' he said. Then he sank into thought.

"The point was that this fellow figured all he had to do to perform quality control was to draw up control charts, so he taught his shop foremen how to construct the charts and they posted the charts everywhere.

"If you think about the role a control chart plays, though, it is clear that it essentially serves as nothing but a mirror. All it does is reflect prevailing conditions. That's it. Pasting hundreds of "mirrors" on the walls or the ceiling or the floor isn't going to guarantee improvements in quality.

"When you look in a mirror and see that your face is dirty, you take a washcloth and wipe your face. That's when the dirt comes off. Looking at your face reflected in a succession of mirrors is utterly pointless unless you do something about it in the form of corrective action."

Dr. Nishibori's admonition made a deep impression on me.

Even today, I sometimes run into young technicians who believe that drawing up control charts is the same thing as quality control. Surely, such people are letting themselves be infatuated by techniques and are not pursuing the true significance of control charts.

Informative Inspections Come to Life Through Action

As I stated earlier, defects will not be reduced unless we first understand the current state of quality and then take appropriate action. Yet control chart methods use sampling to check for abnormalities. Even though this approach may be supported by statistical science, the fact remains that abnormalities appear irregularly and randomly. Since you cannot predict when they will show up, the probability that statistical sampling will find abnormalities at just the right time is far lower than with 100 percent sampling. Moreover, control chart methods as generally practiced involve a considerable time lag between the discovery of an abnormality and the corrective action. That means that it takes a long time before improvements are made. During this period, a substantial number of defects will probably appear.

Thus, the effectiveness of a control chart approach in reducing defects is considerably diluted by a synergism between the time it takes for sampling to turn up abnormalities and the lag between the discovery of such events and corrective action. Indeed, this is surely the main reason that, despite a basic conceptual shift from the old notion of judgment inspections to the innovative idea of informative inspections, it has not been possible to achieve quantum improvements in quality with statistically based methods.

In the final analysis, although statistical science served simply to make methods of inspection more rational, our mastery of its excellent and innovative techniques transformed methods into objectives. We ended up concentrating solely on the applications of technique. As this happened, it seems to me, the basic objectives and functions of informative inspections were simply forgotten.

Pluses and Minuses of SQC Systems

On the plus side, in contrast to the old idea of inspections that distinguished between defective and acceptable items, an appeal to the new, pioneering notion of informative inspections has shown the possibility of defect rate reductions, and this fact has yielded phenomenal developments. Moreover, the pioneering techniques given to us by statistical science are of considerable value. In the planning phase of management, application of analytical techniques such as the experimental planning method and the determination of significant differences has led to real improvements in the establishment of standard work processes and operating procedures. We should also recognize that statistics gives us a highly reliable means for determining appropriate sample sizes for establishing control limits and for finding abnormalities.

At the same time, the method involves several minuses. The first is that the effectiveness of SQC systems as statistical techniques at first led many people to proclaim: "If it doesn't use statistics, it's not quality control." Even today, certain people show the after-effects of this malady.

The beliefs that you cannot carry out quality control without drawing up control charts, or that sampling inspections are rational because they are backed up by statistical science, led people to forget that these are no more than streamlined inspection methods and that they do not make quality assurance any more rational. I think there can be no doubt that the confidence such people had in the powers of statistical science was a bit excessive.

Moreover, the major conceptual advance represented by informative inspections was obscured by the shadow of inductive statistics. As a result, people neglected qualitative improvements in informative inspections, that is, the performance of 100 percent checks or increases in the speed of corrective action.

The use of mathematical techniques such as those of inductive statistics dominated discussions among both scholars and certain theory-oriented technicians who excelled in "desktop" mathematical processing. This frequently ended up alienating shop technicians and front-line supervisors, especially shop foremen, group leaders, and team leaders, who have to bear the responsibility for quality control. I often used to hear shop foremen and group leaders complain that merely hearing the words "quality control" gave them headaches. The fact that quality control efforts in Japan were led by certain highbrow theorists with no real connection to the workplace has been, I suspect, one reason for the tardy pursuit of real quality control systems aimed at zero defects.

Around 1965, I visited C Industries in Nagoya. There, I heard the following story from President Eguchi, on leave from the T Bank:

"About 30 years ago," he said, "one of the directors of my bank started his own company.

"This man's son had a promising future, for he was unusually bright and graduated at the top of his class at N University. At first, he worked for a firm in the Y Automobile group for about 10 years and then his father brought him into his own company, where, after a few years, he was promoted to managing director, with nearly all aspects of production under his jurisdiction.

"About four years ago, this man's son began advocating the massive adoption of QC methods, and he started bringing in consultants from universities and the like. Morning, noon, and night, all he would ever talk about was *kyuu shii* (QC) this and *kyuu shii* (QC) that. Well, recently the whole plant ended up coming to a standstill (*kyuushi*). I mean, QC is fine, but that was a bit extreme. I think the problem was that he was performing QC only in terms of superficial techniques without understanding what true quality control was all about. I'm always warning our technical people to steer clear of that shallow kind of quality control."

This poor fellow's failure served as yet another lesson to me, for he had let himself be carried away by statistical appearances without really understanding the nature of quality control.

Successive Check Systems (SuCS)

The Birth of the Successive Check Method

By 1960, I knew that SQC methods made it possible to lower defect rates dramatically, but I could not rid myself of the nagging thought that there must be some other, more streamlined way to achieve such reductions. In thinking about what that way might be, I observed that the essence of SQC methods had to lie in informative inspections. Drawing courage from the case in which a poka-yoke device had eliminated defects in the spring insertion operation at Yamada Electric, I succeeded in distancing myself to a certain extent from the spell of statistics by realizing that there were ways of reducing defects that lay outside SQC methods. My feeling that SQC systems were overlooking something led me to conclude that such methods suffered from two shortcomings:

1. Abnormalities are found by means of sampling inspections. Yet wouldn't it be better to use 100 percent inspection techniques? The problem is that 100 percent inspections are expensive and they generally take a lot of time and trouble. If low-cost 100 percent inspections could be devised, wouldn't they be preferable? "That's it!" I thought. "That is why effective poka-yoke devices ought to be used!" I determined then and there to design poka-yoke mechanisms.

2. The other point is that a look at SQC methods as they are actually applied shows that feedback and corrective action — the crucial aspects of informative inspections — are too slow to be fully effective.

Theoretically, I thought, the best way to speed up feedback and action would be to have the worker who processes items carry out 100 percent inspections and then immediately take action if he or she found any abnormality. Then I recalled the old rule that holds that objectivity is essential to the performance of inspections. Indeed, this is why, in the past, inspections have had to be performed by independent inspectors, rather than by the workers involved in the actual processing.

A worker who inspects something that he or she has worked on might make compromises on quality or might, through inadvertence, miss defects.

If that is the reasoning, I thought, then it is still not necessary to have independent inspectors. An inspection can be carried out by any worker other than the one who did the processing. If this task is given to the nearest person, then one could have a *successive check system* of the following sort:

1. When A is finished processing an item, he or she passes it on to B at the next process.

2. B first inspects the item processed by A and then carries out the processing assigned to him or her. Then B passes the item on to C.

3. C first inspects the item processed by B and then carries out the processing assigned to him or her. When that work is finished, C passes the item on to D.

4. In this way, each successive worker inspects items from the previous process.

5. If a defect is discovered in an item coming from the previous

process, the defective item is immediately passed back to the earlier process. There, the item is verified and the defect corrected. Action is taken to prevent the occurrence of subsequent defects. The line is shut down while this is going on.

This type of system largely makes up for the deficiencies of SQC methods because it makes it possible to conduct 100 percent inspections, perform immediate feedback and action, and have inspections performed by people other than the workers involved in the processing. This system is all the more effective when poka-yoke devices are applied to it. Indeed, these methods have led to truly significant reductions in defect rates.

Like control chart systems, this successive check system involves a variety of informative inspections. Yet surely this new method represents a conceptual advance over control chart systems. Another advantage of successive check systems is that they can be applied even in cases where sensory inspections are unavoidable.

Examples of Successive Check Systems: Matsushita Electric Industrial Company, Ltd.

From the birth of the concept of successive check systems in about 1960, such systems were applied in a number of plants and yielded one success after another. During this period, I visited Matsushita Electric's Morikawa television division, where the division head, Mr. Kishida, told me of some difficulties his firm was having: "We used to have a process defect rate of around 15 percent in our television assembly operation," he told me. "Control chart methods and vigorous QC Circle activities cut that rate to about 6.5 percent, but defects have leveled off there and we can't figure out how to get the rate any lower."

I explained the successive check method and he promptly agreed when I suggested that he try the approach in his plant. Since the assembly operation had been accompanied by inspection operations, implementation of the new method increased assembly tact time by roughly 10 percent, from 30 seconds to 33 seconds. After one month's implementation of successive check methods, process defects fell from 6.5 to 1.5 percent, and assembly tact time returned to the original 30 seconds on the twenty-third day. Tact time returned to its previous value because checks became simpler as defects gradually decreased, and familiarity made it possible to check items extremely quickly. Although I had at first thought that checks would add time to the procedure, this was because I worried about psychological back-lash involving a need to increase tact time because checks would be performed after the original assembly operation had been completed.

Three months later, the innovations had resulted in stunning success (*Figure 14-3*). Interprocess defects had fallen to 0.06 percent, and defects at the final process to 0.016 percent.

Ordinarily, the implementation of a successive check system leads without exception to a lowering of the defect rate to one-fifth to one-tenth of the previous value in the space of a single month. I often hear factory officials say that such results could never be achieved with SQC methods.

Check Target Selection and Action

Sometimes, however, people have little success with the application of successive check systems. Several points should be kept in mind when dealing with such problems.

Selection of check targets. It is inappropriate to use successive checks to check for too many things. In the final analysis, checking for too many things will undermine the effectiveness of the method, for either nothing will get checked or the number of things workers forget to check will grow.

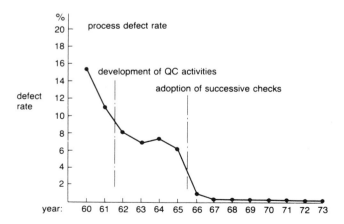

FIGURE 14-3. Effect of Successive Checks

The fact that checking takes time means that eventually some checks will be neglected.

It is appropriate, therefore, to extract major points from statistics on defects discovered at the final process and to limit the number of points checked in each process to two or three. The examination of defect statistics for the purpose of selecting important points to check should take place every two to four weeks.

Important safety points, however, should always be checked, and should be checked last. These include parts such as automobile brakes, in which defects might cause accidents.

Feedback and action. Two extremely important factors in successive checks are the performance of 100 percent checks, and prompt execution of feedback and action.

Successive checks means far more than merely checking items in succession. When defects are discovered, it is critical that workers operating previous processes be alerted promptly so they recognize the defects in question and correct operating conditions accordingly. Defects will never be reduced if the workers involved do not modify operating methods when defects occur. To this end, processing lines are halted while the workers themselves make the necessary corrections. Lines do not move again until those corrections have been made.

In general, managers and workers on the shop floor are loath to shut down lines, but there are three reasons why such measures must be adopted:

1. Shutting down a line makes it possible for managers to identify the offending process rapidly and clearly. They can then exercise effective leadership so that quick and powerful improvements can be implemented.
2. A worker will be that much more attentive to the task in the future because of the responsibility he or she feels for shutting down the line.
3. The fact that defects will cease to be generated after a temporary line shutdown will more than compensate for the loss incurred as a result of the shutdown.

Failing to shut down the line and take corrective action is just the same as subduing the symptoms of appendicitis with ice. The ice will work, but the pain will recur and eventually considerable time will be lost. It is better in the long run to have the appendix removed, because then the symptoms will not return. For reasons such as these, it is extremely important to take basic, thorough corrective action when abnormalities appear.

Checks Based on Sensory Inspections

In cases involving scratches, paint quality, or other issues where judgments must be made by means of sensory inspections, samples of acceptable limits should be made up and judgments made on the basis of comparison with such limit samples. Even then, however, judgments on the margin will be difficult to make.

This is how the problem was handled at V Industries:

1. C checks the operation performed by B at the previous process.
2. At the final process, specialized inspection worker A passes judgment on checks made by C.
3. At the end of each day of operations, A, B, and C meet to examine and discuss the outcomes of that day's checks.

Defects Increase in the Initial
Stage of Successive Checks

I often hear the complaint that defects actually increase in the initial period following the adoption of successive checks. We have to distinguish here between two categories of defects: *interprocess defects*, which are discovered between processes, and *final process defects*, which are discovered at the final inspection of a process. In the initial period, it is nearly always interprocess defects that increase. This is perfectly natural, since defects that had escaped unnoticed in the past are now being discovered. Without exception, however, final process defects will drop by 80 to 90 percent after the first month. As implementation proceeds, interprocess defects will gradually decrease as well.

In general, the implementation of successive checks proceeds as follows:

1. In the first 10 days or so after implementation, interprocess defects increase, but final process defects fall to roughly one-third of their previous level.

2. In the next 10 days, interprocess defects fall to about one-half of their previous level and final process defects drop to roughly one-fifth.

3. In the next 10 days (i.e., after one month), inter-process defects fall to about one-fifth and final process defects to roughly one-tenth of previous levels.

Thus, an initial increase in interprocess defects should actually be a cause for satisfaction because it means that defects that used to slip by unnoticed are now being found.

Consideration for Workers

It is imperative to gain the thorough understanding and compliance of workers in the implementation of successive checks. Failure to do this will undermine interpersonal relations in the shop by creating an atmosphere in which each worker feels as though he or she is always being criticized by the worker at the next process. It is therefore necessary for everyone to understand that inadvertent human errors are more easily detected by others and that workers help one another by checking each other's work.

In the initial phases of successive check implementation at the M Company, a part-time worker, N, was distressed because she had forgotten to attach labels on three occasions in one day. She felt she had caused trouble for everyone else because the line had been shut down each time. "Maybe this job is too much for me," she said. The next day, she stayed home from work.

When this happened, her supervisor promptly went to visit her and assured her that it had not been her fault. He persuaded her to return to the job, and for a month afterwards she did not make a single mistake.

Many workers feel better about checks performed by the next worker down the line because they have the impression that it is more like having friends tell you to be careful than having complaints made about you by specialized inspectors. Workers often say it is better to be warned immediately than to hear complaints long after defective work is done. They support successive checks because their compliance in the identification of defects allows improvements to be made immediately and lowers defects.

Signals to Managers

A group leader at Q Electric once gathered workers at the end of the day because numerous soldering defects were showing up in a chassis assembly process. He warned them several times to be more careful in the soldering operations. Nevertheless, defects did not decrease and, convinced that part-time workers simply did not have the skill required, the group leader more or less gave up.

When successive checks were introduced, the group leader noticed that the conveyor frequently shut down near worker C in process number 3. He therefore stood behind C to observe. He saw that C would press solder against the soldering iron, melt it, and then drop it on the wound portion of lead wires. He explained to C that soldering involved using the soldering iron first to heat the part to be soldered. The solder would melt and flow when the part was sufficiently hot. He then performed the operation himself so that C would understand. From then on, defects were almost completely eliminated.

The group leader who told me this story said that although he had initially thought that part-timers were hopeless because they did not have the necessary skill, it was, in fact, technical leadership that had been lacking. When he realized this, he changed his attitude and, as a result of observations he made in the shop, he discovered a number of similar phenomena. Appropriate leadership eventually reduced defects by 90 percent.

Thus, the fact that a conveyor was stopping in the midst of successive inspections rapidly and accurately signaled the presence of a problem to the manager. Subsequent prompt implementation of effective action led to a reduction in defects.

A Decrease in the Number of Items Held Back for Correction

On a television assembly line at T Industries, inspections used to be carried out at the final process and items to be fixed would be repaired by specialized repair workers.

Since the line was engaged in high-diversity, low-volume production, considerable numbers of items to be repaired accumulated at the final process. This led to frequent model mixing, model errors, and insufficient quantities of finished goods.

The use of successive checks, on the other hand, means that defects are dealt with between processes. No more items are held back and no trouble with model mixing or mismatched quantities ever occurs. The system achieved the further result that a drop in the defect rate means an increase in the number of units produced.

Cases in which Checks Cannot Be Made at the Next Process

Although in principle successive check systems call for checks to be made at the next process, in actual operations this may not be possible. In such cases, one has no choice but to carry out the checks at the nearest possible subsequent process.

When defects are discovered, however, it is imperative to shut down the line right away. The defective item must then be shown to the worker where the defect originated. Once this worker has recognized the problem, he or she can immediately improve processing methods.

The checking of important items, moreover, should be carried out not only by the worker at the next process, but also by the worker at the process after that. This method of "double checking" is extremely effective.

Where the correction of defects requires a long time, an off-line repair worker can do the needed work after the worker where the problem originated has taken a look at the circumstances under which the defect occurred.

It may be necessary, too, to perform successive checks by selecting one item in five (or one in ten) when the operating cycle is unusually rapid.

Basic Principles Underlying Successive Check Methods

Successive check methods rest on the following principles:

- Always conduct 100 percent inspections.
- Judgments about defects are made objectively by a disinterested person.
- When a defect occurs, information to that effect is immediately fed back to the processing worker where the defect originated. That worker then takes stock of the situation and takes corrective action.
- Processing from then on thereby ceases to generate defects.

An Example of Successive Checking

One operation at Orient Technologies involved gluing support braces into the inside corners of television-set cabinets (*Figure 14-4*).

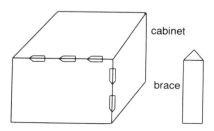

FIGURE 14-4. Brace Attachment

Although 16 such braces had to be glued in, occasionally an inspection worker at the final process would warn that in the course of a day, say, eight cases had been detected in which braces had not been glued in. When this happened, Ms. Takizawa, the very able and spirited worker in charge of the operation, would strongly protest that it was impossible. Even when it was pointed out to her that there were no traces of glue on the defective cabinets, she would not listen, insisting instead that someone must have wiped off the glue at some intermediate process. The adoption of successive checks meant that the worker at the next process was able to indicate missing braces to Ms. Takizawa immediately and return the defective pieces to her. When she examined them then, she saw that, indeed, she had left out some braces.

Now even the strong-willed Ms. Takizawa could not utter a word of rebuttal when she saw braces missing on cabinets she had just sent on to the next process. She realized she had perhaps been a bit overconfident and began paying more attention to the job. From that point onward, no more cabinets showed up with missing braces.

When considerable time used to elapse before cabinets were inspected, Ms. Takizawa had simply been unable to believe that she had left out braces. Now, when cabinets she had just worked on were returned to her and she could verify oversights with her own eyes, she realized that she was capable of errors. Defects were reduced because she then worked more carefully.

Thus, it is 100 times more effective to have defects recognized by the workers themselves than to have them pointed out by a supervisor.

Surely, this example provides a fine explanation of the basic principles involved in successive checks.

Self-Check Systems (SeCS)

Movement Toward Self-Inspection Systems

Although sweeping reductions in defect rates are possible with successive check systems, the nature of informative inspections remains such that rapid feedback and swift action are desirable. For this, it would be ideal to have the actual worker involved conduct 100 percent inspections to check for defects. As I said earlier, however, it has long been held that there are two flaws to be reckoned with: Workers are liable to make compromises when inspecting items that they themselves have worked on, and they are apt occasionally to forget to perform checks on their own.

If it were possible to guard against these flaws, then a self-check system would be superior to a successive check system. In cases where physical, rather than sensory, inspections are possible, so-called poka-yoke devices can be installed within the process boundaries, so that when abnormalities occur, the information is immediately fed back to the worker involved. This makes instant corrective action possible, since it permits abnormalities to be discovered within the processes where they occur rather than at subsequent processes. This sort of self-check system represents a higher-order approach than a successive check system, and its use can cut defect rates even further.

This has been proved by results in many companies, perhaps in part because people have less psychological resistance to discovering abnormal situations themselves than to having them pointed out by others. In addition, being able to see the reality of an abnormal situation with one's own eyes allows one to understand its true causes, and more appropriate and effective countermeasures can be worked out and implemented.

With successive checks, there may be cases in which the actual circumstances of defect generation have already vanished by the time information is relayed back by a worker at the next process. Countermeasures may therefore be inadequate because a worker's confirmation of the facts has to rely on guesswork.

In any event, the use of self-check methods makes possible the extremely rapid achievement of far lower defect rates than with control chart methods.

Self-check systems, however, suffer from the defect that they are difficult to use where the detection of abnormalities depends on sensory methods. Even so, self-check methods can be used in a surprising number of instances if we make efforts to either (1) adopt high-level detection techniques for items that absolutely require sensory inspections, or (2) select basic operating conditions that can be measured physically. This means that, rather than becoming ensnared in present circumstances, it is far preferable for us to consider problems from many angles and actively study ways in which self-check systems can be adopted.

Examples of Self-Check Systems

V Industries. V Industries produced a product called a stem tightener. The 6.5 percent defect rate for this product was high and the company was looking for some way to reduce it.

Operating procedures were as follows:

1. Pour teflon powder into the center of the lower die.
2. Smooth off the die surface to standardize the amount of powder poured in.
3. Press down the upper die to form the product.
4. Expel the product with an expulsion device and remove it from the lower die.
5. Have the expulsion device push the product to a chute.

The problem was that, although inside and outside diameters were reliable, defects would show up in the form of fluctuations in product thickness. The principal cause was that the amount of teflon powder poured into the dies was not uniform. A single worker was in charge of three machines, and since the machines carried out forming operations automatically, this worker occasionally measured and adjusted product thickness. Even so, large numbers of defects continued to be generated.

The improved operation proceeded as described below (*Figure 14-5*). Since the specified thickness for the product was t = 10mm ± O.5mm, the chute for carrying away formed products was equipped as follows:

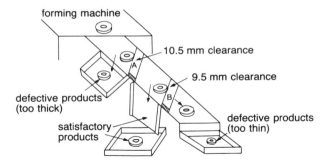

FIGURE 14-5. Stem Tightener Inspection

1. Combination gauge/guide A was attached to the upper end of the chute.
2. The space between gauge A and the chute was 10.5mm.
3. Combination gauge/guide B was attached to the lower end of the chute.
4. The space between gauge B and the chute was 9.5mm.
5. When a formed item is expelled and moves down the chute, products thicker than 10.5mm are unable to pass beneath gauge A and are led by A into a defects bin at the left of the chute.
6. Products thinner than 10.5mm pass underneath A.
7. Products thicker than 9.5mm are led by gauge B into a bin for acceptable parts to the left of the chute.
8. Parts that are thinner than 9.5mm pass underneath gauge B and are led to the defects bin in the middle.
9. When defective products show up in either defective parts bin, they come in contact with limit switches that notify the worker that a defect has occurred by stopping the line and sounding a buzzer.
10. When this happens, the worker hurries to the machine, finds the cause of the defect, and then fixes it. Machine operations start up again after repairs have been completed.

The cause of thickness defects lay in fluctuations in the amounts of teflon powder poured in. The principal reasons for this were that:

- So-called bridging in the materials hopper meant variations in amounts of teflon poured in.
- Blockages in the mesh of the box-type vibrating sieve used for pouring powder into the die caused variations in the amounts of powder falling into the die.

The following improvements were made:

- A device to prevent bridging was mounted on the materials hopper.
- A W-shaped flat spring was installed in the middle of the box-type vibrating sieve. Vibrations cause it to clean the die constantly and mesh blockage no longer occurs.

As a result, V Industries was able to reduce the previous 6.5 percent defect rate to 0.4 percent, that is, to one-fifteenth of its former figure. A number of actions were important in attaining this strikingly low defect rate:

- 100 percent inspections are performed.
- Feedback and action take place as soon as defects occur.
- The new system prevents the occurrence of serial defects by promptly shutting down machines and taking corrective action whenever a single defect occurs.
- Suitable countermeasures can be devised because the circumstances surrounding defect generation are clearly visible.

SOURCE INSPECTIONS: INSPECTIONS THAT ELIMINATE DEFECTS

Source inspections can be described as inspection methods that, rather than stimulating feedback and action in response to defects, are based on the idea of discovering errors in conditions that give rise to defects and performing feedback and action at the error stage so as to keep those errors from turning into defects.

Zero QC systems can be set up by combining these source inspections with 100 percent inspections and immediate feedback and action. In terms of practical measures to achieve this end, the use of poka-yoke devices is extremely effective. Indeed, it is poka-yoke methods that first make it possible to bring about zero defects.

The Significance of Source Inspections

Many people maintain that it is impossible to eliminate defects from any task performed by humans. This view stems from the failure to make a clear separation between errors and defects. Defects arise because errors are made; the two have a cause-and-effect relationship.

I claim that it is impossible to eliminate all errors from any task performed by humans. Indeed, inadvertent errors are both possible and inevitable. Yet errors will not turn into defects if feedback and action take place at the error stage. In this way, I am advocating the elimination of defects by clearly distinguishing between errors and defects, that is, between causes and effects. This is the principal feature of source inspections.

The problem can be visualized in the following way. Management systems in the past have carried out control or management in large cycles:

- An error takes place (cause).
- A defect occurs as a result.
- This information is fed back.
- Corrective action is taken accordingly.

In source inspections, however, control or management is carried out in small cycles:

- An error takes place (cause).
- Feedback is carried out at the error stage, before the error turns into a defect.
- Corrective action is taken accordingly.

Zero defects are achieved because errors do not turn into defects, and management cycles are extremely rapid.

In general, we can imagine five situations in which defects occur:

1. Cases in which either inappropriate standard work processes or inappropriate standard operating procedures are established at the planning stage. An example of this might be the setting of unsuitable heat-treatment temperatures. Since all products become defective in this sort of situation, real operations can not begin, of course, until these conditions are corrected.

2. Cases in which actual operations show excessive variation even though standard methods are appropriate. An example might be the occurrence of occasional defects owing to excessive play in machine bearings. Here, too, operations can begin after proper maintenance has been performed.
3. In cases where sections of raw materials are damaged or material thicknesses fluctuate excessively, thorough inspections must be carried out when such materials are received.
4. In cases where friction in machine bearings results in excessive play or worn tools throw off measurements, overall tool management and maintenance need to be carried out.
5. Some defects clearly occur in cases of inadvertent errors by workers or machines, for example, when chips clog parts. Such events are unpredictable and occur randomly, which makes them difficult for sampling inspections to capture. Here, 100 percent inspections are indispensable.

The various situations described above recall something I have already said. The reduction in the defect rate at Arakawa Auto Body from 3.5 percent to 0.01 percent in the space of two years resulted from the adoption of source inspections, self-checks, successive checks, and poka-yoke devices. This fact proves, does it not, that the majority of defects are of the inadvertent error type (5)?

Most of the remaining 0.01 percent of defects are those involving dirt, scratches, or other things that are difficult to eliminate. The above methods completely do away with mismatched assemblies, missing parts, and similar defects.

Thus, the most effective strategies for reaching zero defects are using source inspections to move through management cycles at the level of causes, and using source inspections in combination with 100 percent inspections and poka-yoke devices to speed up feedback and action.

Examples of Source Inspection

A vacuum cleaner packaging operation. Mr. Shimizu, the head of the Production Technology Department at Matsushita Electric's Vacuum Cleaner Division, once told me that parts occasionally turned out to be missing at the final packaging process for finished vacuum cleaners. He was annoyed by this because products with parts missing were sometimes even shipped to customers. I immediately went to the plant and observed the packaging operation. The operation proceeded as follows:

- About 10 small accessories and an instruction manual were placed in a cardboard carton, along with larger items such as the body of the vacuum cleaner and the hose.
- When packing was completed, the top was closed and sealed with plastic tape.
- The fully packed carton was then weighed on a scale set up on a nearby roller conveyor.
- When the weight was too low, the carton would be reopened and checked for missing parts. Any missing parts were then added.

The problem was that the accuracy level of the scale did not make it possible to detect the omission of small parts. Vacuum cleaners missing such parts were occasionally sent to customers and this resulted in complaints.

"I thought of using a more accurate scale," said Mr. Shimizu, "but I hesitated because of the high cost."

After observing the operation for a while, I turned to Mr. Shimizu and said I thought that the basic idea behind the method he used was wrong.

"What! The basic idea is wrong? What are you talking about?" he answered.

"The method you're using tries to carry out inspections after defects have already occurred," I explained. "Why don't you make your inspections in such a way that you prevent defects from happening in the first place?"

Mr. Shimizu is extremely bright and he caught on immediately.

"Yes," he said, "I get it. I'll change the operation right away."

The improved operation proceeded as follows:

- Bowed springs were installed in front of boxes containing small parts so that every time a part is removed from a box, a spring is pressed and a limit switch is activated (*Figure 14-6, A*).
- A spring is provided on the holder in the box containing instruction booklets. The movement of a hand taking an instruction booklet pushes the spring and trips a limit switch (*Figure 14-6, B*).

- Thus, the movement involved in taking each small part trips a limit switch and for each motion a green signal lamp lights up (*Figure 14-6, C*).
- If a part is missing, a stopper does not descend, the packing carton halts, and a buzzer sounds (*Figure 14-6, D*). When the part not indicated by a green lamp is added, the stopper descends.
- Gummed tape is then applied and the carton is shipped out.

After these improvements were made, defects were eliminated and the operation has continued with zero defects for several years since.

A. Bowed Spring Poka-yoke

B. Instruction Booklet Poka-yoke

C. Instruction Booklet Insertion Lamp

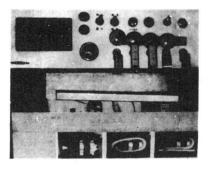

D. Conveyor Stopper

FIGURE 14-6. **Improvements in Vacuum Cleaner Packaging Operation**

Bending cover edges. This operation involved bending one edge of a cover used in an automobile. Right and left covers were the same shape, the only differences being that on right-hand covers a hole was on the right and on left-hand covers it was on the left. This led workers occasionally to bend the wrong edges of covers.

Sometimes one cover in every several dozen was defective in this way. The operation was improved as follows (*Figure 14-7*):

- For right-hand covers, a sensor that activates a limit switch was installed at the position of the right-hand hole.
- For left-hand covers, a sensor that activates a limit switch was installed at the position of the left-hand hole.
- When the edge of a right-hand cover is to be bent, a switch causes current to flow to the right-hand limit switch sensor. When the edge of a left-hand cover is to be bent, current flows to the left-hand limit switch.
- If a part is positioned backwards, the part presses against the sensor, causes a buzzer to sound, and switches off power to the bender. When this happens, the machine will not operate even when the start button is pushed.

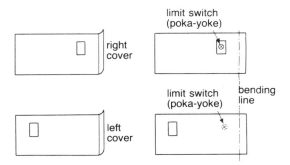

FIGURE 14-7. Poka-Yoke Device for Bending Cover Edges

These improvements resulted in the elimination of defects, and for the first time, the operation became one that even novices could perform flawlessly.

Carburetor assembly. In this operation, a small ball valve was inserted in an automobile carburetor and then a cap was installed. Defects sometimes occurred, however, when workers forgot to insert ball valves before installing caps. Function tests at a subsequent process would uncover gasoline leaks and the unit would have to be reassembled after it was taken apart and a ball valve inserted. The operation was improved as follows (*Figure 14-8*):

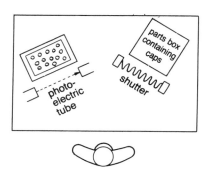

FIGURE 14-8. Poka-Yoke Device for Guaranteeing Ball Valve Insertion

- A photoelectric switch was installed in front of a box containing ball valves.
- A shutter was attached to the front of a box containing caps.
- When a worker's left hand reaches into the box to take out a ball valve, the movement trips the photoelectric switch and the shutter for the cap box opens. Unless the worker reaches into the valve box, the shutter on the cap box will not open and caps cannot be removed.

This made it impossible for a worker to perform the operation if he or she had forgotten to take out a ball valve. Not a single instance of missing ball valve insertion has shown up in the several years since these improvements were made.

Seat assembly. Seat assembly operations at Arakawa Auto Body took the form of so-called mixed production, with seats for Coronas, Corollas, Celicas, Carinas, and other models all moving along the same line. This meant that workers had to pay extraordinarily careful attention to attaching the appropriate fittings to each seat. Even so, incorrect parts were occasionally attached.

The following improvements were made:

- Small foil disks were pasted to the lower portions of kanban according to the model involved.
- Kanban insertion racks were set up, with a reflector-type photoelectric switch for each model mounted on the front.
- When the kanban arrives along with a seat body, a worker takes the kanban and inserts it in the kanban insertion rack. This causes a lamp to light on the front of the parts box containing fittings for the model indicated. At the same time, the shutter for only that box opens (*Figure 14-9*).
- The worker then takes parts out of the box indicated by the lamp and attaches them to the seat.
- Tact time is 30 seconds. If 20 seconds elapse and no parts are removed from the box, a buzzer sounds and seats are prevented from moving to the next process because a conveyor stopper is not withdrawn. (When a seat comes in contact with the stopper, furthermore, the assembly conveyor shuts down.)
- Since no shutters open except the one for the correct parts box, it has become impossible to attach incorrect fittings to seats.

Even on a mixed production line handling a variety of models, the above improvements eliminated model mismatches and made it

FIGURE 14-9. Poka-Yoke Device for Attachment of Seat Fittings

possible for workers to perform the operation without anxiety. Incorrect parts were not attached to seats even when regular workers were absent and other workers substituted for them. This method is known at Arakawa as the *passport system*, and it has proven to be a considerable success in a number of applications.

The examples cited above share several common features:

- Each makes use of a source inspections approach in which the idea is to discover errors at their source and then carry out feedback and action before the errors turn into defects.
- The use of poka-yoke devices allows information concerning the appearance of defects to be fed back immediately, and prompt corrective action is then taken. In addition, 100 percent inspections are used.
- In general, the cost of constructing poka-yoke devices came to ¥30,000 ($150) or less. In expensive cases it was no more than ¥100,000 ($500) or so.

The use of source inspections and poka-yoke devices has made it possible to go for several years without the occurrence of a single defect.

When these ideas are applied to machine maintenance, breakdowns can be eliminated as well. For example, a thermistor attached to the bearing section of a machine might set off a buzzer and shut down the machine whenever the temperature exceeded 20° C. This would protect against breakdowns involving "baking."

In such situations, the approach is to distinguish between abnormalities (or problems) and breakdowns, and then to run through control cycles at the causal stage by discovering abnormalities where they occur and carrying out feedback and action. By preventing breakdowns from occurring even when abnormalities show up, this conceptual approach makes it possible to make zero breakdowns a reality. In this area as well, poka-yoke methods can be very effective.

THE ESTABLISHMENT OF A POKA-YOKE SYSTEM

As I have explained so far, poka-yoke systems involve carrying out 100 percent inspections and requiring immediate feedback and action when errors or defects occur. This approach therefore neatly solves the problems posed by the old-fashioned belief that 100 percent inspections take too much trouble and cost too much.

Because of the considerable effect obtained by actually installing poka-yoke devices, however, many people are under the false impression that simply putting in such devices will eliminate defects.

Yet in the final analysis, a poka-yoke system is a means and not an end. Poka-yoke systems can be combined with successive checks or with self-checks, and can fulfill the needs of those techniques by providing 100 percent inspections and prompt feedback and action. Successive checks and self-checks, however, can function only as informative inspections, in which feedback and action take place after a defect has occurred. In fact, they make the occurrence of at least one defect inevitable. Of course, in cases where repairs can be made it looks as though no defects occurred, but in an absolute sense, these methods are inherently unable to attain zero defects.

It follows that source inspections and poka-yoke measures must be combined if one wishes to eliminate defects. It is the combination of source inspections and poka-yoke devices that makes it possible to establish a Zero QC system.

Thus, in spite of the fact that poka-yoke methods themselves are extremely effective, final results will depend considerably on the inspection system with which poka-yoke methods are combined. Insofar as is possible, it is imperative to try to combine source inspections and the poka-yoke system, and the use of poka-yoke methods with self-checks or successive checks should be limited to instances constrained by technical or financial impediments.

One must never forget, finally, that the poka-yoke system refers to a means and not to an end.

SAMPLING INSPECTIONS AND 100 PERCENT INSPECTIONS

To summarize, the persistence of defects in production activities creates the need to find and eliminate those defects. Since it is impossible to zero in on defects automatically, defects will not be found unless 100 percent of the items involved are inspected. Generally speaking, acceptable items are overwhelmingly more numerous than defective ones, so this sort of 100 percent inspection entails considerable "wasted" work. In addition, 100 percent inspections require a great deal of trouble and high labor costs.

These problems have given rise to a technique called sampling inspection, backed by the scientific discipline of inductive statistics. In this approach, highly reliable inspections that take little trouble and are of the same level as 100 percent inspections can be carried out by means of sample sizes indicated on acceptable quality level (AQL) charts; the size of the sample depends on how often defects occur.

According to the extremely logical AQL approach, the relative sample size can be low when the defect rate is high, and relative sample size is increased when the defect rate is low. This method lowers both the cost and the bother of inspections considerably.

Yet even when sample size is determined by the proportion of defects, the defects occur at random intervals. If sampling methods call for one item in 25, for example, or if sampling is random, it is extremely difficult to match sampling with the occurrence of abnormalities or defects.

This is because the fundamental approach of sampling inspections is based on probability theory and does not account for one occurrence in 100,000 or one in one million.

Thus such methods may reduce defects, but they can never eliminate them. It used to be thought that 100 percent inspections would raise inspection costs because they require considerable work. Now, however, the use of poka-yoke devices makes for trouble-free and low-cost inspections. This means that so-called sampling inspections have lost their *raison d'être* and the fact that they are backed by scientific statistics becomes meaningless.

Naturally, the possible use of sampling inspections as a second-best strategy should be considered in situations where the application of poka-yoke measures would be extremely difficult, but it should be understood that these are not the method of choice.

I would like readers to free themselves from blind faith in the sampling inspection as a superior and extremely rational method, and I want to stress the importance of understanding clearly that no matter how rational a means of inspection it may be, a sampling inspection is not necessarily appropriate from the point of view of zero-defects-oriented quality assurance. This is especially true in modern automated assembly processes, for even one rare defect can cause an automatic machine to break down or can cause constant temporary shutdowns. Furthermore, since inspection itself is a wasteful act, it is wasteful to set up independent inspection processes. It is important to keep in mind that inspection processes should be attached to work processes so as to eliminate the need for a separate inspection process.

MODEL CHANGES AND ZERO DEFECTS

A new-model television set was to be assembled at the Ibaraki Division of A Electronics. On this occasion, Mr. Yamagata, head of the Manufacturing Department, gathered his front-line supervisors and told them what he expected of them.

"We are going to assemble 30,000 of the new-model television sets," he told them, "but initially we are going to make just 50 of them. I want things done so that absolutely no defects are passed on to subsequent processes. Not only that, if a defective item is discovered by a successive check or a self-check, I want it sent back to the previous process immediately and allowed to move forward only after the defect has been corrected.

"While you are working on this," he concluded, "I don't want you to be concerned with output levels or with labor costs."

All conceivable poka-yoke devices were installed and self-check and successive check routines were adopted.

Progress toward the daily production target of 1,000 sets was steady:

> First day: 285 sets
> Second day: 473 sets
> Third day: 815 sets
> Fourth day: 978 sets
> Fifth day: 1,012 sets

Daily production after the fifth day exceeded the target of 1,000, and by the end of the month the previously unimaginable production figure of 1,270 sets had been achieved.

In the past, the idea had been to maintain production volumes, and so items had been sent along regularly to subsequent processes. This meant that products needing repair piled up at the final process and there, pressed by the volume of repairs needed, skilled workers worked overtime to correct errors. They were so overworked that occasionally defective products were shipped out and then claims would come back to the company. The new method, however, was tremendously successful and no claims were made involving television sets manufactured through the use of this "IT system."

Later, at an IE institute held in Utsunomiya, I happened to hear a talk given by Mr. Ohta, the foreman actually in charge of this experiment.

"I really resisted it," Mr. Ohta told me, "when we were told we couldn't have any defects in the assembly of those 30,000 new-model television sets. I would have said it simply wasn't possible.

"Since they told us that we only had to try the new methods with 50 sets and that output didn't matter, I decided to give it a try.

"In starting the assembly work, we fixed all of the defects that showed up initially and then corrected any problems we had with parts. For errors in operating methods, we put an experienced leader in charge of five workers and he both provided guidance on operating methods and rapidly set up poka-yoke devices. All this led to unexpectedly good results, and we're much more confident now about future model changes."

Listening to Mr. Ohta made me think that it was like taking contaminated blood from a newborn infant and replacing it with healthy blood. The baby would develop a little more slowly at first, but before long things would go smoothly and it would grow into a strong, healthy child.

Any company that deals with model changes has to display new lines of products in its outlets, so there is a tendency to concentrate on raising production figures, to work nights and overtime to "get the numbers right." Yet it is methods like this that lead to greater success, methods that are not bound to output numbers and are aimed at preventing defects from occurring.

Indeed, K Electric in Kyushu used this system with tremendous success when it had to accommodate a model change in home stereo equipment and output was not rising.

INSPECTIONS AND AUTOMATION

As I mentioned earlier, the head of manufacturing of the American L Company — a firm making inroads in Japan by producing door locks for the Japanese firm H Technologies — came and visited the

Osaka plant of M Metals and Mining, a company that manufactures the same door locks in Japan. After he had toured the plant and various preliminaries had been gotten out of the way, the L Company representative was told proudly by Mr. Kurozu, the plant manager, that at M Metals and Mining, all finished products were inspected automatically by machine so that not a single defective item was sent on to customers. The American silenced Mr. Kurozu by responding that his company used poka-yoke methods to carry out source inspections, self-checks, and successive checks at each process and that absolutely no defective items moved from one process to the next, so they did not need special inspections at the final process to keep defective goods from being sent to customers.

Ultimately, the fact that the L Company used automated inspection equipment for judgment inspections may have had the advantage of cutting labor costs by eliminating inspection personnel, but there was no way it could be expected to reduce or eliminate defects.

We see, then, that reducing inspection personnel and reducing or eliminating defects are entirely different issues. Whether defects will be reduced or eliminated depends on the kind of inspection methods used, not on whether the inspections are or are not automated.

Automation can be applied to source inspections, to informative inspections (including control chart methods, successive checks, and self-checks) or to judgment inspections. But the automation of inspections is ultimately a matter of economizing on labor; it has no connection with the lowering of defect rates.

If automation has any effect at all on defect reduction, it may make it possible to conduct 100 percent inspections and thus prevent the shipment of defective goods to customers. It may also allow all abnormalities to be detected and therefore increase the frequency of feedback and action. But that is all.

Recently, I met the director of the N Association's publishing division and he told me that the managing director of the D Company had said that defects would not be reduced unless inspections were automated. I remember feeling that there are many people in the world who, failing to understand that inspection automation and defect rate reduction are different issues, still cling to the delusion that automation will reduce defects.

15

Using Poka-Yoke Systems

POKA-YOKE SYSTEM FUNCTIONS

A poka-yoke system possesses two functions: it can carry out 100 percent inspections and, if abnormalities occur, it can carry out immediate feedback and action. The effects of poka-yoke methods in reducing defects will differ depending on the inspection systems with which they are combined: source inspections, self-checks, or successive checks.

TYPES OF POKA-YOKE SYSTEMS

Poka-yoke systems fall into regulatory function categories, depending on their purposes, and setting function categories, according to techniques they use.

Poka-yoke Regulatory Functions

Two regulatory functions are performed by poka-yoke systems: control methods and warning methods.

Control Methods

These are methods that, when abnormalities occur, shut down machines or lock clamps to halt operations, thereby preventing the occurrence of serial defects. Such methods have a more powerful regulatory function than do those of the "warning" type discussed below, and maximum efficacy in achieving zero defects is obtained by the use of these control-type systems.

Although I have defined control methods as ones that shut down machines to halt operations, the shutting down of machines is by no means the only possible strategy, as the following example illustrates.

The Stereo Equipment Division of A Electronics had an insertion machine that automatically inserted parts such as transistors and diodes into printed circuit boards. The machine would stop when pitch errors occurred in the insertion of bent parts legs into the circuit boards, or when insertion mistakes cropped up because legs were crooked. This had the effect of drastically lowering the machine's work rate. This was the stage things were at when I spoke to the head of the Manufacturing Department.

"In a fully automated system," I told him, "When an abnormality shows up, the mechanism itself has the capacity to detect the trouble and take steps to deal with it.

"In contrast, the 'preautomation' approach I am advocating has the mechanism itself detect the trouble, but then human beings take steps to deal with it. Both methods recognize that abnormalities will occur. After all, there is no machine in the world that will operate 100 years without any abnormal situations arising.

"The abnormal situations in your case are so-called isolated defects. They can also be fixed, so we're not talking about a machine where abnormalities continue to occur just because one error shows up.

"If that's the case, why not make a mark on the board when an abnormality occurs and let the machine continue to operate? The problem boards can be automatically spotted and separated from the good ones. The trouble can be resolved by hand and the machine is not shut down. Wouldn't this sort of approach improve the work rate and be more profitable in the end?"

Methods for the operation were promptly revised and a 30 percent increase in the work rate was achieved.

Thus, control methods do not always imply shutting down machines. A variety of strategies is available.

This example describes an approach taken when isolated defects occurred. It was also a case in which the abnormalities could be corrected. If we were dealing with a case in which abnormalities kept on occurring, that is, a case of serial defects, then, of course, it would be necessary to use a method that shut down the machine. In a case such as that of unfinished holes resulting from a broken punch, a control method should be used and the machine shut down.

Warning Methods

These methods call abnormalities to workers' attention by activating a buzzer or a light. Since defects will continue to occur if workers do not notice these signals, this approach provides a less powerful regulatory function than control methods.

In cases where workers' attention is captured by means of light, blinking lights can attract attention more powerfully than steady ones. Ultimately, this method is effective only when workers take notice, and the passive aspect of light signals makes it necessary to regulate placement, intensity and color, etc. On the other hand, sound can actively call out to people, but since it cannot be effective if it is drowned out by other noises in the workplace, it is necessary to regulate volume, tone, and intermittency.

There are a surprising number of cases, too, in which it is more effective to change musical scales or timbres than to turn up the volume. In this sense, there are frequently situations where good results can be obtained through the use of music box type tones. Light and sound can also be used in combination with one another.

In any event, control methods display far more powerful regulatory effects than do warning methods, so control-type measures should be used as much as possible. The use of warning methods may be considered either where the impact of abnormalities is slight or where technical or economic factors make the adoption of control methods extremely difficult.

Poka-Yoke Setting Functions

The setting functions of poka-yoke systems can be divided into three categories: contact methods, fixed-value methods, and motion-step methods.

Contact Methods

Methods in which sensing devices detect abnormalities in product shape or dimension by whether or not contact is made between the products and the sensing devices are called contact methods.

Example: Preventing errors in brake wire clamp mounting.
The fact that both left- and right-handed brake wire clamp mounting

jigs could be set into a bridge occasioned errors in which left and right parts would be mixed up (*Figure 15-1*).

Example: Ensuring the presence of hardware mounting screws in television cabinets. The construction of cabinets for television sets at Daito Woodworking, Ltd. included the task of attaching four hardware fittings for the television tube in the front frame, securing each of the fittings with four screws, and then applying tape over the top of the fittings.

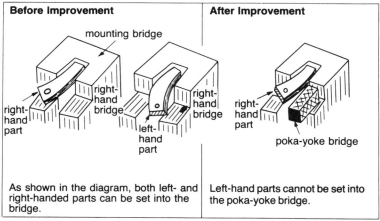

Before Improvement	After Improvement
As shown in the diagram, both left- and right-handed parts can be set into the bridge.	Left-hand parts cannot be set into the poka-yoke bridge.

Effects: Confusion of left and right parts was reduced to zero.

FIGURE 15-1. **Preventing Erroneous Brake Wire Clamp Mounting**

Sixteen screws were attached in all, and on rare occasions one or more screws would be left out. Since tape was then applied over the top of the fittings, such errors were not found when the units were shipped to the parent company and only came to light in the assembly process (*Figure 15-2*).

Mr. Morikawa of Daito made the following improvements:

- Sixteen limit switches were mounted on the jig underneath the sites where screws were to be attached to the frame.
- After glue has been applied to the four side sections and they are joined to form the frame, pneumatic cylinders press them together and each of the fittings is secured with four screws.

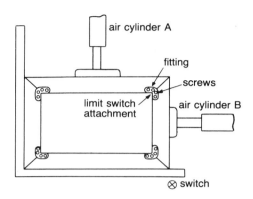

air cylinder A

fitting

screws

limit switch
attachment

air cylinder B

⊗ switch

FIGURE 15-2. Screws and Poka-Yoke Device

- In the event that even a single screw is missing, the otherwise completed frame cannot move to the next operation because a switch will not have been turned.

Adopting this strategy made it impossible to make defective cabinets, and no more instances of missing screws occurred.

Fixed-Value Methods

With these methods, abnormalities are detected by checking for the specified number of motions in cases where operations must be repeated a predetermined number of times.

Example: Ensuring application of insulation tape. At the O Plant, insulation tape was applied to television cabinets in 10 places. In the past, 8cm strips of insulation tape had been lined up on a rod and these would be taken off as needed and applied to the cabinet. Sometimes strips were not applied, however, so the following poka-yoke approach was adopted (*Figure 15-3*).

Strips of tape were first applied to the rod in groups of 10, so that if a worker failed to apply one strip to the cabinet, he or she would quickly notice that one of that group of 10 remained on the rod. From that point onward, workers never neglected to apply all 10 strips.

Next, sets of legs for television sets were manufactured and then packed in cardboard cartons of 50 sets each. An assembly instruction

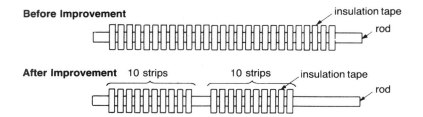

FIGURE 15-3. Insulation Tape and Poka-Yoke Device

sheet had to be inserted in each small box containing a set of legs, but the parent company warned that occasionally these instruction sheets were missing. To deal with this problem, the following poka-yoke procedure was devised:

- Instruction sheets are counted and separated into groups of 50 beforehand.

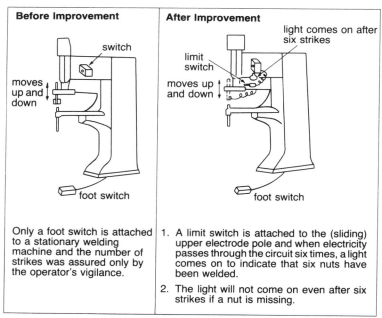

Effect: nut welding defects were eliminated
Cost: ¥7,000 ($35)

FIGURE 15-4. Device to Ensure the Welding of Nuts

- A packet of 50 instruction sheets is taken out each time a new carton is packed.
- If any instruction sheets remain after a carton is packed, then one or more of the small boxes is missing a sheet. When this happens, the packed items are checked. This put an end to complaints from the parent company.

Example: Ensuring the welding of nuts. Although six nuts had to be attached in a welding process, nuts were occasionally left out (*Figure 15-4*).

Motion-Step Methods

These are methods in which abnormalities are detected by checking for errors in standard motions in cases where operations must be carried out with predetermined motions. These extremely effective methods have a wide range of application, and the possibility of their use should by all means be examined when poka-yoke setting functions are considered.

Example: Ensuring the attachment of labels. Workers sometimes failed to apply labels and this error would be discovered at an inspection process (*Figure 15-5*).

The examples show that a wide variety of poka-yoke methods can be devised.*

DETECTION METHODS FOR POKA-YOKE SYSTEMS

Below are simple explanations of the functions of the various detection methods.

Contact Detection Methods

Limit switches, microswitches. These confirm the presence and position of objects and detect broken tools, etc. Some limit switches are equipped with lights for easy maintenance checks.

---

* Editor's note: Dr. Shingo's *Zero Quality Control: Source Inspection and the Poka-yoke System* (Cambridge: Productivity Press, 1986) includes many more examples from a number of companies.

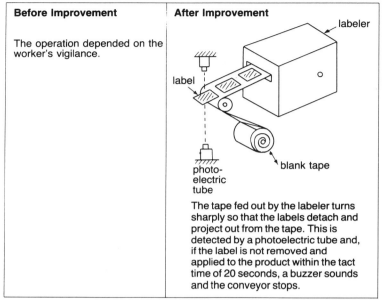

Before Improvement	After Improvement
The operation depended on the worker's vigilance.	The tape fed out by the labeler turns sharply so that the labels detach and project out from the tape. This is detected by a photoelectric tube and, if the label is not removed and applied to the product within the tact time of 20 seconds, a buzzer sounds and the conveyor stops.

Effect: label application failures were eliminated.
Cost: ¥ 15,000 ($75)

FIGURE 15-5. Device to Ensure Attachment of Labels

Touch switches. Activated by a light touch on their antenna sections, touch switches can detect object presence, position, breakage, dimensions, etc., with high sensitivity.

Differential transformers. When put in contact with a product, a differential transformer picks up changes in the degree of contact as fluctuations in lines of magnetic force, thus enabling it to detect objects with a high degree of precision.

Trimetrons. A dial gauge forms the body of a trimetron, and limit values can easily be set on the plus and minus sides as well as at the true position. This is a convenient detection device because these limits can be selected electronically, allowing the device to both detect the acceptability of measurements and exclude them (*Figure 15-6*).

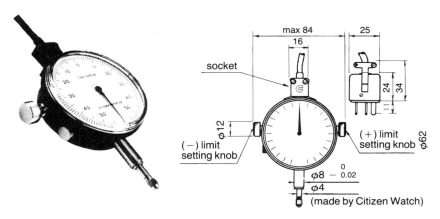

FIGURE 15-6. Trimetron

Liquid level relays. These can detect liquid levels without using floats.

Contactless Detection Methods

Proximity switches. These systems respond to changes in distances from objects and to changes in lines of magnetic force. For this reason, they must be used with materials susceptible to magnetism.

Photoelectric switches (transmission types and reflection types). Photoelectric switches include transmission types, in which a beam transmitted between two photoelectric switches is interrupted, and reflection types, which make use of reflected light beams. Photo-electric switches are widely used for nonferrous items, and reflection

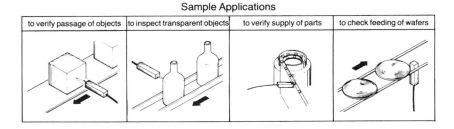

FIGURE 15-7. Photoelectric Switches — Sample Applications

types are especially convenient for distinguishing color differences. They can even judge welds and the like by means of color differences (*Figure 15-7*).

Beam sensors (transmission types and reflection types). These detection systems make use of electron beams. Beam sensors, too, include transmission and reflection types (*Figures 15-8* and *15-9*).

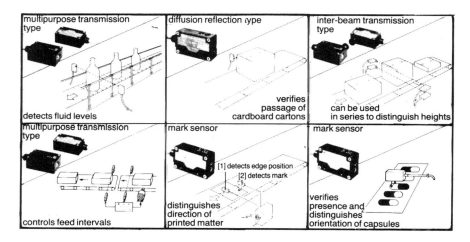

FIGURE 15-8. Beam Sensors

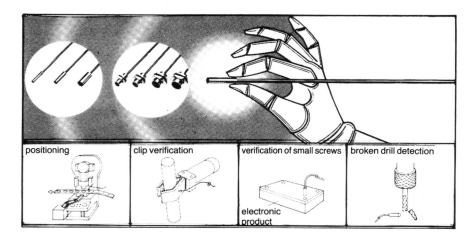

FIGURE 15-9. Proximity Beam Sensors

Fiber sensors. These are sensors that use optical fibers (*Figure 15-10*).

Area sensors. The majority of sensors detect only linear interruptions, but area sensors can detect random interruptions over a fixed area (*Figure 15-11*).

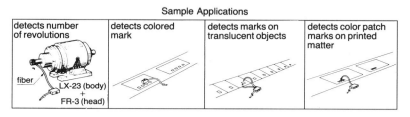

FIGURE 15-10. Fiber Sensors — Sample Applications

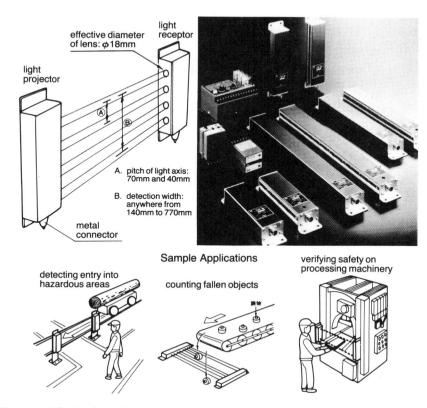

FIGURE 15-11. Area Sensors

Positioning sensors. These are sensors that detect positioning
Figure 15-12).

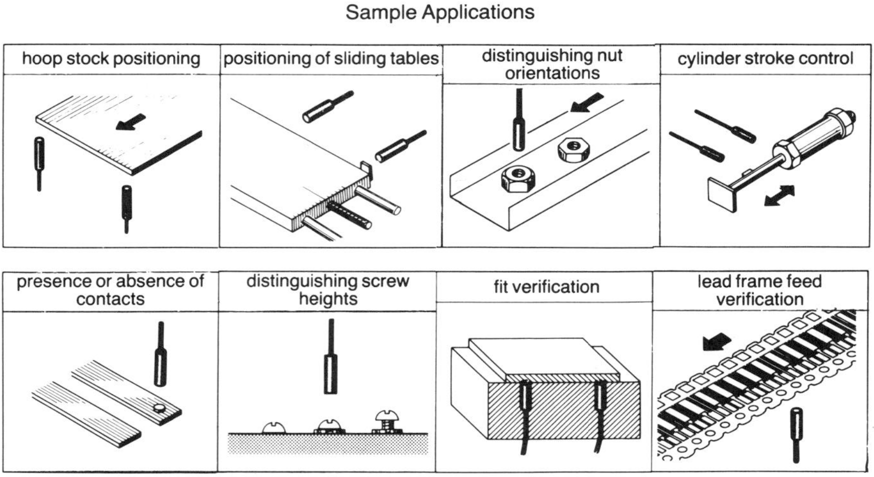

Sample Applications

FIGURE 15-12. Positioning Sensors — Sample Applications

Dimension sensors. These are sensors that detect whether dimensions are correct (*Figure 15-13*).

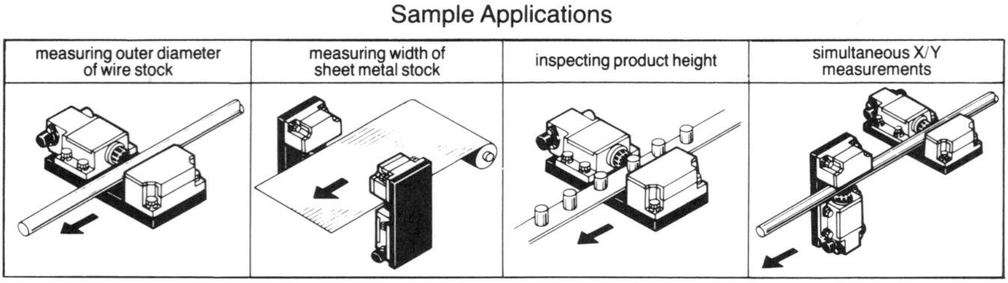

Sample Applications

FIGURE 15-13. Dimension Sensors — Sample Applications

Displacement sensors. These are sensors that detect warping, thickness, and level heights (*Figure 15-14*).

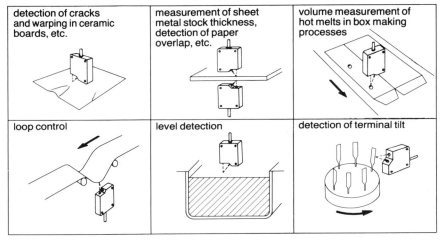

FIGURE 15-14. Displacement Sensors — Sample Applications

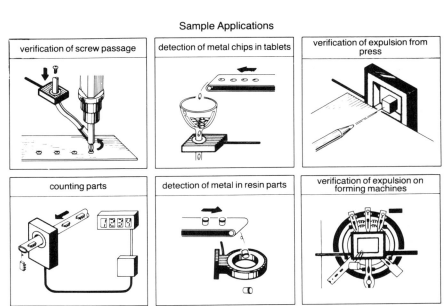

FIGURE 15-15. Metal Passage Sensors — Sample Applications

Metal passage sensors. These can detect whether or not products have passed by and can sense the presence of metal mixed in with resin materials (*Figure 15-15*).

Color marking sensors. These are sensors that detect colored marks or differences in color (*Figure 15-16*).

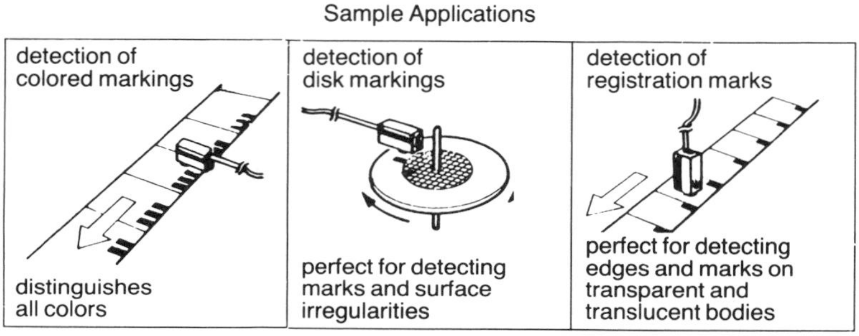

Sample Applications

detection of colored markings	detection of disk markings	detection of registration marks
distinguishes all colors	perfect for detecting marks and surface irregularities	perfect for detecting edges and marks on transparent and translucent bodies

FIGURE 15-16. Color Marking Sensors — Sample Applications

Vibration sensors. These can detect the passage of goods, the position of welds, and snapped wires (*Figure 15-17*).

Sample Applications

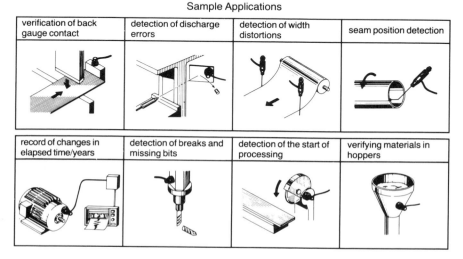

verification of back gauge contact	detection of discharge errors	detection of width distortions	seam position detection
record of changes in elapsed time/years	detection of breaks and missing bits	detection of the start of processing	verifying materials in hoppers

FIGURE 15-17. Vibration Sensors — Sample Applications

Double-feed sensors. These are sensors that detect two products fed at the same time (*Figure 15-18*).

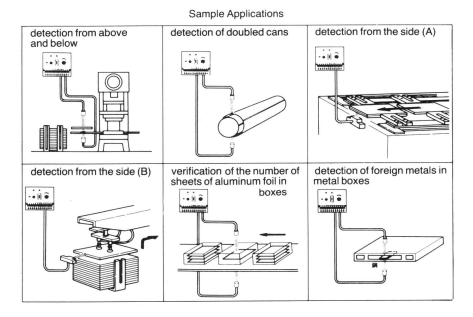

Sample Applications

| detection from above and below | detection of doubled cans | detection from the side (A) |
| detection from the side (B) | verification of the number of sheets of aluminum foil in boxes | detection of foreign metals in metal boxes |

FIGURE 15-18. Double-Feed Sensors — Sample Applications

Methods for Detecting Pressure, Temperature, Electric Current, Vibration, Numbers of Cycles, Timing, and Information Transmission

Detection of pressure changes. The use of pressure gauges or pressure-sensitive switches permits detection of oil pipe flow interruptions, etc.

Detection of temperature changes. Temperature changes can be detected through the use of thermometers, thermostats, thermistors, thermocouples, etc. These can be used to check surface temperatures of dies, electronic parts, and motors; to perform machine maintenance checks; and for all other kinds of industrial temperature measurement control.

Detection of electrical current fluctuations. Meter relays are extremely convenient for being able to control the causes of defects by detecting the occurrence of electric currents.

Time and timing detection. Timers, delay relays, timing units, and time switches can be used for these purposes.

Measures for the transmission of information regarding abnormalities. Either sound or light can be used, but whereas sound actively captures workers' attention, defects may continue to be generated if a worker fails to notice a light. The use of color somewhat improves the attention-getting capacity of a steady light, but the summoning power of a blinking light is far greater still.

Above, I have described a variety of detection devices in widespread use. Detection methods and capacities have been rapidly improving of late and I hope that people do their own research and actively gather data so such devices may be used appropriately.

EXAMPLES OF POKA-YOKE SYSTEMS

Inspection Method		Setting Function		Regulative Function		Company Name
Source Inspection	●	Contact Method	●	Control Method	●	Hosei Brake Industries, Ltd.
Informative Inspection (self)		Constant Value Method		Warning Method		**Proposed by**
Informative Inspection (successive)		Motion-Step Method				Naoteru Ochiai

Theme	Preventing Painting of the Wrong Vehicle Model Identification Color (Painting Mistakes)

Before Improvement

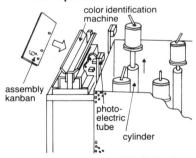

1. Defects cropped up that involved identifying paint color errors and items left unpainted.

2. A worker checked a kanban (tag) and then selected a paint container for painting.

After Improvement

color identification machine

assembly kanban

photo-electric tube

cylinder

The placement of holes punched in an assembly kanban identifies vehicle body type and indicates the specified color to the worker by using air cylinders to raise the correct container. To guard against unpainted items, photoelectric tubes verify the removal of paint containers.

assembly kanban

Effects	Painting errors involving the wrong color or the failure to apply paint were eliminated.	Cost	approx. ¥ 150,000 ($750)

FIGURE 15-19. Example 1

Inspection Method		Setting Function		Regulative Function		Company Name
Source Inspection	●	Contact Method	●	Control Method	●	Hosei Brake Industries, Ltd.
Informative Inspection (self)		Constant Value Method		Warning Method		**Proposed by**
Informative Inspection (successive)		Motion-Step Method				Toshihiro Nabeta

Theme Preventing Upside-Down Welding of Plates

Before Improvement

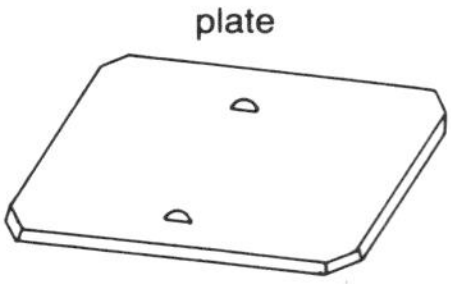

plate

1. Welding defects due to upside-down positioning of plates occasionally occurred in a hardware projection welding process.
2. Although welding was done after a check was made to ensure that the side of a plate with welding projections was on top when the plate was positioned on the welding jig, sometimes a plate would inadvertently be set upside down and then welded.

After Improvement

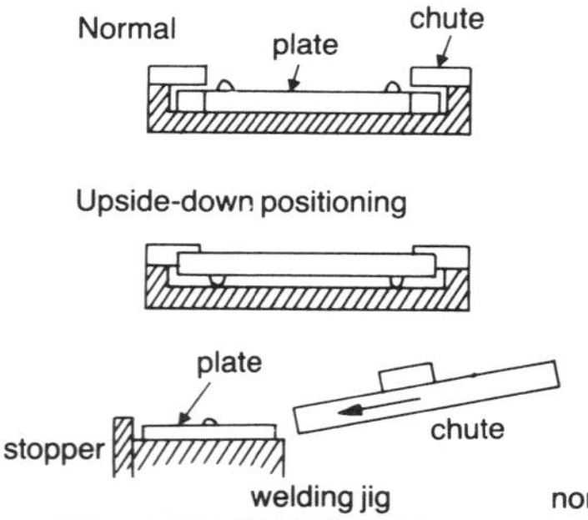

Normal   chute   plate

Upside-down positioning

plate   chute   stopper   welding jig

1. When a plate is positioned on the jig, a chute prevents the finished product from proceeding if the plate is upside down.
2. A plate that is upside down hits a block on the top of the chute and cannot be positioned in the jig.

normal   upside down

Effects	Cost
Upside down plate weldings were eliminated.	¥ 500 ($2.50)

FIGURE 15-20. Example 2

Inspection Method		Setting Function		Regulative Function		Company Name
Source Inspection	●	Contact Method		Control Method		Arakawa Auto Body Industries, Ltd./Sarunage Plant
Informative Inspection (self)		Constant Value Method	●	Warning Method	●	**Proposed by**
Informative Inspection (successive)		Motion-Step Method				

Theme	Preventing the Omission of Spot Welding

Before Improvement

Workers would sometimes forget the number of spot welds to be made when the order of operations changed.

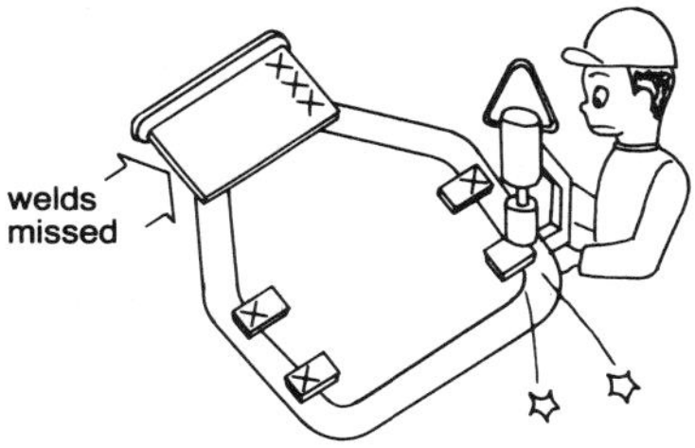

welds missed

After Improvement

1. A control board counter detects the number of welds and operates clamps.

2. The control board counts whenever the portable spot welder is operated and clamps are loosened only when the count reaches 10.

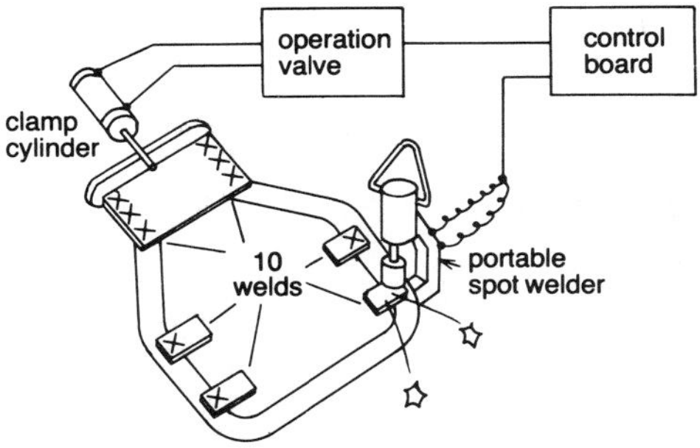

operation valve

control board

clamp cylinder

10 welds

portable spot welder

Effects Defects due to insufficient spot welds dropped from two per month to zero.	**Cost** ¥ 8,500 ($42.50)

FIGURE 15-21. Example 3

Inspection Method		Setting Function		Regulative Function		Company Name
Source Inspection		Contact Method		Control Method		Saga Tekkohsho Co., Ltd./ Fujisawa Plant
Informative Inspection (self)		Constant Value Method		Warning Method		**Proposed by**
Informative Inspection (successive)		Motion-Step Method				Katsuhiko Miura

Theme	Eliminating Bolts with Uncut Grooves

Before Improvement

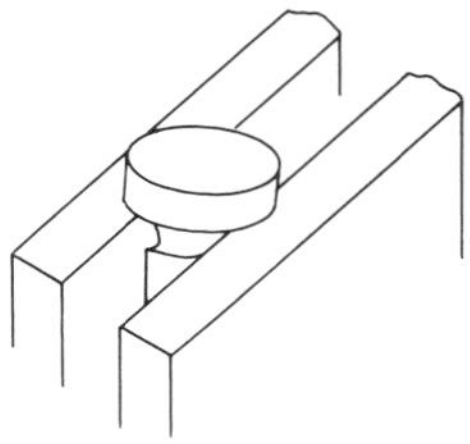

1. In the automated cutting of grooves under bolt heads, uncut items would very infrequently creep in because of chucking defects on the machine.

2. Such defects were uncovered during visual inspections after processing. (judgment inspection)

After Improvement

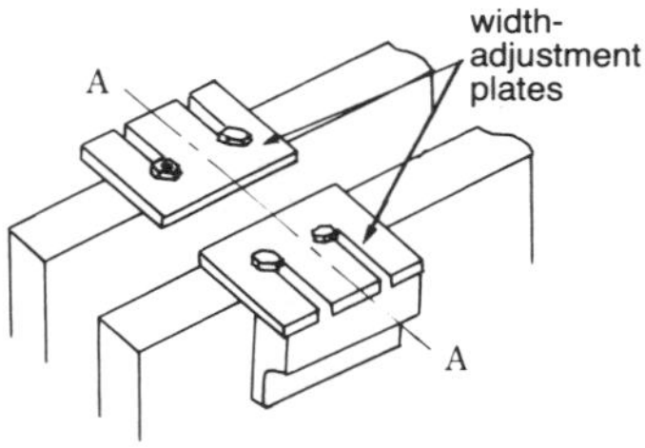

width-adjustment plates

A

A

A-A' cross-section

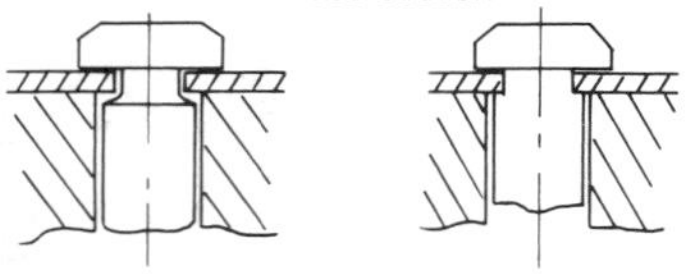

1. A poka-yoke device was installed on the top of the chute leading to the product holder.

2. Plates adjusted to match the width of bolts with grooves under their heads were set so as to halt the outflow of uncut items. A bolt caught on this device sets off a buzzer, which allows chucking errors to be corrected.

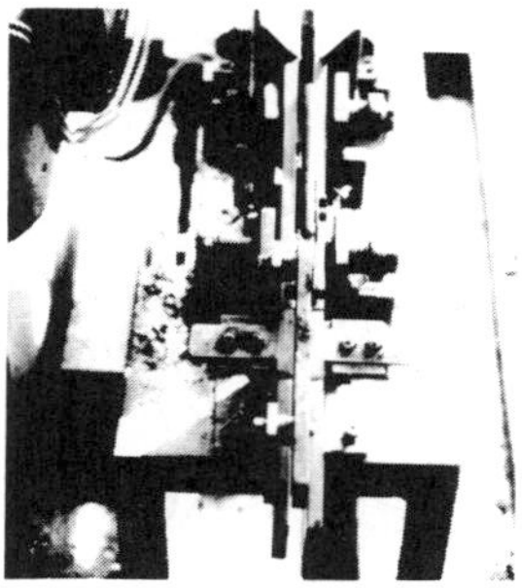

Effects	After installation, the inclusion of bolts with uncut grooves was eliminated.	Cost	¥ 15,000 ($75)

FIGURE 15-22. Example 4

SECTION THREE

*A Revolution in Manufacturing: The SMED System**

* The readings in this section are excerpted entirely from
  Dr. Shingo's *A Revolution in Manufacturing: The SMED
  System* (Cambridge: Productivity Press, 1985).

INTRODUCTION

It always requires some physical or mental effort to end one task and begin another. In production, this operation of changeover is often referred to as a *setup*, and is frequently both time-consuming and expensive. In 1776, Adam Smith, in his book *Wealth of Nations*, wrote of the dampening effect lost time had on productivity:

> The advantage which is gained by saving the time commonly lost in passing from one sort of work to another is much greater than we should at first view be apt to imagine it. It is impossible to pass very quickly from one kind of work to another that is carried on in a different place, and with quite different tools.... This cause alone must always reduce considerably the quantity of work which [a worker] is capable of performing.[1]

Because of the time and expense of changing from one operation to another, manufacturers have always had strong incentives to make long production runs to amortize the initial cost of setup. This had several bad effects, one of which was recognized by Karl Marx in 1867, when he wrote in *Das Kapital*,

> An artificer, who performs one after another the various fractional operations in the production of a finished article, must at one time change his place, at another his tools. The transition from one operation to another interrupts the flow of his labor, and creates, so to say, gaps in his working day. These gaps close up so soon as he is tied to one and the same operation all day long; they vanish in proportion as the changes in his work diminish. The resulting increased productive power is owing either to an increased expenditure of labor-power in a given time — *i.e.*, to increased intensity of labor — or to a decrease in the amount of labor-power unproductively consumed. The extra expenditure of power, demanded by every transition from rest to motion, is made up for by prolonging the duration of the normal velocity when once acquired. On the other hand, constant labor of one uniform kind disturbs the intensity and flow of a man's animal spirits, which find recreation and delight in mere change of activity.[2]

---

[1] Adam Smith, *An Inquiry into the Nature and Causes of the Wealth of Nations*, edited by Edwin Cannan, University of Chicago Press, 1976, p. 12.

[2] Robert Tucker, Ed., *The Marx-Engels Reader*, W.W. Norton & Co., NY, 1972, p. 278.

Another undesirable effect of the long production run is the huge inventory of products it builds up. This is expensive for a number of reasons. In his book *Toyota Production System*, Taiichi Ohno wrote,:

> The greatest waste of all is excess inventory. If there is too much inventory for the plant to store, we must build a warehouse, hire workers to carry the goods to the warehouse, and probably buy a carrying cart for each worker.
>
> In the warehouse, people would be needed for rust prevention and inventory management. Even then, some stored goods still rust and suffer damage. Because of this, additional workers will be needed to repair the goods before removal from the warehouse for use. Once stored in the warehouse, the goods must be inventoried regularly. This requires additional workers. When the situation reaches a certain level, some people consider buying computers for inventory control.[3]

In February of 1913, Ford W. Harris, an engineer at Westinghouse Electric and Manufacturing Company and later a patent lawyer and consultant, wrote an article in *Factory, the Magazine of Management* entitled "How Many Parts to Make at Once." The paper examined the question of the most economical quantity to make at one time, or the "Economic Order Quantity" (EOQ). The EOQ is the quantity which most properly balances the cost of setup with the cost of holding inventory built up by a production run until that inventory is depleted and the next production run is begun.

For seventy-five years the concept of the EOQ has been taught to production managers, and the thesis propounded that long production runs are needed to amortize the cost of setup. But what if the setup time could be reduced to minutes or seconds, instead of the customary hours? Would it be possible for the EOQ to be reduced to one item, so that a profit could be made by manufacturing one item at a time? These are questions that Toyota management asked of Dr. Shingo in 1969.

In the following selection of readings, you will find his answers. You will read about his Single-Minute Exchange of Die (SMED) system — a comprehensive methodology that has often reduced

---

[3] Taiichi Ohno, *The Toyota Production System: Beyond Large-Scale Production*, Productivity Press, Cambridge, MA, 1988, p. 54.

setup times which previously took hours to less than ten minutes. As Dr. Shingo quite rightly claims, a careful study of these ideas will enable anyone to reduce setup times to less than ten minutes in many situations.

Indeed, on a recent plant tour, an operations management student in my class (familiar with SMED through only a single lecture) pointed out to some astonished production managers how to lower the setup time on one of their bottleneck machines from two hours to a few minutes. I should add that although this student happens to be a clever young woman, cleverness is not a prerequisite for implementing SMED. As you will see, all that's needed is a little common sense and some familiarity with the ideas contained in this section and elaborated upon further in *A Revolution in Manufacturing: The SMED System.*

16

Introduction to SMED

I was very impressed during a recent visit to the U.S. by the fact that many American industries are interested in Japanese production systems — in particular, Just-In-Time (JIT) and Total Quality Control (TQC) — and are attempting to integrate these systems into their operations.

It goes without saying that JIT is very effective in industrial management, but JIT is an end, not a means. Without understanding the practical methods and techniques that form its core, JIT has no meaning in and of itself.

I firmly believe that the SMED system is the most effective method for achieving Just-In-Time production.

In my experience, most people do not believe that a four-hour setup time can be reduced to only three minutes. In fact, when presented with this claim, most people will maintain that it is impossible. The SMED system, however, contains three essential components that allow the "impossible" to become possible:

- A basic way of thinking about production
- A realistic system
- A practical method

A complete understanding of all three facets of SMED will make it possible for virtually anyone to apply the SMED system, with fruitful results, to any industrial setting.

I am confident that the SMED system will be of great help in revolutionizing existing production systems, and sincerely hope that you will not only come to understand the essence of SMED, but will be able to utilize it effectively in your workplace.

When I ask about the major difficulties encountered in the many factories I visit, the response is usually brief: diversified, low-volume production. When I dig a little deeper and inquire why diversified, low-volume production constitutes a problem, the main difficulty generally turns out to be the setup operations required — calibrations, switching of tools or dies, etc. Frequent setups are necessary to produce a variety of goods in small lots.

Even if their number cannot be reduced, however, the setup time itself can be cut down. Think of the productivity improvement that could be attained if a setup operation requiring three hours could be reduced to three minutes! This has, in fact, become possible with the implementation of single-minute setup.

Single-minute setup is popularly known as the SMED system, SMED being an acronym for Single-Minute Exchange of Die. The term refers to a theory and techniques for performing setup operations in under ten minutes, that is, in a number of minutes expressed in a single digit. Although not every setup can literally be completed in single-digit minutes, this is the goal of the system described here, and it can be met in a surprisingly high percentage of cases. Even where it cannot, dramatic reductions in setup time are usually possible.

A host of books with such titles as *Quick Die Changes* and *The Instant Setup* has appeared recently in Japan. Japanese industrial engineers have long understood that reducing setup time is a key to developing a competitive industrial position. Most of these books, however, do not go beyond mere description of techniques. They present the know-how without explaining *why* the techniques work. These manuals are applicable as long as the examples they discuss match the situation at hand. When they do not, application is difficult.

In this section, I endeavor to present you with both practical examples and the theory behind them. Even dissimilar industries with dissimilar machines should then be able to apply the principles of SMED to their own production processes, with substantial improvements in productivity and lead time resulting.

In the following chapters, you will find:

- The conceptual stages underlying SMED
- Practical methods derived from this conceptual framework
- Illustrations of practical techniques

At this point, I would like to summarize the traditional wisdom concerning setup time improvement. It consists of three basic ideas:

- The skill required for setup changes can be acquired through practice and long-term experience.
- Large-lot production diminishes the effect of setup time and cuts down on man-hours. Combining setup operations saves setup time and leads to increased efficiency and productive capacity.
- Large-lot production brings inventory increases. Economic lots should be determined and inventory quantities regulated accordingly.

These ideas were once thought to constitute the basis for rational production policies. In fact, they conceal an important blind spot: the unspoken assumption that setup time itself cannot undergo drastic reduction. With the adoption of the SMED system, the economic-lot approach simply collapses.

Why have setup improvements not been pursued more vigorously before now? The answer is that setup procedures are usually dealt with on the spot and depend on the skills of workers on the shop floor. Managers have found refuge in the apparent rationality of the economic-lot-size concept and have not taken the trouble to pursue the matter further — chiefly, I believe, because they have been indifferent. Industrial engineers bear a special responsibility in this regard.

It has been argued forcefully in the past that diversified, low-volume production is extremely difficult and that high-volume production of fewer kinds of items is more desirable. Of course, high-volume production necessarily gives rise to inventory, which managers have traditionally regarded as a necessary evil. However, this line of thinking does not hold water. Whether production is to be diversified and low-volume, or more homogeneous and high-volume, depends on both the market (demand) and production conditions (supply).

Even when demand calls for high diversity and low volume, if several orders are combined, large lots become possible and setup frequency can be reduced. But bear in mind, this solution gives rise to excess inventory.

On the other hand, when demand calls for little diversity and high volume, the supply side can respond with numerous repetitions of small-lot production. Inventory is minimized, but the number of setup operations increases.

In this way the characteristics of demand can be separated from those of supply. Even if high-volume production is desired in order to amortize capital equipment, we must keep in mind that this is a function of demand and cannot form the basis of a theory of production (supply). Moreover, there is an unfortunate tendency to confuse high-volume production with large lot sizes, and hence to delude ourselves into thinking that because high volume is good, large lot sizes are similarly desirable. We need to recognize this problem and make clear the distinction between these two concepts.

Furthermore, while it is true that the number of setups cannot be reduced when we are engaged in diversified, small-lot production, it is still possible to reduce setup time dramatically. Consequently, even in small-lot production, the effects of setup time can be greatly diminished and inventory can be cut back significantly.

So far, we have seen that production planning as commonly practiced confuses high volume with large lots. This approach, which assumes that excess inventory will inevitably be created, stands in contrast to the concept of *confirmed production* in which excess inventory is eliminated and small lots are produced on the basis of orders actually received.

Surely this will become the model for production planning in the future. Instead of producing goods that *ought* to sell, factories will produce only goods that have already been ordered. This idea represents a revolution in the concept of production. Indeed, I believe that the SMED system marks a turning point in the history of economic progress. What is often referred to as the Toyota production system will be seen as the first pioneering implementation of this new concept.

It took nineteen long years to develop the SMED system. It began while I was conducting an improvement study for Toyo Industries in 1950. I realized for the first time that there are two kinds of setup operations: *internal setup* (IED, or inside exchange of die), which can be performed only when a machine is shut down, and *external setup* (OED, or outside exchange of die), which can be done while the machine is running. A new die can be attached to a press, for example, only when the press is stopped, but the bolts to attach the die can be assembled and sorted while the press is operating.

In 1957, a dramatic improvement in the setup operation for a diesel engine bed planer at Mitsubishi Heavy Industries foreshadowed an astonishing request I would receive from the Toyota Motor Company in 1969. Toyota wanted the setup time of a 1,000-ton press — which had already been reduced from four hours to an hour and a half — further reduced to three minutes! Having studied setup phenomena for many years, I was excited by this challenge and had a sudden inspiration: internal setup changes could be converted to external ones. In a flash, a whole new way of thinking dawned on me.

I mention this to illustrate a point. The SMED system is much more than a matter of technique; it is an entirely new way of thinking about production itself.

The SMED system has undergone much development in various sectors of Japanese industry, and has started to spread around the world. America's Federal-Mogul Corporation, Citroen in France, and the H. Weidmann Company in Switzerland have all used SMED to achieve substantial productivity improvements. In any country, positive results will be obtained when the theory and techniques of SMED are understood and suitably applied.

17

Setup Operations in the Past

SOME DEFINITIONS OF TERMS

Small, Medium, and Large Lots

Although discussions of setup procedures often mention small, medium, and large lots, these terms are not precise and are, in fact, rather vague. For the sake of convenience, this book will use the following classification as a rough guide:

Small lot: 500 units or fewer
Medium lot: 501 to 5,000 units
Large lot: more than 5,000 units

Excess Inventory and Excess Anticipated Production

With a promised delivery date coming up fast, it would be awkward to find defective goods causing a shortage in the quantity ready for shipment. To avoid such a shortage, 330 items might be produced to satisfy an order for 300. If only twenty turn out, in fact, to be defective, then ten unnecessary items remain. If the order is not repeated, these leftover goods must be discarded; often they are kept in inventory with the hope of receiving another order for them. This stock, resulting from the production of too many goods, is called *excess inventory*.

Another type of surplus, *excess anticipated production*, results when intermediate or finished goods are produced before they are actually needed.

Everyone will agree that it is wasteful to dispose of surplus goods, and most managers do their best to avoid excess inventory. Strangely enough, however, goods that are produced before they are needed — excess anticipated production — often are not thought of as particularly undesirable. Indeed, some relief is often felt that a deadline has not been missed.

Here the terms *stock* and *inventory* will usually refer to excess anticipated production. The term *excess inventory* will be used to refer to production quantities which, for one reason or another, are larger than the actual number of units needed to fill orders.

TRADITIONAL STRATEGIES FOR IMPROVING SETUP OPERATIONS

Many factory managers consider diversified, low-volume production to be their single greatest challenge. This view, however, confuses characteristics of supply with those of demand. From the standpoint of demand, diversified, low-volume production means that many kinds of products are desired, and the quantity of any given kind is low.

To overcome the problems posed by diversified production, some companies have opted simply to produce only a few kinds of products and then try to stimulate a sufficient demand for them. Volkswagen is a case in point. For a long time, Volkswagen manufactured only one type of car, the famous "Bug."

In today's world of diversified demand, this strategy has met with limited success. Indeed, in recent years Volkswagen has had to develop a full line of cars. More generally, it will become increasingly difficult for the automobile industry to slow the pace of diversification as it attempts to stimulate new demand with frequent model changes. And as production diversifies, the quantity of each model will inevitably decrease.

We should, however, note one important characteristic of demand: the distinction between one-time and repeat orders. One-time orders will always pose a problem because they always require special setup changes. For repeat orders — even if each individual order is small — the number of setups can be reduced by combining several lots into one. Unfortunately, this solution gives rise to waste by producing too much too soon.

Corresponding to the demand characteristics noted above, the supply side (production) requires numerous setup operations for diversified production and small lots.

Although numerous setup operations must be carried out in a diversified production system, several possibilities arise when we look at the problem in terms of the setup itself.

First, there may be *common setup elements*. Although the products may differ, the dimensions of the tools and parts used in processing may remain constant. On a visit to a Volkswagen plant, I remember being impressed by their use of common setup elements. Although a model change had necessitated a change in the shape of the instrument panels, the fixtures were the same as the old ones: There was no change whatsoever in production operating conditions. In situations like this, setup problems are considerably reduced.

Second, there may be *similar setup elements*. Sometimes the products differ, but the basic shape of, for example, the chuck remains constant. If it is still round, and only the diameter differs, then the only setup change required is adjusting the dimension of the chuck claws. A setup in this kind of situation is extremely simple.

By focusing on common and similar setup elements, by classifying these elements, and by choosing the right machine for each task, it is possible to reduce setup difficulties dramatically, even if the number of setups remains the same.

Small-lot production suffers from the disadvantage that as soon as one operation begins to develop momentum, production has to move on to the next one. Strategies such as the following should be considered to deal with this problem:

- Eliminate the need for guesswork as much as possible by improving operations.
- Simplify operations through division of labor and attempts to minimize the effects of shifting work rhythms.

If demand allows for anticipatory production, small lots can be combined into larger ones, thus reducing the number of setups.

At any rate, the problem facing factories is not diversified, low-volume production, but rather production involving multiple setups and small lots. We need to evaluate the problem correctly and then consider effective strategies for dealing with it.

Strategies Involving Skill

In traditional manufacturing operations, efficient setup changes require two things:

- *Knowledge* relating to the structure and function of the machinery and equipment, as well as a thorough acquaintance with tools, blades, dies, jigs, etc.
- *Skill* in mounting and removing these items, and also in measuring, centering, adjusting, and calibrating after trial runs.

As a result, efficient setups require highly skilled workers, and although a simple machine may pose no problems, the specialized knowledge of a "setup engineer" (sometimes referred to simply as a "setup man") is called for when the machinery is complex.

While the setup engineer is engaged in the setup, the machine operator normally performs miscellaneous duties as the engineer's assistant, operates another machine, or in some cases simply waits. All of these activities, however, are inefficient.

It is generally and erroneously believed that the most effective policies for dealing with setups address the problem in terms of skill. Although many companies have setup policies designed to raise the skill level of the workers, few have implemented strategies that lower the skill level required by the setup itself.

Strategies Involving Large Lots

Setup operations have traditionally demanded a great deal of time, and manufacturing companies have long suffered from the extreme inefficiency this causes. A marvelous solution was found to this problem, however: increasing lot size.

If a large order is received, large-lot production will pose no particular problems because the effect of setup time is slight when divided by the total operating time for the lot, and setup time has only a small effect on the work rate.

For diversified, low-volume orders, on the other hand, the impact of setup time is much greater. When demand takes the form of repeated diversified, low-volume orders, lot sizes can be increased by combining several orders and producing in anticipation of demand. If lot sizes are increased, the ratio of setup time to the number of operations can be greatly reduced (*Table 17-1*).

Setup Time	Lot Size	Principal Operation Time Per Item	Operation Time	Ratio (%)	Ratio (%)
4 hrs.	100	1 min.	$1\,\text{min.} + \dfrac{4 \times 60}{100} = 3.4\,\text{min.}$	100	
4 hrs.	1,000	1 min.	$1\,\text{min.} + \dfrac{4 \times 60}{1,000} = 1.24\,\text{min.}$	36	100
4hrs.	10,000	1 min.	$1\,\text{min.} + \dfrac{4 \times 60}{10,000} = 1.024\,\text{min.}$	30	83

TABLE 17-1. **Relationship Between Setup Time and Lot Size — I**

As *Table 17-1* shows, increasing the lot size from 100 to 1,000 units leads to a 64 percent reduction in production man-hours. When lot size is increased by another factor of ten, however, to 10,000 units, the related decrease in man-hours is only 17 percent. In other words, increasing the size of a small lot leads to a relatively large decrease in man-hours, but as size increases the rate of reduction in man-hours decreases. Similarly, the gains from increasing lot size are greater for long setup times than for shorter ones (*Table 17-2*).

Despite this law of diminishing returns, the rate of reduction rises whether the setup time is four hours or eight. The greater the setup time, the more effective are the results of increasing the lot size.

Setup Time	Lot Size	Principal Operation Time Per Item	Operation Time	Ratio (%)	Ratio (%)
8 hrs.	100	1 min.	$1\,\text{min.} + \dfrac{8 \times 60}{100} = 5.8\,\text{min.}$	100	
8 hrs.	1,000	1 min.	$1\,\text{min.} + \dfrac{8 \times 60}{1,000} = 1.48\,\text{min.}$	26	100
8 hrs.	10,000	1 min.	$1\,\text{min.} + \dfrac{8 \times 60}{10,000} = 1.048\,\text{min.}$	18	71

TABLE 17-2. **Relationship Between Setup Time and Lot Size — II**

Moreover, increasing lot size by a factor of ten amounts to combining ten setup operations into one. The result is a substantial increase in the work rate and in production capacity (*Table 17-3*).

Setup Time	Setup Time Saved	Work Day	Days Saved
4 hours	4 × 9 = 36 hours	8 hours	4.5
8 hours	8 × 9 = 72 hours	8 hours	9

TABLE 17-3. **Relationship Between Setup Time and Lot Size — III**

Plant managers always welcome the double benefit of this considerable increase in productive power and reduction in needed manhours. Indeed, we might well imagine that this is the principal reason for favoring large-lot production on the shop floor. With traditional setup procedures, large-lot production seems the easiest and most effective way to minimize the undesirable effects of setup operations.

Economic-Lot Strategies

Large-lot production in response to large orders is fine, but most large-lot production in fact results from combining repeated orders for small volumes of goods, giving rise to excess anticipated production. Inventory is often called a necessary evil, since there are so many advantages associated with it. Nonetheless, we must bear in mind that no matter how "necessary" it may appear, an evil is still an evil.

Let us take another look at the pros and cons of large-lot production:

Advantages

- Since the ratio of setup time to main operation is lower, apparent operating man-hours are reduced.
- Combining setup operations reduces the number of setups, increases the work rate, and increases productivity proportionately.
- The existence of inventory facilitates load leveling.

- Inventory serves as a cushion, alleviating problems when defects show up or machinery breaks down.
- Inventories can be used to fill rush orders.

Disadvantages

- Capital turnover rates fall, increasing interest burdens.
- Inventory itself does not produce added value, so the tremendous physical space it occupies is entirely wasted.
- Inventory storage necessitates the installation of racks, pallets, and so forth, all of which increase costs. When inventories grow too large, special rack rooms or the like are installed and automated stock entry and retrieval becomes possible. Some companies pride themselves on their automated inventory control, boasting that any item can be retrieved in three minutes or so. This in turn requires managerial man-hours for taking inventory. Although all of this has been called "rationalization," in reality it is the rationalization of waste rather than its elimination.
- The transportation and storage of stock requires handling man-hours.
- Large lots entail longer lead times. As a result, discrepancies arise with respect to projected demand. This leads to internal inventories and discarded parts. Furthermore, long lead times can mean that new orders are delayed and deadlines are missed.
- Stocks must be disposed of whenever model changes take place, either by selling them at a discount or by discarding them.
- Inventory quality deteriorates over time. Rust, for example, leads to needless costs. As stocks become dated, their value diminishes.

Given these advantages and disadvantages, one can see that large-lot production generally lowers costs associated with long setup times, but raises costs by enlarging inventories. This relationship is shown graphically in *Figure 17-1*, where a curve representing setup effects (P) and a straight line representing inventory (S) intersect at point E, which scholars call the economic lot size. This is the point at which the advantages and disadvantages of setup and inventory balance out.

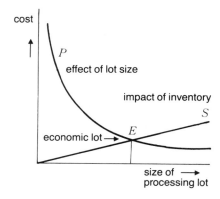

FIGURE 17-1. The Economic Lot Size

A Blind Spot in the Economic-Lot Concept

There is no doubt that the concept of economic lot size is entirely correct in theory. Yet this concept conceals an enormous blind spot: the unspoken assumption that drastic reductions in setup time are impossible.

If a four-hour setup were reduced to three minutes — and adoption of the SMED system has actually made this possible — then even without increasing lot size, the ratio of setup hours to the main operation could be made extremely small. This being so, attempts to mitigate the effects of setup time by producing in large lots would be without value.

As an example, let us examine the effect of increasing the lot size by a factor of ten on an operation whose setup time is three minutes (*Table 17-4*). In this case, the reduction in man-hours will be only

Setup Time	Lot Size	Principal Operation Time Per Item	Total Operation Time Per Item (Including Setup)	Ratio (%)
3 min.	100	1 min.	$1 \text{ min.} + \dfrac{3}{100} = 1.03 \text{ min.}$	100
3 min.	1,000	1 min.	$1 \text{ min.} + \dfrac{3}{1,000} = 1.003 \text{ min.}$	97

TABLE 17-4. Relationship Between Setup Time and Lot Size — IV

three percent. Furthermore, since ten lots are combined, the savings in setup time resulting from combining lots will be:

$$3 \text{ minutes} \times (10 - 1) = 27 \text{ minutes}$$

If we let one workday equal eight hours, the reduction is a mere 0.06 day. Suppose, however, that the setup time was previously four hours. Cutting this time to three minutes will result in a tremendous rise in both work rate and productive capacity. In addition, inventory can be kept at a minimum since there will be no obstacle to small-lot production: The question of economic lot size will not even be an issue. This is why it has been said recently that with the development of SMED, the concept of economic lots has disappeared from the profit-engineering agenda.

In fact, the very notion of economic lots was an evasive measure and in no way a positive approach to improving production. Moreover, since SMED can substantially reduce the level of skill required for setups, the need for skilled setup workers is largely eliminated. This has exploded once and for all the myth that the best way to deal with setup problems is through skill and large-lot production.

18

Fundamentals of SMED

THE HISTORY OF SMED

The Birth of SMED

In the spring of 1950, I conducted an efficiency improvement survey at Toyo Kogyo's Mazda plant in Hiroshima, which at the time manufactured three-wheeled vehicles. Toyo wanted to eliminate bottlenecks caused by large body-molding presses — presses of 350, 750, and 800 tons — that were not working up to capacity. I immediately conducted an on-site inspection, and then made the following request of the section manager in charge of manufacturing: "Will you let me do a week-long production analysis with a stopwatch so I can get an idea of the work these big presses do?"

He replied that it would be a waste of time: He already knew that the presses were the cause of the bottlenecks and had assigned his most skilled and conscientious employees to work on them. He had the three presses working around the clock and felt that the only way to improve productivity further was to buy more machines, which is exactly what he hoped top management would do.

"That sounds pretty bad," I said. "But listen, let me do an analysis anyway. If it turns out that there's no other way to eliminate the bottlenecks, then I'll advise management to buy the machines." With that argument, I was finally permitted to conduct a fact-finding survey.

On the third day, there was a die change on the 800-ton press. Workers removed the old die and then started rushing about all over the place. I asked the operator what was going on. He replied, "One of the mounting bolts for the new die is missing. I was sure they were all with the die, but I can't find the last one and I've been looking all over for it."

"When you find it," I said, "you'll come back to the die, won't you? I'll wait for you here."

"All right," he replied. "Having you around here gives me the jitters, anyway."

I sat down by the machine and waited. After more than an hour, the operator rushed back, drenched with sweat and brandishing a bolt in his right hand. "Ah," I said, "You've found it!"

"No," he answered. "I didn't actually find it. I borrowed a long die bolt from the next machine over there. I cut it to make it shorter, then threaded it. That's what took so long. It wasn't easy, I can tell you!"

I said a few words of sympathetic encouragement, but a sudden thought started me worrying. "You cut it to the right length for this machine, but what are you going to do when you have to set up the machine you took it from? Does this kind of thing go on all the time?"

"No," he replied, "I wouldn't say it happens all the time. It's just something that gives us trouble now and then."

As *Figure 18-1* shows, the large press was actually engaged in the main manufacturing operation for less than three percent of that entire day.

It dawned on me at that point that setup operations were actually of two fundamentally different types:

- *Internal setup* (IED), such as mounting or removing dies, that can be performed only when a machine is stopped
- *External setup* (OED), such as transporting old dies to storage or conveying new dies to the machine, that can be conducted while a machine is in operation

Preparing the bolts was an external operation. It was senseless to stop the operation of an 800-ton press because a bolt was missing. All we had to do was establish an external setup procedure: verifying that the necessary bolts were ready for the next setup.

We established a process for thoroughly sorting all the bolts and putting the necessary ones in boxes. We also improved the entire procedure by performing all possible aspects of the setup externally. This raised efficiency by about 50 percent, and the bottleneck was dissipated. Ever since this episode, I have made it a policy to distinguish clearly between internal and external setup.

Thus the newly born SMED concept took its first steps at Toyo Kogyo.

The Second Encounter

In the summer of 1957, I was asked to do a study at the Mitsubishi Heavy Industries shipyard in Hiroshima. When I asked the plant manager, Matsuzo Okazaki, what the problem was, he told me that a large, open-sided planer used to machine diesel engine beds was not working up to capacity and that he wanted to streamline the operation.

After doing a production analysis, I realized that the marking-off procedure for centering and dimensioning the engine bed was being conducted on the planer table itself. This reduced the operating rate tremendously. As I discussed this with Mr. Okazaki, an idea came to me quite suddenly: "Why not install a second planer table and perform the setup operation on it separately?" That way, we could switch tables as we shifted from one lot to the next, and there would be a significant reduction in the amount of time the planing operation was interrupted for each setup. Mr. Okazaki agreed to this change on the spot.

On my next visit to the factory I found that the extra planer table had been completed. This solution resulted in a 40 percent increase in productivity. Mr. Okazaki and I were ecstatic and toasted one another on our accomplishment, yet even now I regret one thing. If I had grasped at the time the overwhelming importance of converting an internal setup to an external one, the SMED concept would have been perfected some dozen years sooner.

The Third Encounter

In 1969, I visited the body shop at Toyota Motor Company's main plant. Mr. Sugiura, the divisional manager, told me they had a 1,000-ton press that required four hours for each setup change. Volkswagen in Germany had been performing setups on a similar press in two hours, and management had given Mr. Sugiura clear instructions to better that time.

Content of Operation / Machine	Setup — Preparation After-Adjustment	Main Operation — Essential Operation	Main Operation — Auxiliary Operation	Margin Allowances — Hygiene	Margin Allowances — Fatigue	Margin Allowances — Oper.	Margin Allowances — Workplace	Important Points for Reexamination — Preparation & After-Adjustment			Important Points for Reexamination — Workplace Allowances		
									sec.	%		sec.	%
800-ton press / Main Operator	47.0%	3.0%	24%	1.0%	5.0%	6.0%	14.0%	die transportation	869	3.5	material transport.	574	2.3
								securing die	2940	11.7	waiting crane	776	3.1
								adjusting	5475	21.7	material cooling	902	3.6
								removing die	1789	7.2	assist adjacent press	34	0.1
								miscellaneous	610	2.4	miscellaneous	1162	4.6
750-ton press / Main Operator	46.3	4.27	23.6	0	1.84	7.34	16.65	die transportation	1469	5.3	material transport.	2231	8.3
								securing die	2033	8.2	waiting crane	356	1.4
								adjusting	5968	23.5	misc.	1599	6.4
								removing die	307	1.2			
								misc.	1963	7.9			
750-ton press / Assistant	23.5	0	15.8	0	13.2	4.9	42.6	die transportation	1633	6.5	loading & unloading (material & products)	3711	14.8
								preparing and securing part	727	2.9	waiting for preparation & after-adjustment	5635	22.0
								adjusting	1912	7.6	waiting for main operation	701	2.8
								removing die	507	2.0	misc.	380	1.5
								misc.	224	1.0			
300-ton press / Main Operator	40.0	9.0	27.0	0	2.0	13.0	9.0	die transportation	2000	7.9	material transport.	105	0.6
								securing die	2849	11.3	waiting crane	1220	4.8
								adjusting	3424	13.6	misc.	56	0.2
								removing die	799	7.2			
								misc.	1699	6.7			

FIGURE 18-1. Production Analysis of a Large Press

Together with the foreman and plant manager, I set about seeing what could be done. We took special pains to distinguish clearly between internal and external setup (IED and OED), trying to improve each separately. After six months we succeeded in cutting setup time to ninety minutes.

We were all pleased with this success, but when I revisited the body shop the following month, Mr. Sugiura had some rather startling news for me. Management had given him orders to further reduce setup time, to less than three minutes! For an instant I was dumbfounded at this request. But then an inspiration struck: "Why not convert IED to OED?"

A number of thoughts followed in rapid succession. On a conference-room blackboard I listed eight techniques for shortening setup times. Using this new concept, we were able to achieve the three-minute goal after three months of diligent effort. In the hope that any setup could be performed in under ten minutes, I named this concept "single-minute exchange of die," or SMED. SMED was later adopted by all Toyota plants and continued to evolve as one of the principal elements of the Toyota production system. Its use has now spread to companies throughout Japan and the world.

Mr. Taiichi Ohno, formerly a vice president at Toyota Motor Company and now a consultant, wrote about SMED in an article entitled "Bringing Wisdom to the Factory," which appeared in the journal *Management*, published by the Japan Management Association, in June 1976:

> Until some ten years ago, production in our firm took place as much as possible during regular working hours. Changes of cutters, drills and the like were relegated to the noon break or the evening. We had a policy of replacing the cutters after every fifty items. Yet as production has risen over the past decade or so, machine operators have often begrudged the time needed for these changes. For the multigrinder in particular, replacing the numerous cutters and drills took half a day. Since afternoon production would stop whenever a replacement was made on a week day, workers were forced to work temporary shifts on the following Sunday.
>
> This was uneconomical and therefore unacceptable. Since we also wanted maintenance to be done during working hours, we began to study the question of how setup changes could be performed in a very short period of time. Shigeo Shingo, of the Japan Management Association, was advocating "single-minute setup changes" and we felt that this concept could be of great service to us. It used to be that after

spending half a day on setup, the machine might be used for only ten minutes. Now, one might think that since the setup took half a day, production ought to continue for at least that long. This, however, would have left us with a lot of finished products we could never sell. We are now looking into cutting setup times down to a matter of seconds. Of course this is easier said than done. Somehow, though, we must reduce the amount of time needed for setup changes.

This passage underscores the impact of setup time reductions on the improvement of production activities as a whole.

The development of the SMED concept took nineteen years in all. It came about as the culmination of my ever-deepening insight into the practical and theoretical aspects of setup improvement. The finishing touches were stimulated by Toyota Motor Company's requirement that we reduce setup time on a 1,000-ton press from four hours to ninety minutes.

I would like to stress that SMED is based on theory and years of practical experimentation. It is a scientific approach to setup time reduction that can be applied in any factory to any machine.

BASIC STEPS IN THE SETUP PROCEDURE

Setup procedures are usually thought of as infinitely varied, depending on the type of operation and the type of equipment being used. Yet when these procedures are analyzed from a different viewpoint, it can be seen that all setup operations comprise a sequence of steps. In traditional setup changes the distribution of time is often that shown in *Table 18-1*.

Let us examine each of these in greater detail.

Operation	Proportion of time
Preparation, after-process adjustment, and checking of raw material, blades, dies, jigs, gauges, etc.	30%
Mounting and removing blades, etc.	5%
Centering, dimensioning and setting of other conditions	15%
Trial runs and adjustments	50%

TABLE 18-1. **Steps in the Setup Process**

Preparation, after-process adjustment, checking of materials, tools, etc. This step ensures that all parts and tools are where they should be and that they are functioning properly. Also included in this step is the period after processing when these items are removed and returned to storage, machinery is cleaned, etc.

Mounting and removing blades, tools, parts, etc. This includes the removal of parts and tools after completion of processing and the attachment of the parts and tools for the next lot.

Measurements, settings, and calibrations. This step refers to all of the measurements and calibrations that must be made in order to perform a production operation, such as centering, dimensioning, measuring temperature or pressure, etc.

Trial runs and adjustments. In these steps, adjustments are made after a test piece is machined. The greater the accuracy of the measurements and calibrations in the preceding step, the easier these adjustments will be.

The frequency and length of test runs and adjustment procedures depend on the skill of the setup engineer. The greatest difficulties in a setup operation lie in adjusting the equipment correctly. The large proportion of time associated with trial runs derives from these adjustment problems. If we want to make trial runs and adjustments easier, we need to understand that the most effective approach is to increase the precision of the preceding measurements and calibrations.

SETUP IMPROVEMENT: CONCEPTUAL STAGES

The conceptual stages involved in setup improvements are shown in *Figure 18-2*.

Preliminary Stage: Internal and External Setup Conditions Are Not Distinguished

In traditional setup operations, internal and external setup are confused; what *could* be done externally is done as internal setup, and machines therefore remain idle for extended periods. In planning how to implement SMED, one must study actual shop floor conditions in great detail.

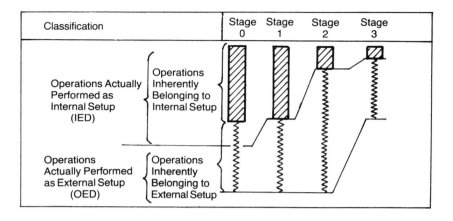

Classification		Stage 0		Stage 1		Stage 2		Stage 3	

FIGURE 18-2. Conceptual Stages for Setup Improvement

A *continuous production analysis* performed with a stopwatch is probably the best approach. Such an analysis, however, takes a great deal of time and requires great skill.

Another possibility is to use a *work sampling study*. The problem with this option is that work samples are precise only where there is a great deal of repetition. Such a study may not be suitable where few actions are repeated.

A third useful approach is to study actual conditions on the shop floor by *interviewing workers*.

An even better method is to *videotape* the entire setup operation. This is extremely effective if the tape is shown to the workers immediately after the setup has been completed. Giving workers the opportunity to air their views often leads to surprisingly astute and useful insights. In many instances these insights can be applied on the spot.

At any rate, even though some consultants advocate in-depth continuous production analyses for the purpose of improving setup, the truth is that informal observation and discussion with the workers often suffice.

Stage 1: Separating Internal and External Setup

The most important step in implementing SMED is distinguishing between internal and external setup. Everyone will agree that preparation of parts, maintenance, and so forth should not be done while the machines are stopped. Nonetheless, it is absolutely astounding to observe how often this is the case.

If instead we make a scientific effort to treat as much of the setup operation as possible as external setup, then the time needed for internal setup — performed while the machine is off — can usually be cut some 30 to 50 percent. Mastering the distinction between internal and external setup is thus the passport to achieving SMED.

Stage 2: Converting Internal to External Setup

I have just explained that normal setup times can be reduced 30 to 50 percent by separating internal and external setup procedures. But even this tremendous reduction is insufficient to achieve the SMED objective. The second stage — converting internal setup to external setup — involves two important notions:

- Re-examining operations to see whether any steps are wrongly assumed to be internal
- Finding ways to convert these steps to external setup

Examples might include preheating elements that have previously been heated only after setup has begun, and converting centering to an external procedure by doing it before production starts.

Operations that are now performed as internal setup can often be converted to external setup by re-examining their true function. It is extremely important to adopt new perspectives that are not bound by old habits.

Stage 3: Streamlining All Aspects of the Setup Operation

Although the single-minute range can occasionally be reached by converting to external setup, this is not true in the majority of cases. This is why we must make a concerted effort to streamline each elemental internal and external setup operation. Thus stage 3 calls for a detailed analysis of each elemental operation. The following examples are drawn from successful applications of stages 1, 2, and 3.

- At Toyota Motor Company, the internal setup time of a boltmaker — which had previously required eight hours — was cut to fifty-eight seconds.
- Mitsubishi Heavy Industries, the internal setup time for a six-arbor boring machine — which had previously required twenty-four hours — was reduced to two minutes and forty seconds.

Stages 2 and 3 do not need to be performed sequentially; they may be nearly simultaneous. I have separated them here to show that they nonetheless involve two distinct notions: analysis, then implementation.

19

Techniques for Applying SMED

Now that you know the concepts involved in setup improvement, let us take a look at some practical techniques corresponding to the conceptual stages.

PRELIMINARY STAGE: INTERNAL AND EXTERNAL SETUP ARE NOT DISTINGUISHED

In traditional setup operations, several kinds of waste recur:

- Finished goods are transported to storage or the next batch of raw materials is moved from stock after the previous lot has been completed and the machine has been turned off. Since the machine is off during transportation, valuable time is lost.
- Blades, dies, etc., are delivered after internal setup has begun, or a defective part is discovered only after mounting and test runs. As a result, time is lost removing the part from the machine and starting over again. As with the transportation of raw materials or finished goods, waste can occur *after* processing. Parts that are no longer needed are transported to the tool room while the machine is still turned off.
- With jigs and gauges, a jig may be replaced because it is not accurate enough and repairs have not been made; bolts cannot be found; a bolt is no good because the nut is too tight; or no blocks of the appropriate thickness can be found.

You can probably think of many other instances where shortages, mistakes, inadequate verification of equipment, or similar problems have occurred and led to delays in setup operations.

Traditionally, managers and manufacturing engineers have failed to devote their full abilities to the analysis of setup operations.

More often than not, they assign setup to the workers, and assume that because their workers are conscientious, they will do their best to perform setups as quickly as possible. In other words, the problem of setup time is left to be resolved on the shop floor. Surely this attitude is one of the main reasons why, until recently, no great progress has been made in improving setup operations.

STAGE 1: SEPARATING INTERNAL AND EXTERNAL SETUP

The following techniques are effective in ensuring that operations that can be conducted as external setup are, in fact, performed while the machine is running.

Using a Checklist

Make a checklist of all the parts and steps required in an operation. This list will include:

- Names
- Specifications
- Numbers of blades, dies, and other items
- Pressure, temperature, and other settings
- Numeric values for all measurements and dimensions

On the basis of this list, double-check that there are no mistakes in operating conditions. By doing this beforehand, you can avoid many time-consuming errors and test runs.

The use of a so-called *check table* is also very handy. A check table is a table on which drawings have been made of all the parts and tools required for a setup. The corresponding parts are simply placed over the appropriate drawings before the internal setup is begun. Since a single glance at the table will tell the operator whether any parts are missing, this is an extremely effective visual control technique. The only limitation on the usefulness of the check table is that it cannot be used to verify the operating conditions themselves. Nonetheless, it remains a valuable adjunct to the checklist.

It is very important to establish a specific checklist and table for each machine. Avoid the use of general checklists for an entire shop:

they can be confusing, they tend to get lost, and because they are confusing they are too frequently ignored.

Performing Function Checks

A checklist is useful for determining whether all the parts are where they should be, but it does not tell whether they are in perfect working order. Consequently, it is necessary to perform function checks in the course of external setup.

Failure to do this will lead inevitably to delays in internal setup when it is suddenly discovered that a gauge does not work right or a jig is not accurate. In particular, inadequate repairs to presses and plastic molds are sometimes discovered only after test runs have been completed. In this event, molds that one has already taken the trouble to mount on a machine must be removed and repaired, thus increasing setup time substantially.

One frequent problem is repairs that are anticipated, but take longer than expected. The operation is begun before repairs are completed. When defective goods show up as a result, the die is hurriedly removed, and further repairs are made, interrupting production. It is always important to finish repairs before internal setup is begun.

Improving Transportation of Dies and Other Parts

Parts have to be moved from storage to the machines, and then returned to storage once a lot is finished. This must be done as an external setup procedure, in which either the operator moves the parts himself while the machine is running automatically, or another worker is assigned to the task of transportation.

One factory I worked with conducted setup operations on a large press by extracting the die on a moving bolster. A cable was attached to the die, which a crane then lifted and conveyed to the storage area. I suggested a number of changes to the shop foreman:

- Have the crane move the new die to the machine beforehand.
- Next, lower the old die from the moving bolster to the side of the machine.

- Attach the new die to the moving bolster, insert it in the machine, and begin the new operation.
- After that, hook a cable to the old die and transport it to the storage area.

"That's no good," the foreman argued. "Cables would have to be attached twice, and that's inefficient."

"But," I replied, "it takes four minutes and twenty seconds to transport the old and new dies to and from the machine. If the press were put into operation that much earlier, you could manufacture about five extra units in the time you would save. Which is preferable, attaching the cables only once or producing five extra products?" The foreman agreed right away that he had been looking at the setup operation the wrong way, and the new system was implemented immediately.

This example illustrates a tendency of people on the shop floor to be distracted by small efficiencies while overlooking bigger ones. Considered on a deeper level, it shows the need for front-line managers to understand internal and external setup thoroughly.

STAGE 2: CONVERTING INTERNAL TO EXTERNAL SETUP

Preparing Operating Conditions in Advance

The first step in converting setup operations is to prepare operating conditions beforehand. We will illustrate this method with a number of examples.

Trial Shots on Die-Casting Machines

Trial shots are usually performed as part of the internal setup of die-casting machines. Cold dies are attached to the machine and gradually heated to the appropriate temperature by injecting molten metal. The first casting is then made. Since the material injected during the heating process will produce defective castings, items from the first casting must be remolded.

If gas or electric heat were used to preheat the mold, however, good castings would result from the first injections into the mounted and preheated die. Generally speaking, this method can cut internal setup time by about thirty minutes. In addition to increasing productivity, it will reduce the number of poor castings that must be remelted.

At one die-casting facility, a special rack was built on top of a holding oven installed at the side of a die-casting machine. Dies to be used in the following operation were preheated by heat dissipated from the holding oven.

Using recycled heat to preheat the dies killed two birds with one stone. The only expense the company incurred was the cost of building a special rack strong enough to hold the dies (*Plate 20-1*).

PLATE 19-1. Preheating of Dies

Thread Dyeing

At a fabric manufacturing plant, dyeing operations had been conducted by immersing a rack holding a number of threads in a dyeing vat and then heating the vat with steam. This was a very time-consuming operation, because it took quite a while for the vat to reach the right temperature.

The solution to this problem involved setting up a second vat. The auxiliary vat was filled with dye and preheated while the previous lot was being processed. When the first lot was completed, a valve was opened in the auxiliary vat and the preheated dye was allowed to flow into the dyeing vat. It thus became possible to eliminate the delay caused by heating the dye. This solution also had the effect of improving product quality by producing crisper colors.

Previously, there had been only one thread rack for each vat. When a lot was finished, the thread was removed from the rack, and a second lot of thread was installed on it. We were able to further reduce setup time by installing a second rack that was preloaded and switched with the first as soon as processing of the first lot was completed.

By combining this new procedure with the improvement in dye heating, we were able to more than double the operating rate of the dyeing operation.

The improved operation thus took place as follows:

- Prepare a rack by placing new thread on it.
- After dyeing, remove the rack bearing the dyed thread and clean the vat.
- Fill the vat with preheated dye from the auxiliary vat and begin the dyeing process.
- While the dyeing operation is in process, remove the thread which has already been dyed in the previous lot.

Plastic Vacuum Molding

Plastic vacuum molding is normally carried out in four steps:

- Join a movable mold with a fixed mold.
- Pump out air to form a vacuum in the mold.
- Inject resin.
- Open the mold and remove the finished product.

Vacuum molding is successful only when a nearly complete vacuum has been created in the mold; this means that a great deal of time is spent on the second step. A combined system, as described in *Figure 19-1*, helps solve this problem:

1. Install a vacuum tank with a capacity roughly 1,000 times the volume of the mold.
2. Connect the mold to the vacuum tank and open the escape valve. This will cause the pressure in the mold to drop by a factor of about 1,000 within one second.

3. Close the valve connecting the mold to the vacuum tank and turn on the pump to suck out any remaining air.
4. Begin the next injection. When it is completed, close the valve between the mold and the pump.
5. Simultaneously connect the vacuum tank to the pump and remove the air that has entered the tank.
6. Continue expelling the air from the tank until the injection is completed, open the mold to remove the finished product, and close the mold again.

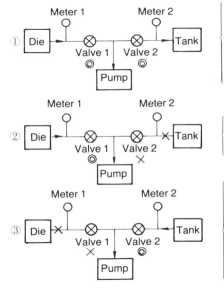

Valves 1 and 2 are opened simultaneously after die is closed; air in die moves to tank

Close valve 2 when valves 1 and 2 read the same; pressure inside die will fall to 1/1001

Expel air remaining in die with pump at 1/1001 atm.

After injection, close valve 1

Open valve 2 to connect tank and pump

Expel air from tank in external operation

Since vacuum pumps aspirate by volume, tank interior should be compressed as much as possible. After aspiration, volume should be enlarged again.

FIGURE 19-1. A Combined System

This combined system offers many advantages. Air inside the mold is not simply sucked out during internal setup. Once it moves to the vacuum tank, it is expelled during external setup. This efficient method of creating a vacuum in the mold clearly distinguishes between internal and external setup.

Continuous Materials Method

In a spring manufacturing plant, a spool-changing operation had been performed when the end of each roll of spring stock was reached. As shown in *Figure 19-2*, it was possible to eliminate the internal setup operation in changing spools by joining the spring stock at the end of one lot, A_1, to the next spool, A_2. Thus, a new spool would automatically begin when the end of the old spool was reached.

When the spring stock is narrow and thin, long lengths can be wound onto wide spools, since kinks will not occur even when up to ten bands of stock are welded together.

The end of A_1 is welded to the start of A_2

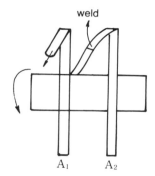

FIGURE 19-2. Continuous Materials Method

A Temporary Spring Stock Holder

In this example of a progressive type press, a forklift brought each roll of spring stock and positioned it when the end of the previous roll was reached. An insufficient number of forklifts, however, meant frequent delays while waiting for raw materials to arrive.

The solution here was to build a spool holder (*Figure 19-3*) on which the next roll of stock was held ready for processing. At the end of one processing run, a worker would simply push the roll into position from its temporary holder. No time was wasted waiting for materials.

Function Standardization

Anyone can appreciate the appeal of standardizing setup operations. One way this can be done is by standardizing the sizes and dimensions of all machine parts and tools, but this method, called *shape*

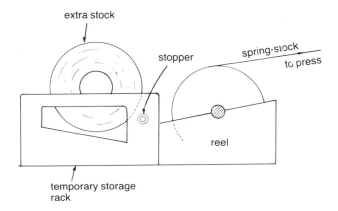

FIGURE 19-3. Temporary Spring Stock Holder

standardization, is wasteful: Dies become larger to accommodate the largest size needed, and costs rise because of unnecessary "fat."

In contrast, *function standardization* calls for standardizing only those parts whose functions are necessary from the standpoint of setup operations. With this approach, dies need not be made larger or more elaborate, and costs rise only moderately.

To implement function standardization, individual functions are analyzed and then considered one by one. That is, general operations are broken down into their basic elements, for example clamping, centering, dimensioning, expelling, grasping, and maintaining loads. The engineer must decide which of these operations, if any, need to be standardized. He must then distinguish between parts that can be standardized and parts that necessitate setting changes.

Although there are many ways to replace a mechanical arm — from the shoulder, elbow, wrist, fingertip, or only the fingernail — the most cost-efficient procedure is to replace the smallest part that includes the part needing replacement.

Efficient function standardization requires that we analyze the functions of each piece of apparatus, element by element, and replace the fewest possible parts. The examples below illustrate the principle of function standardization.

Function Standardization of a Press Die

In the setup procedure for a press, adjusting shut height requires a great degree of skill. It is widely believed, furthermore, that this operation must be performed as part of internal setup. Yet given two die heights of 320 mm (die A) and 270 mm (die B), shut height adjustments would be unnecessary in changing from die A to die B if shims or blocks 50 mm thick were placed under die B to raise it to a height of 320 mm (*Figure 19-4*). Once this has been done, the height of the attachment edges on die A will be 30 mm, while those on die B will be 80 mm.

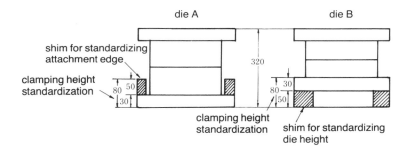

FIGURE 19-4. Standardized Height of Die and Attachment Edge

Thus if 30 × 30 × 50 mm shims are welded to the attachment edges of die A, the same clamping bolts can be used for both dies. Since the equalizing blocks are standardized, handling can be simplified by welding the blocks to the clamp. This also eliminates the trouble of having to search for a block of the proper height or having to store blocks of varying dimensions. The dies can be attached to the machine with only a special clamp and bolts. Both setup and management of the dies are made easier.

Bottom Centering Jig

In another setup, the shanks found on some small press dies give rise to a troublesome operation. To align the ram hole and shank, the worker inches the ram downward and adjusts the position of the die by sight. Suppose that a centering jig is mounted on the far side of the machine, and the distance from the center of the shank hole to the centering jig is 350 mm. If the distance from the center of the die shank to the far edge of the die is 230 mm, then a 120-mm centering jig will be attached to the far side of the die. A V-shaped projection is made in the middle of the fixed centering jig and a corresponding V-shaped depression is cut in the movable jig. If the top jig is made to fit snugly in the bottom one, the holes in the ram and the shank will align automatically. There will be no need to inch the ram downward and the shank can be engaged very simply.

Multipurpose Die Sets

Dies are used for two general purposes: to make objects of various shapes, and to bear loads. By standardizing the external part of a die and designing it so that the metal die set can be inserted and withdrawn like a cassette, manufacturers have achieved setup times as short as twenty seconds. This approach is particularly useful with small press dies.

Attaching Instrument Panels

I have already mentioned being impressed by the cleverness of Volkswagen engineers. Although the exterior of the instrument panel for a new model had been redesigned, the new instrument panel was attached in precisely the same way as the old one. The operation itself had not changed. This, too, is a good example of function standardization.

Using Intermediary Jigs

In the processing of many items, two standardized jig plates of the appropriate size and shape can be made. While the workpiece attached to one of the plates is being processed, the next workpiece is centered and attached to the other jig as an external setup procedure. When the first workpiece is finished, this second jig, together with the attached workpiece, is mounted on the machine. This standardized jig plate is called an "intermediary jig."*

---

* Editor's Note: Companies may have different names for this, *e.g.* "master shoe."

Countersinking a Hole in Bearing Metal

This operation involved countersinking the upper surface of an oil hole in bearing metal. Previously a drill had been attached to a drill press at a predetermined angle, then pressed against the bearing metal to start cutting. Since the countersinking depth had to be precise, once the drill had started cutting into the metal, measurements were made with a micrometer and the degree of drill protrusion was often adjusted.

We improved this operation by making an additional standardized drill holder. The drill attached to the holder was clamped in place after the precise degree of protrusion was gauged. Whenever it was necessary to replace drills, the setup was completed merely by pushing the holder into the taper hole of the drill press. As a result, even an inexperienced worker could replace drills, and do it quickly (*Figure 19-5*).

STAGE 3: STREAMLINING ALL ASPECTS OF THE SETUP OPERATION

After going through stage 1 (separating internal and external setup) and stage 2 (converting internal to external setup), you can proceed to make sweeping improvements in elemental setup operations.

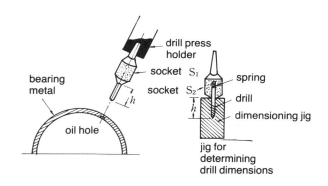

FIGURE 19-5. **Countersinking a Hole in a Bearing Metal**

Radical Improvements in External Setup Operations

Improvements in the storage and transportation of parts and tools (including blades, dies, jigs, and gauges) can contribute to streamlining operations, although by themselves they will not be enough.

In the case of medium-sized press dies, advanced equipment is available for storing and moving parts and tools. The rack room is one such arrangement, in which dies are stored on three-dimensional racks, and automated equipment is used to store the dies and send them off on conveyors to the appropriate machines. This kind of automated storage system reduces the number of man-hours needed for external setup, but does not represent an improvement in internal setup. Consequently, it does not directly help us achieve the SMED objective, and should be used only when control of a large number of unwieldy dies is very difficult.

Radical Improvements in Internal Setup Operations

The techniques described in the following chapter can lead to sweeping improvements in internal setup.

20

Applying SMED
to Internal Operations

IMPLEMENTATION OF PARALLEL OPERATIONS

Operations on plastic molding machines, die-casting machines and large presses invariably involve work both at the front and at the back of the machine. When a single person performs these operations, movement is continually being wasted as he walks around the machine.

Parallel operations involving more than one worker are very helpful in speeding up this kind of work. With two people, an operation that took twelve minutes will be completed not in six minutes, but perhaps in four, thanks to the economies of movement that are obtained.

When a parallel operation is being performed, special attention must be given to avoiding unnecessary waiting. Indeed, a poorly conceived parallel operation may result in no time savings at all (*Table 20-1*).

The most important issue in conducting parallel operations is safety. Each time one of the workers has completed an elemental operation, he must signal the other worker or workers. Sometimes this can be done by shouting, but in a noisy place like a factory shouts are often inaudible and confusing. It is preferable to signal with a buzzer or whistle, having agreed in advance on signals for "go ahead" and "wait."

In another variation, a worker at the back of the machine presses a button when his operation is completed. This lights a "confirmation board" at the front of the machine. After checking it, the worker in front is free to start the machine.

Task	Time (sec)	Worker 1	Worker 2	Buzzer
1	15	Lower ram (to bottom dead point).	Prepare to remove rear bolts.	
2	20	Remove front mounting bolts securing upper die.	Remove rear mounting bolts securing upper die.	Yes
3	30	Raise ram (to top dead point).	Turn press switch off.	Yes
4	20	Remove bolster setting pins.	Prepare to remove mounting bolts securing lower die.	
5	60	Move bolsters.	Remove mounting bolts securing lower die.	
6	20	Attach cable to transport metal die.	Attach cable to transport metal die.	
7	20	Hoist.	Move metal die for mounting.	
8	30	Position metal die.	Position metal die.	
9	20	Tighten front bolts securing lower die.	Tighten rear bolts securing lower die.	
10	50	Move bolster.		Yes
11	30	Set pins for bolsters.	Move crane.	
12	30	Set ram at bottom dead point.	Adjust ram stroke.	Yes
13	50	Tighten front mounting bolts securing upper die.	Prepare to tighten rear bolts securing upper die.	
14	20	Raise ram (to top dead point).	Tighten rear bolts securing upper die.	Yes
15	15	Test die action of empty press.	Check switches and meters. Set pressing lever.	Yes
16	40	Insert material and process.	Check for safety and quality, etc.	
	Total time 470 sec. (7 min. 50 sec.)	Problems to watch for: (1) Twisted or severed cables or strands. (2) Vertical movement of dies while they are being exchanged. (3) Presence of any hazard on floor.	Actions to be confirmed: (1) Tightening of bolts. (2) Switch (on or off). (3) Bolster pin setting. (4) Meter. (5) Quality check.	OK On

TABLE 20-1. Procedural Chart for Parallel Operations

Better safety can also be achieved by using an interlock mechanism that prevents operation of the machine from the front unless the worker at the back has tripped a release switch.

Managers often say that insufficient manpower prevents them from conducting parallel operations. With the SMED system this problem is eliminated because only a few minutes' assistance will be needed, and even unskilled workers can help, since the operations are simple ones. Assistance might be given by the operator of an automatic machine, by someone taking advantage of a lull between operations, or by a shift supervisor. With a little ingenuity, any number of methods can be found.

Even when the number of man-hours needed for setup operations is unchanged, parallel operations will cut elapsed time in half. This is a powerful tool for bringing setup times down to the single-minute range.

THE USE OF FUNCTIONAL CLAMPS

A functional clamp is an attachment device serving to hold objects in place with minimal effort. For example, the *direct attachment method* is used to secure a die to a press (*Figure 20-1*). A bolt is passed through a hole in the die and attached to the press bed. If the nut has fifteen threads on it, it cannot be tightened unless the bolt is turned fifteen times. In reality, though, it is the last turn that tightens the bolt and the first one that loosens it. The remaining fourteen turns are

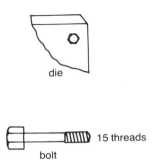

FIGURE 20-1. Direct Attachment Method and Bolt

wasted. In traditional setups, even more turns are wasted because the length of the bolt exceeds that of the part to be attached. Moreover, fifteen threads on the bolt mean that fifteen threads' worth of friction will be required to oppose the clamping resistance when the nut is fastened.

If the purpose of a bolt is simply to fasten or unfasten, its length should be determined so that only one turn will be needed. The bolt will then be a functional clamp.

One-Turn Attachments

The following are examples of functional clamps that can fasten or unfasten objects with only one turn.[1] I have frequently challenged plant managers to adopt this technique. I like to tell them that they will be allowed one turn per screw during setup, but that they will be fined 100,000 yen ($413)[2] for every additional turn.

The Pear-Shaped Hole Method

The problem here involved a large vulcanizing pan. Products were packed into the pan. The lid was then closed and secured with sixteen bolts, using a direct attachment method. The large number of bolts was needed to withstand considerable pressure. The operation took quite a long time because tightening required turning each bolt about thirty times. Opening the lid took a long time as well, and similarly required thirty turns for each of sixteen nuts. The movements needed to find and pick up loose nuts set down by the side of the pan made this a bothersome operation. Even though a few minutes had been saved by the use of an air-driven nut runner, the operation was still a nuisance.

To improve this setup, the bolt holes in the lid were made into pear-shaped holes (*Figure 20-2*) so that each nut could be loosened in one turn.

When all sixteen bolts had been loosened, the lid was turned counterclockwise by one bolt diameter. This brought the nuts to the

---

[1] Editor's Note: Some people find that one turn of a standard thread bolt is insufficient and that specially designed threads are needed for this purpose.

[2] Editor's Note: Presently, 100,000 yen is worth close to $700.

large ends of the holes. The lid could now be removed immediately by a crane. To fasten the lid, the reverse process was carried out, and a single turn was sufficient to tighten the nuts. It was no longer necessary to remove the nuts from the bolts, so the process of searching for nuts was eliminated. In the old method, bolt and nut combinations changed with each setup; the new method solved this problem as well.

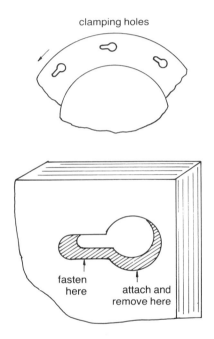

FIGURE 20-2. Pear-Shaped Holes for Clamping

The U-Shaped Washer Method

In this operation, wire was wound around the core of a motor. When winding was completed, the operation was carried out in the following sequence:

1. Loosen and remove clamping nut.
2. Remove washer.
3. Remove finished core.
4. Attach washer.

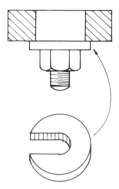

FIGURE 20-3. The U-Shaped Washer

5. Turn nut and clamp.
6. Begin next winding operation.

This operation was streamlined by replacing the washer with a U-shaped one (*Figure 20-3*).

The resulting sequence was as follows:

1. When winding is finished, stop the machine and loosen nut by one turn.
2. Slide off U-shaped washer.
3. Remove core with the nut in place (this is possible because the inside diameter of the core exceeds the outside diameter of the nut).
4. Slide U-shaped washer back on.
5. Fasten with one turn of the nut.
6. Begin next winding operation.

Using a U-shaped washer thus simplified the operation considerably. This example provides further evidence that fastening and unfastening can be readily performed with a single turn.

The U-shaped washer method was also very successful when applied to the attachment and removal of replacement gears on a gear-cutting machine.

The Split Thread Method

While doing some consulting work in the U.S. for Federal-Mogul Corporation, I commented that screws could be fastened or unfastened with a single turn. "Since one turn is all that is needed," I said, "let's agree that on my next visit you'll pay me a $1,000 penalty for each additional turn you use." Having extracted this promise, I returned to Japan.

When I revisited the plant six months later, a single-turn method had been implemented successfully. This is how it worked (*Figure 20-4*):

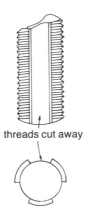

threads cut away

FIGURE 20-4. **The Split Thread Method**

1. Grooves were cut along the length of the bolt to divide it into three sections.
2. Corresponding grooves were cut in the threads of the female screw.
3. In the attachment process, insertion was accomplished by aligning the ridges of the bolt with the grooves of the female screw. The bolt was then simply slipped all the way into position.
4. The bolt was then tightened by a one-third turn.

In this particular case, the area of effective friction was preserved by lengthening the female screw.

The U-Slot Method

A U-shaped slot was cut in the attachment edge of a die. By inserting the head of the bolt into a dovetail groove on the machine bed, then sliding the bolt into the U-slot of the die, it became possible to fasten the die with one turn of the nut. This method guarantees a very strong attachment (*Figure 20-5*).

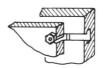

Figure 20-5. The U-Slot Method

In one instance, problems were caused by washers slipping off and falling. This was solved by spot-welding the washers and nuts together. This U-slot method can often be used to improve setups where direct clamping has been used previously. It must be pointed out, though, that a single screw turn is not sufficient for fastening when the U-slot pieces are not of uniform thickness.

The Clamp Method

As we have already pointed out, direct attachment methods often require many screw turns. One widely used alternative is the clamp method. In this technique, the die is secured by tightening the bolt on a clamp that presses down on the die (*Figure 20-6*).

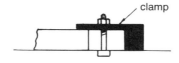

Figure 20-6. The Clamp Method

This method, like the U-slot method, is useful only if all the items to be fastened are of uniform thickness. If thicknesses vary, the engineer will first have to standardize the parts to be attached.

We have now seen various methods that make it possible for a screw to attach or release a die with a single turn. The key to developing attachment techniques lies in recognizing that the role of engaged threads is to maintain friction corresponding to the clamping pressure.

In the past, whenever an object needed to be secured, it was immediately assumed that it would be attached with screws, yet no thought whatsoever was given to the number of times the screws would have to be turned. Surely this point needs to be reconsidered. It is also important to recognize that screws and bolts are by no means the only way to attach objects.

One-Motion Methods

The concept of securing an object with a single motion lies behind a number of devices, including:

- Cams and clamps
- Wedges, tapered pins, and knock pins
- Springs

The elasticity in springs can be used to secure objects. Springs are usually used in pincer-type or expansion mechanisms. One company, however, applied spring elasticity in a simple operation to secure the replacement gears on a gear-cutting machine (*Figure 20-7*). In this application:

- A semicircular groove was cut along the length of the gearshaft.
- Spring-mounted check pins with semicircular heads were installed at three points around the inside circumference of a clamping device.
- Where screws had been used in the past, the check pins of the new clamping device gripped the shaft from the side. When the correct position was reached, the check pins engaged the groove and clamping action was achieved.

This extremely simple clamping device made it possible to attach and remove replacement gears more quickly and easily. At the time I worried that the gears, which had previously been attached with screws, might come off if held in place only by springs. In fact, this has never happened.

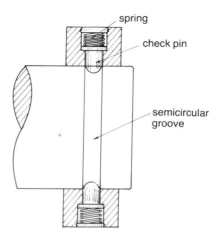

FIGURE 20-7. Spring Stops

Magnetism and Vacuum Suction

Magnetism and vacuums are very convenient when the entire surface of the workpiece is to be machined and there is no room for attachment devices. When suction is used, care must be taken that the surfaces are smooth and no air can leak out.

Interlocking Methods

We tend to assume that some sort of fastener is needed whenever an object is to be secured. On the contrary, in many circumstances it is enough to simply fit and join two parts together.

Direction and Magnitude of Forces

Very effective methods of securing objects can be found by considering the directions in which forces are needed and the magnitude of force needed in each direction.

For instance, in one operation, six stoppers were screwed to each of the six spindles of a boring machine. The operation was a nuisance because the screws had to be turned in extremely cramped conditions. After completing an on-site inspection of the operation, I asked the section chief what the function of the stoppers was.

"We need them," he replied, "for setting positions during processing."

"Look," I told him, "there are three directions in space: left-to-right, front-to-back, and up-and-down. Since the stopper is engaging the opposite spindle, left-to-right and up-and-down movement are both prevented, aren't they?"

"The problem is front-to-back movement," he said.

"The stopper obviously bears a force from the opposite direction," I replied. "Since it is engaged, it will be supported by the end of the spindle. The remaining difficulty is determining how much force is required to remove it." I suggested that pulling off the stopper should involve, at most, enough force for the head of the workpiece to catch on the stopper face when covered with oil. In that case, there would be no need to use screws. We improved the operation as follows (*Figure 20-8*):

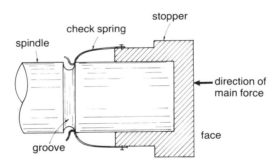

FIGURE 20-8. Securing a Stopper

- Threads were removed to make cylindrical fits.
- Circumferential semicircular check grooves were cut near the ends of the spindles.
- Springs were attached at three places around the edge of each stopper. When a stopper was fitted on a spindle, the springs and groove would engage and the spring tension would prevent the stopper from coming off.

The stoppers were attached merely by fitting them onto the spindles, thereby greatly simplifying the operation. An analysis of the directions and magnitudes of the necessary forces had led to the adoption of this simple method.

Analysis of the forces involved in attaching press dies also made it possible to improve setup by switching from threaded clamps to an interlocking method.

In short, effective improvements can be made by studying actual clamping functions rather than by assuming that threaded fasteners will suffice for everything.

ELIMINATION OF ADJUSTMENTS

As already explained, adjustments and test runs normally account for as much as 50 percent of setup time. Eliminating them, therefore, will always lead to tremendous time savings. Note that elimination of adjustments means just that — *elimination* — not just a reduction in the time given over to them.

Test runs and adjustments are necessitated by inaccurate centering, dimensioning, etc., earlier in the internal setup procedure. It is extremely important to recognize that adjustments are not an independent operation. To eliminate them, we must move back a step and improve the earlier stages of internal setup.

Fixing Numerical Settings

Eliminating adjustments requires, above all, abandoning reliance on intuition in setting machines for production. Intuitive judgments may have some sort of statistical validity, but they remain inexact and do not have the same precision as constant value settings.

In my frequent visits to factories, I often tell the foremen: "Since you are so convinced of the value of determining settings by intuition, do it three times on the same machine. If you get the same results each time, then there's no problem. If you get good results only twice, then the method has to be abandoned."

"Why," I am asked, "is three times all right, but not twice?" To this I reply that although three plums on a slot machine is a winning combination, two plums alone are worthless. This gets a laugh, but it also underscores an important point: As long as settings are made on the basis of intuition, there is no way to avoid test runs.

The initial step in doing away with adjustments is to make calibrations. When intuition prevails, there is no way for fixed amounts to be represented. Calibrations overcome that problem. Everyone knows what it means to "set the dial at five," and the same value can be set the next time. It is possible, moreover, for other people to set the machine to the same value.

Although graduated scales in themselves have a positive impact, they by no means eliminate adjustments completely. Still, the use of graduated scales will lead to significant improvements in setups involving a wide range of possible settings.

Visual calibration readings generally yield accuracies to 0.5 mm. When greater accuracy is required, calipers will permit another magnitude of precision. Installing a dial gauge makes it possible to take readings on the order of 0.01 mm, and even greater accuracy can be obtained with numerical control devices. The use of the digital method is also satisfactory in this respect. Measurement devices for numerical settings have been greatly refined in recent years, so improvements can often be secured simply by installing a sufficiently accurate measurement tool for the task at hand.

In one application, a magnescale was used for dimensioning on a woodworking double sizer. This dramatically increased accuracy and allowed faster setup time than the previous method, in which parallels were set by sight.

Imaginary Center Lines and Reference Planes

When setup is actually being performed on a machine, no center lines or reference planes are visible. They must be found by trial and error, which can be a lengthy process.

The distinction between *setting* and *adjusting* is not fully appreciated in most factories. Many people are under the impression that adjustments are a necessary evil in setup procedures. Workers pride themselves on how frequently, cleverly, and quickly they can make adjustments. This is indeed a skill — an important one — but we must not lose sight of improvements that can make the adjustments unnecessary. We must recognize clearly that setting and adjusting are completely different functions. Our goal should be to design measures based on settings, not adjustments. A highly effective approach is to substitute visible center lines and reference planes for imaginary ones. This approach is applicable to drill presses, milling machines, and all other machine tools.

The Least Common Multiple System

The Least Common Multiple (LCM) System may be thought of as a technique for eliminating adjustments. It is a powerful method based upon a simple concept of arithmetic. The name refers to the notion of providing a number of mechanisms corresponding to the least common multiple of various operating conditions. The workers then perform only the functions required for a given operation. This can greatly enhance the speed of setup operations.

A slogan arising from this method is: *Leave the mechanism alone, and modify only the function.*

One-Touch Exchange of Plastic Forming Molds

This example comes from an operation for molding television dials. Notable features of the production process included the following:

- It was necessary to change molds because two parts being made, A and B, required different types of resins.
- The large orders for these parts required the use of one machine for a solid month.
- To avoid excess inventory of one part or the other, lots were alternated daily. This led to an enormous amount of setup time.

The improvements described below successfully dealt with this situation.

- As shown in *Figure 20-9*, four dies — A_1, A_2, B_1, B_2 — were cut in a single die block.

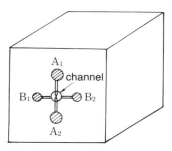

FIGURE 20-9. **A One Touch Exchange Die**

- The flow of resin was directed into A_1 and A_2 when part A was produced, and into B_1 and B_2 when part B was produced, simply by rotating the central resin channels 90°.

This made it possible for setup changes and resin switches to be performed in five minutes or so. By raising productivity and drastically reducing inventories, this method succeeded in killing two birds with one stone.

Inspecting Steering Wheels for Wobble

Toyota used a special device for inspecting molded steering wheels. A jig fitting the steering wheel of each car model — Crown, Corolla, Corona, and Celica — was mounted in the center of this device. Setting the central jig required great accuracy.

Since this was beyond the abilities of the part-time workers charged with inspection, a shift supervisor handled the setup. He turned it back to the workers only after repeated centering and adjusting had allowed him to align the jig. In addition to requiring a high level of skill, this operation kept workers idle during the centering procedure. A quality control (QC) circle assigned to study the problem came up with the following suggestions (*Figure 20-10*):

- Build a box-shaped inspection bench.
- On its four faces mount the special center jigs for each car model, one to each surface, making sure that the jigs do not wobble at all.

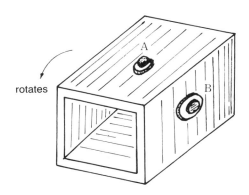

FIGURE 20-10. A Rotating Jig for Wobble Inspection

- In the actual operation for, say, the Corona, turn up the appropriate face of the inspection bench and hold it in place with a stopper.

With this procedure, there was no need to center each jig every time an operation changed. Furthermore, the setup operation could be performed easily, quickly and independently by a part-time worker.

Countersink Boring of Motor Core Shafts

This operation involved using a drill to countersink a hole for a stationary screw in a motor core shaft. Since the cores were of eight different lengths, stoppers had to be repositioned each time the operation changed. This required repeated test runs and adjustments, following this procedure:

- The stopper was loosened and repositioned.
- Measurements were made and a preliminary setting was established.
- A test run was conducted. If unsuccessful, it was followed by further adjustment.
- When the correct measurements had been made, the stopper was tightened and the operation began.

With the improvement shown in *Figure 20-11*, the entire operation was vastly simplified:

- Stopper plugs of eight heights were made and mounted on a single plate.
- When the operation changed, all that had to be done was to rotate the plate to set the stopper at the desired height. The plate was then secured.

This arrangement eliminated the need for adjustment or test runs. While the old method had produced three or four substandard products each time, this new technique reduced that number to zero.

Setup on a Multishaft Drill Press

In this operation holes were made in clutch parts at either four or six points. Because every change in the type of workpiece required a new drill holder setting, the setup time was considerable.

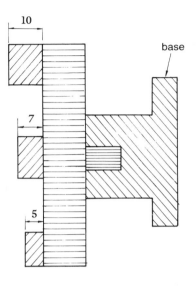

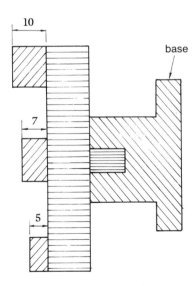

FIGURE 20-11. A Rotary Stopper

Two holders were added so that a total of eight holders permitted both four-drill and six-drill configurations (*Figure 20-12*). When four holes were to be drilled, drills were mounted in the holders for the four-hole configuration and the other four holders were left empty. When six holes were to be drilled, drills were mounted in the holders for the six-hole configuration and the remaining two holders were left empty. This made it possible to shift between the two combinations merely by inserting or removing drills.

The result was the elimination of setup change adjustments and a setup which could be performed in about two minutes.

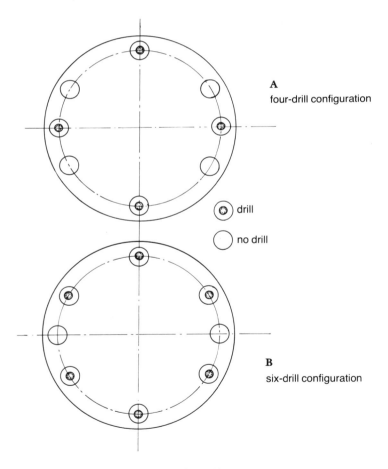

A
four-drill configuration

drill

no drill

B
six-drill configuration

FIGURE 20-12. Setup on a Multishaft Drill Press

Positioning Washing Machines

Automatic mounting is an intermediate process in washing machine assembly. In this process, positioning stoppers are installed on a pallet where the machine is to be set. In this example, there were four models, and each change required replacing the stoppers.

This operation was modified by placing in the corners of the pallet four stoppers that were made to rotate automatically just before the assembly began (*Figure 20-13*). The widths and depths of the washing machine models varied, and the rotating stoppers were made with notches corresponding to these differences. They could be turned easily to the proper position.

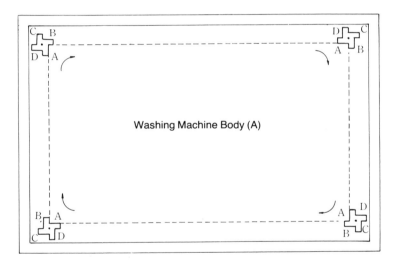

Washing Machine Body (A)

FIGURE 20-13. Positioning Washing Machine Bodies

This change made setup quite simple and eliminated the need for human labor. Small-lot production was adopted, and no problems arose in spite of the increased number of setups.

Changing Limit Switches

This example concerns an operation in which a limit switch controlled the end point of machining for making shafts. Since there were five types of shafts involved, the switch needed to be moved among five locations. Every time a position was changed, a number of steps were followed. First, the switch was moved. Test runs were then conducted to verify that the switch was at the proper location. When it was not, adjustments were made. Its position was then rechecked. With this system, as many as four readjustments had to be made.

The operation was improved as follows (*Figure 20-14*):

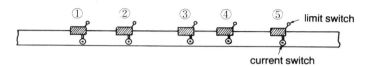

<small>Figure 20-14.</small> **Changing Limit Switches**

- Five switches were installed — one at each of the five sites.
- An electric switch was provided to supply current to each of the five limit switches.
- To activate, for example, the third limit switch, only the third electric switch was turned on; no current flowed to the other switches, which remained off. This system functioned similarly for all the other limit switches.

This arrangement made it possible to perform setup changes simply by flipping a switch. It demonstrates the successful application of the "one-touch" concept. Using this technique, it became possible to change limit switches in less than one second.

The large number of examples of the Least Common Multiple system has been presented for two reasons. The first is that with this system, extremely easy, yet extraordinarily effective improvements are possible. The second is that these examples can be applied in a variety of situations if the engineer will only take the trouble to modify them according to the conditions in his plant.

It is important to recognize that the LCM system rests on two fundamental principles:

- Make settings, not adjustments.
- Change only functions; leave mechanisms as they are.

Undoubtedly many improvements can be made by examining your own operations in the light of this concept. I fervently hope that many important improvements in production will result from using this approach.

Mechanization

Only after every attempt has been made to improve setups using the methods we have already described should mechanization be considered. Bear in mind that the many basic techniques we have covered so far will often serve to reduce a two-hour setup to one requiring about three minutes. Mechanization may then further reduce the time by another minute or so.

Avoid the mistake of jumping into mechanization from the start, however. There is a simple reason for this. Mechanizing an inefficient setup operation will achieve time reductions, but it will do little to remedy the basic faults of a poorly designed setup process. It is much more effective to mechanize setups that have already been streamlined.

21
Basic Examples of SMED

The SMED system can be applied to many types of machines. Following are examples involving plastic forming machines.

Switching Resins

When changing from resin A to resin B, the volume of resin A in the hopper just prior to completing the first operation is proportional to the number of shots remaining. Any excess is removed. Resin B is then introduced. This ensures that when the change is made, most of the resin in the nozzle will be resin B. The changeover is thus streamlined and little of resin A is wasted (*Figure 21-1*). A daily plan of operations is drawn up so that work proceeds from lighter to darker colored resins. When changing resins, it is necessary to follow this order, for example:

- Transparent
- White
- Yellow
- Red
- Black

This simple approach minimizes the effects of dye contamination.

Changing Hoppers

Cleaning the interiors of hoppers for resin or dye changes is quite a chore. This is especially so on large hoppers that have dryers attached. One effective technique here is to devise hopper liners. This way, instead of cleaning the hoppers, one simply changes the liner.

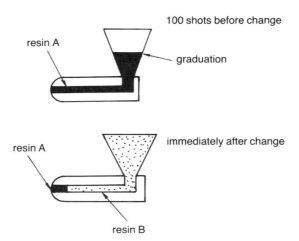

FIGURE 21-1. Changing Resins

Preferable to this, however, is the "floating dryer" I developed for one company. By suspending and drying resin in a stream of hot air, it is possible to dry in five minutes items that used to take an hour to heat and dry.

Since only one shot's worth of resin needs to be dried per cycle, only five to ten shots of resin need to be kept in the hopper. As long as a regular supply is made from the raw materials vat, a very small hopper will suffice and cleaning is simplified. The operation becomes even simpler when the hopper is switched with a new spare hopper.

At the S Pen Company, hopper cleaning and changing operations are carried out in a very simple way. A small dual hopper is spun around and a new hopper is used. This way hoppers can be specialized for use with individual resins and dyes. The handling operations are simple because the small hoppers have capacities of only about 100 mm × 200 mm.

Cleaning Out Nozzles

Cleaning out nozzles is the most annoying problem in changing resins. Resins adhering to the nozzles' inner walls and to screw surfaces remain there and mix in with the next batch of resin, thus contaminating the colors. Eventually, the old resin is flushed away, but when this takes too long, a suitable purging agent must be used. How to speed up this operation is a problem requiring further study.

Die Preheating

When a die needs to be preheated, one extremely effective method is to use a steam generator and circulate hot water through the coolant channels to actually heat the die. Another common method is to use electric heaters.

In a case similar to that of die preheating, a considerable amount of internal setup time used to be spent making forty electrical connections on a hot runner die after the die was mounted on the machine. By preparing another connecting jig, connecting it in advance to the next die and plugging it in, substantial reductions in internal setup time were secured. Here again is an example of the use of an intermediary jig.

The examples presented so far can also be applied to other machine tools, forging machines, casting machines, painting and woodworking machines, etc. My experience has led me to the firm conviction that SMED can be achieved in all cases by applying the conceptual framework and corresponding practical techniques.

22
Effects of SMED

In this chapter we discuss time savings achieved and other effects of applying the SMED system.

TIME SAVED BY APPLYING SMED TECHNIQUES

Table 22-1 shows time reductions achieved by around 1975, when the SMED system was beginning to gain ground. In the last ten years reductions have been even greater; the average setup now takes one-fortieth (2½ percent) of the time originally required.

OTHER EFFECTS OF SMED

Stockless Production

It is true, of course, that inventories disappear when high-diversity, low-volume orders are dealt with by means of high-diversity, small-lot production. Yet the multiplicative effects of the high-diversity component, on the one hand, and the small-lot component, on the other, lead inevitably to a substantial increase in the number of setup operations that must be performed. Cutting setups that used to take two hours to three minutes with SMED, however, changes the situation considerably. The SMED system offers the only path to both high-diversity, small-lot production and minimal inventory levels.

Moreover, when a system of production that minimizes inventories is adopted, the following collateral effects can be expected:

- Capital turnover rates increase.
- Stock reductions lead to more efficient use of plant space. (For

No.	Company	Capacity (in tons)	Before Improvement	After Improvement	1/n
Presses (single-shot dies)					
1	K Auto	500 t-3 machines	1 hr 30 min	4 min 51 sec	1/19
2	S Auto	300 t-3 machines	1 hr 40 min	7 min 36 sec	1/13
3	D Auto	150 t	1 hr 30 min	8 min 24 sec	1/11
4	M Electric	"	2 hr 10 min	7 min 25 sec	1/18
5	S Electric	"	1 hr 20 min	5 min 45 sec	1/14
6	M Industries	"	1 hr 30 min	6 min 36 sec	1/14
7	A Auto Body	"	1 hr 40 min	7 min 46 sec	1/13
8	K Industries	100 t	1 hr 30 min	3 min 20 sec	1/27
9	S Metals	"	40 min	2 min 26 sec	1/16
10	A Steel	"	30 min	2 min 41 sec	1/11
11	K Press	"	40 min	2 min 48 sec	1/14
12	M Metals	"	1 hr 30 min	5 min 30 sec	1/16
13	K Metals	"	1 hr 10 min	4 min 33 sec	1/15
14	T Manufacturing (dies for springs)	80 t	4 hr 0 min	4 min 18 sec	1/56
15	M Ironworks	"	50 min	3 min 16 sec	1/15
16	H Engineering	50 t	40 min	2 min 40 sec	1/15
17	M Electric	"	40 min	1 min 30 sec	1/27
18	M Electric	"	50 min	2 min 45 sec	1/18
19	H Press	30 t	50 min	48 sec	1/63
20	K Metals	"	40 min	2 min 40 sec	1/15
21	Y Industries	"	30 min	2 min 27 sec	1/12
22	I Metals (multiple dies)	"	50 min	2 min 48 sec	1/18
23	S Industries (progressive dies)	150 t	1 hr 40 min	4 min 36 sec	1/22
24	K Metals	100 t	1 hr 50 min	6 min 36 sec	1/17
25	M Electric	100 t	1 hr 30 min	6 min 28 sec	1/14
				Average	1/18

TABLE 22-1. Time Reductions Achieved by Using SMED

Company	Capacity (in tons)	Before Improvement	After Improvement	1/n
Presses (single-shot dies)				
K Auto	500 t-3 machines	1 hr 30 min	4 min 51 sec	1/19
S Auto	300 t-3 machines	1 hr 40 min	7 min 36 sec	1/13
D Auto	150 t	1 hr 30 min	8 min 24 sec	1/11
M Electric	"	2 hr 10 min	7 min 25 sec	1/18
S Electric	"	1 hr 20 min	5 min 45 sec	1/14
M Industries	"	1 hr 30 min	6 min 36 sec	1/14
A Auto Body	"	1 hr 40 min	7 min 46 sec	1/13
K Industries	100 t	1 hr 30 min	3 min 20 sec	1/27
S Metals	"	40 min	2 min 26 sec	1/16
A Steel	"	30 min	2 min 41 sec	1/11
K Press	"	40 min	2 min 48 sec	1/14
M Metals	"	1 hr 30 min	5 min 30 sec	1/16
K Metals	"	1 hr 10 min	4 min 33 sec	1/15
T Manufacturing	80 t	4 hr 0 min	4 min 18 sec	1/56
(dies for springs)				
M Ironworks	"	50 min	3 min 16 sec	1/15
H Engineering	50 t	40 min	2 min 40 sec	1/15
M Electric	"	40 min	1 min 30 sec	1/27
M Electric	"	50 min	2 min 45 sec	1/18
H Press	30 t	50 min	48 sec	1/63
K Metals	"	40 min	2 min 40 sec	1/15
Y Industries	"	30 min	2 min 27 sec	1/12
I Metals	"	50 min	2 min 48 sec	1/18
(multiple dies)				
S Industries	150 t	1 hr 40 min	4 min 36 sec	1/22
(progressive dies)				
K Metals	100 t	1 hr 50 min	6 min 36 sec	1/17
M Electric	100 t	1 hr 30 min	6 min 28 sec	1/14
			Average	1/18

Plastic Forming Machines					
26	M Manufacturing	140 ounces	6 hr 40 min	7 min 36 sec	1/53
27	TM Manufacturing	100 ounces	2 hr 30 min	8 min 14 sec	1/18
28	Y Manufacturing	"	1 hr 50 min	4 min 36 sec	1/24
29	N Rubber	"	2 hr 30 min	6 min 28 sec	1/23
30	N Rubber	50 ounces	2 hr 0 min	4 min 18 sec	1/28
31	T Industries	"	1 hr 20 min	6 min 46 sec	1/12
32	TT Industries	"	1 hr 10 min	7 min 36 sec	1/9
33	N Chemicals	20 ounces	40 min	3 min 45 sec	1/11
34	D Plastics	10 ounces	50 min	2 min 26 sec	1/19
35	GA Electric	"	50 min	6 min 45 sec	1/7
36	S Lighting	"	40 min	3 min 38 sec	1/11
37	Y Synthetics	"	40 min	2 min 48 sec	1/14
38	W Company (Switzerland)	50 ounces	2 hr 30 min	6 min 0 sec	1/25
				Average	1/20
Die-cast Molding Machines					
39	M Metals	250 t	50 min	6 min 24 sec	1/8
40	T Die Casting	"	1 hr 20 min	7 min 46 sec	1/10
41	S Manufacturing	"	1 hr 10 min	5 min 36 sec	1/13
				Average	1/10
				Overall Average	1/18

TABLE 22-1. Time Reductions Achieved by Using SMED (continued)

example, the manager of a Citroen factory told me that twenty-two days' worth of inventory had been reduced to eight days' worth after SMED was adopted. He said this made the planned construction of a new building unnecessary.)

- Productivity rises as stock handling operations are eliminated. (Production in the Citroen plant cited above rose 20 percent.)
- Unusable stock arising from model changeovers or mistaken estimates of demand is eliminated.
- Goods are no longer lost through deterioration.
- The ability to mix production of various types of goods leads to further inventory reductions.

Increased Machine Work Rates and Productive Capacity

If setup times are drastically reduced, then the work rates of machines will increase and productivity will rise in spite of an increased number of setup operations.

Elimination of Setup Errors

Setup errors are reduced, and the elimination of trial runs lowers the incidence of defects.

Improved Quality

Quality also improves, since operating conditions are fully regulated in advance.

Increased Safety

Simpler setups result in safer operations.

Simplified Housekeeping

Standardization reduces the number of tools required, and those that are still needed are organized more functionally.

Decreased Setup Time

The total amount of setup time — including both internal and external setup — is reduced, with a consequent drop in man-hours.

Lower Expense

Implementing SMED increases investment efficiency by making possible dramatic increases in productivity at relatively little cost. The cost of setups for small, single-shot metal press dies runs about 30,000 yen–50,000 yen ($124-$206) in Japan and is about the same for plastic molding machine dies (*Figure 22-1*).

Operator Preference

Since adoption of SMED means that tooling changes are simple and quick, there is no longer any reason to avoid them.

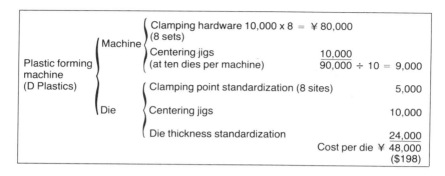

FIGURE 22-1. Cost of Implementing SMED

Lower Skill Level Requirements

The ease of tooling changes eliminates the need for skilled workers.

I once observed a setup operation for helical gears on a gear-cutting machine at a Citroen plant in France. By using SMED, an unskilled worker in charge of the machine was able to complete in seven minutes and thirty-eight seconds an operation which previously had taken a skilled specialist about an hour and a half to perform.

As the plant manager and I returned to the office after observing this operation, he said to me, "You know, I saw something odd recently. A worker was wiping his machine with oil. This setup used to be handled by a specialist, so that while the setup was going on the regular machine operator would go off to some other machine and do something else. Since workers would take turns handling various machines, no one felt that any particular machine was his own. That's why up until now you would never see a worker taking care of the machine he was handling.

"Lately, though, machine operators have been able to perform setup changes themselves and they spend a month at a time concentrating on the operation of a single machine. This gives them a feeling of responsibility for their machines. I'm sure that's why they're now oiling and taking care of the equipment."

When I heard this, I realized that consideration for the feelings of workers was just as important in France — or anywhere else — as it is in Japan.

Reduced Production Time

Production periods can be shortened drastically. Generally speaking, the following three strategies have proven effective.

Eliminate waiting for processes. The greatest delays in production are caused not by inspection or transportation, but by time spent waiting for the processing of one lot to be completed before another lot can be processed.

The ratio of time devoted to processing and to waiting for processes is frequently of the following order:

Waiting for processes : Processing
                  60 : 40
                  80 : 20

If the waiting periods could be eliminated, production time could be cut by as much as two-fifths. This can be accomplished by standardizing both processing quantities and processing times — that is, by equalizing the number of units processed in each operation, and by making the processing time in each operation the same.

Standardizing processing quantities can be accomplished fairly easily; the real problem lies in standardizing processing times. This is because machines used for individual operations are not necessarily of equal capacities. Processing time standardization seems to be impossible, for example, when the daily production capacity of machine A, used in Process 1, is 3,000 items, while that of B, the machine used in Process 2, is only 2,500 items. In a situation like this, there is a tendency to try to balance things out by installing another B machine.

Another important concept is applicable here, however: *The quantities produced should be the quantities needed.* If the required daily output is 2,000 items, there is no need to bring the capacity of machine B into line with that of machine A, since one B machine has sufficient capacity to process the daily amount needed. Consequently, the capacities of machines A and B should both be brought into line with required daily output. This still leaves a disparity between the capacities of machines A and B, however — a disparity that can be handled by adopting *a full work control system.*

A full work control system would fulfill the following functions in the given example:

- It sets up a buffer before machine B.
- It halts operation of machine A (the previous process) when twenty products accumulate in the buffer.
- It resumes operation of machine A when there are five products in the buffer.

In this way, process flows can be standardized using minimum cushion amounts. It is important to bear in mind, however, that while machines can be idle, workers must not be, because the cost of manpower is generally far higher than the cost of amortizing machines. Thus, it can be extremely effective to have several machines engaged in waiting operations so that workers will always have machines to take charge of.

Eliminate waiting for lots. Much time is lost when intermediary and raw materials must wait for processing of an entire lot to be completed. These delays can be eliminated only by establishing "transport lots" of one item each, so that each item moves to the subsequent process as soon as it has undergone processing. It is necessary, in other words, to adopt what might be termed "single-item-flow" operations. As shown in *Figure 22-2*, all the intervals between processes will now take the time needed to process one item. If single-item-flow operations are established for, say, ten processes, overall lot processing time can be cut by 90 percent.

On the other hand, processing a lot of 1,000 items will require 1,000 transport operations. Various strategies must be devised to deal with this, such as improving plant layout so as to simplify transportation, and finding convenient transportation procedures, for example, using conveyors.

Produce in small lots. Production time can be cut 90 percent by engaging in small-lot production, for example, by dividing lots of 1,000 into lots of 100, and by using standardized processing times and single-item-flow operations.

This leads, however, to a tenfold increase in the number of setup operations that must be performed. Through the use of SMED, production times can be shortened considerably even when the number of setups increases, since, for example, if a setup time that used to take two hours is cut to three minutes, ten repetitions of the setup will still take only thirty minutes.

(A) Improvement of Process Delays

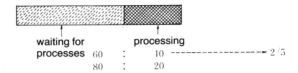

waiting for   processing
processes   60   :   10   - - - - - - - - - - - - → 2/5
         80   :   20

(B) Improvement of Lot Delays

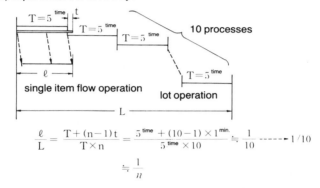

$$\frac{\ell}{L} = \frac{T+(n-1)t}{T\times n} = \frac{5^{\text{time}}+(10-1)\times 1^{\text{min.}}}{5^{\text{time}}\times 10} \doteqdot \frac{1}{10} \quad ----- \rightarrow 1/10$$

$$\doteqdot \frac{1}{n}$$

(C) Small Lot Production

lot size ⟶ 1/10 - - - - - - - - - - - - - - → 1/10

total $= 2/5\times 1/10 \times 1/10 = 1/250$

Strategy	Proportion of Previous Time	Percentage of Previous Time
Waiting for processing	2/5	40%
Waiting for lots	1/10	10%
Small lot production	1/10	10%
Total production time	1/250	.4%

FIGURE 22-2. Reducing Production Time

Combining the savings in production time attainable by employing the three strategies described above leads to dramatic results (*Figure
22-2, bottom*).

At the washing machine division of M Electric, the completion
of everything from blanking a washing machine body on a press to
press forming, welding, painting, and assembling is carried out in a
mere two hours by means of standardized processing times and
single-item-flow operations. This achievement is based on the approach outlined above.

For the first time, moreover, SMED makes it possible to perform
the several daily changeovers required by the adoption of a "divided
production scheme," in which the same items are produced every day
in small lots.

Production lead times are drastically cut by the use of methods
such as this. As a result:

- Production can take place after orders are received, rather
  than before.
- Even before orders are confirmed, production can begin on
  the basis of reliable information about incoming orders.
- Rush orders can be dealt with promptly.
- It is easy to meet delivery dates.

In this instance, SMED has not only reduced production times
dramatically, it has also reduced both work in process and stocks of
finished products.

Increased Production Flexibility

In addition to shortening production times, the adoption of
SMED facilitates product changeovers, thereby making it possible to
respond rapidly to changes in demand and substantially increasing
manufacturing flexibility.

Elimination of Conceptual Blind Spots

I once heard the following from Ashton Marcus, Vice President
of Omark Industries of Portland, Oregon:

> Omark has always wanted to reduce inventories, but little ever came of
> the idea because smaller lots and more setup changes meant lowered

productivity. We had always assumed that a setup change had to be performed by a specially skilled worker and that it had to take several hours. It wasn't just that we had resigned ourselves to several-hour setups; we never even questioned them.

Even though it sounded logical, I had my doubts when I read in your book, *Study of the 'Toyota' Production System,* that our setup changes could be completed in less than ten minutes. Nevertheless, several of our operations accepted the challenge, and they separated internal setup and external setup, shifted internal setup to external setup, and eliminated adjustments.

As a result, one operation was able to reduce to one minute and thirty seconds a setup operation which had previously taken two hours.

The results were similar in other pilot programs, and improved setup times gained momentum in other operations. Reductions of as much as 98 percent of previous times in some locations allowed them to move to small-lot production. In half a year total company inventory was reduced over 25 percent, and productivity in those locations rose 30 percent.

I keep thinking of how our biggest problem had been the presence of a conceptual blind spot which kept us resigned to the idea that the setup change was a long operation requiring a skilled worker.

Conceptual blind spots of this sort may surely be found in other companies as well.

New Attitudes

A revolution in thinking makes the impossible possible. At a SMED seminar, participants from Hitachi, Ltd. and Bridgestone Tire made observations of the following sort:

In putting SMED into practice, the thing I was most keenly aware of was making the impossible possible.

Frankly, I didn't believe that setups that used to take two or three hours could be completed within nine minutes. After actually trying it, though, I found that it was indeed possible. I figured that it was no good just to keep telling myself that it couldn't be done. Instead, I tried to think of ways to make it work. The important thing, I kept telling myself, was to take up the challenge. Gradually I realized that what I had always thought to be impossible could, in fact, be done.

Nowadays, when someone in our company makes a suggestion, expressions such as "that can never work" or "that's impossible" are taboo. When reminded that SMED had in fact proved to be possible, we think again and find that a surprising number of things can be accomplished when we accept challenges in a positive way. At any rate, despite a tendency to assume that something can't be done, we find an unexpectedly large number of possibilities when we give some thought to how it might be possible to do it.

Here we see that the major cause of success has been the change in peoples' perceptions after they witnessed the effects of SMED firsthand.

Revolutionized Production Methods

In the past, many people believed that mass production was a good thing. Since large orders are a good thing, it was reasoned, large-lot production is also a good thing. This belief, however, derives from a confusion of the terms involved.

It is true, indeed, that large orders are advantageous in many ways. They hasten the amortization of machinery and dies and simplify management, thereby lowering management costs. Yet large orders constitute an area in which the buyer has the power to decide and the producer is without the authority to make choices. The only choice left to the producer is whether to conduct large-lot or small-lot production.

Of course, since producers prefer large-lot production, they can combine small orders into larger ones. These larger orders, however, will be apparent orders, not real ones. What we think of as a large order — say, an order for 30,000 cars in the space of ten days — is really nothing more than a real demand for 30,000 cars in thirty days which, for the sake of convenience, we have compressed into ten days. When the 30,000 cars produced in ten days are delivered, either the client or the dealers will have to keep them as inventory.

Even with such a large order, inventories would be greatly reduced if production were spread over thirty days. Managers have always assumed, however, that anticipatory production was the right way to go. They have thought, unconsciously, that anticipatory production was the *only* kind of production. In the end, anticipatory production — which we euphemistically refer to as "planned production" — is essentially nothing more than production based on guesswork. Of course, we do our utmost to improve the reliability of our guesswork by conducting large-scale market surveys and seeking the counsel of experts, but guesswork will always be guesswork. We cannot expect it to coincide 100 percent with actual demand. A cool summer, for example, will tend to result in unsold summer clothing, and stocks of winter goods rise during a warm winter. Moreover, long-range forecasting will always be necessary to plan for future materials, equipment and manpower needs.

When production is linked directly to actual demand, however, it becomes possible to use small-lot production to produce the minimum necessary, cut lead times to a minimum, and respond immediately to changes in demand. These benefits will surely eliminate the motivation to cling to traditional large-lot production.

It is true that large-lot production has some undeniable advantages:

- Efficiency rises and skills improve quickly, since the same operation is performed repeatedly.
- Work rates rise because few setups are needed.

The impact of these advantages is lessened considerably, however, when the SMED system is employed: Needed levels of skill are reduced by means of improved and simplified operations, setups are simplified, and setup times are cut drastically.

In any case, the belief used to be widely held that mass production is good and inventory is a necessary evil. Now, with the realization that large orders and large-lot production are separate phenomena with separate advantages, we should recognize that large orders are indeed desirable, but they should be met by small-lot production. Managers who are responsible for production must recognize that the proper strategy is to make only what can be sold.

The single indispensable condition for making this strategy succeed is the adoption of SMED, for two reasons: SMED makes it possible to respond quickly to fluctuations in demand, and it creates the necessary conditions for lead time reductions.

The time has come to bid farewell to the long-standing myths of anticipatory production and large-lot production. We must also recognize that flexible production can come about only through SMED.

In this sense, it is a great pleasure to see recognition of the need for the SMED concept reflected in recent machine advertisements. They now treat as a selling point the fact that changes on such-and-such a machine can be made in three minutes or so. I believe that the theory and practice of SMED constitute a key that is about to open the door to a new concept of production.

About the Author

CAREER: 50 YEARS IN FACTORY IMPROVEMENT

First Period: Private Enterprise

1909 Born in Saga City, Saga-Pref., Japan, on January 8.

1924 While studying at Saga Technical High School, reads and is deeply impressed by Toshiro Ikeda's *The Secret of Eliminating Unprofitable Efforts,* said to be a translation of Taylor's thesis.

1930 Graduates from Yamanashi Technical College with a degree in mechanical engineering; goes to work for the Taipei Railway Factory.

1931 While a technician in the casting shop at the Taipei Railway Factory, observes worker operations and feels the need for improvement. Reads accounts of the streamlining of operations at Japan National Railways plants and awakens to the need for rational plant management.

Reads Taylor's *The Principles of Scientific Management* and, greatly impressed, decides to make the study and practice of scientific management his life's work.

Reads and studies many books, including the works of Yoichi Ueno and texts published by the Japan Industrial Association.

1937 For two months beginning September 1, attends the First Long-Term Industrial Engineering Training Course, sponsored by the Japan Industrial Association, the precursor of the Japan Management Association. Is thoroughly instructed in the "motion mind" concept by Ken'ichi Horikome.

1943   Transfers to the Amano Manufacturing Plant (Yokohama) on orders from the Ministry of Munitions. As Manufacturing Section Chief, applies flow operations to the processing of depth mechanisms for air-launched torpedoes and raises productivity by 100%.

Second Period: The Japan Management Association

1945   On orders from the Ministry of Munitions, transfers to Ishii Precision Mfg. (Niigata), a maker of similar air-launched torpedo depth mechanisms, for the purpose of improving factory operations.

With the end of the war in August, accepts a post at Yasui Kogyo (Kita Kyushu) starting in April 1946 and moves to Takanabe-cho in Miyazaki Prefecture. Stops by Tokyo at this time and visits Isamu Fukuda at the Japan Management Association, where he is introduced to Chairman of the Board Morikawa. Is asked to participate temporarily in a plant survey to improve operations at Hitachi, Ltd.'s vehicle manufacturing facility at Kasado. Afterwards enters the service of the Japan Management Association.

1946   When asked by a survey team member during process analysis at the Hitachi plant how to treat times when goods are delayed while waiting for cranes, realizes that "processes" and "operations," which had previously been thought to be separate and parallel entities, form a "network of processes and operations" — a systematic, synthetic whole. Reports this finding at a Japan Management Association technical conference.

Invents a method of classifying like operations by counting non-interventions while studying the layout of a Hitachi, Ltd. woodworking plant.

1948   Elucidates the "true nature of skill" in *A Study of 'Peko' Can Operations* at Toyo Steel's Shitamatsu plant.

Between 1948 and 1954, takes charge of Production Technology Courses. Also runs production technology classes at companies.

At a production technology course held at Hitachi, Ltd.'s Fujita plant, begins to question the nature of plant layout. Studies and reflects on the problem.

1950 Perfects and implements a method for determining equipment layout based on a coefficient of ease of transport at Furukawa Electric's Copper Refinery in Nikko.

Analyzes work at a press at Tōyō Kōgyō and realizes that a setup operation is composed of "internal setup" (IED) and "external setup" (OED). This concept will become the first stage of SMED.

1954 Morita Masanobu from Toyota Motor Co., Ltd. participates in a production technology course at Toyoda Automatic Loom and achieves striking results when he returns to his company. This occasions a series of productivity technology courses inaugurated in 1955. By 1982, eighty-seven sessions of the course had been held, with approximately 2,000 participants.

1955 Observes multiple machine operations at the first production technology training course at Toyota Motor Corp. and is impressed by the separation of workers and machines.

1956 From 1956 to 1958 takes charge of a three-year study of Mitsubishi Shipbuilding's Nagasaki shipyards. Invents a new system for cutting supertanker assembly from four months to three and then to two. This system spreads to Japanese shipbuilding circles and contributes to the development of the shipbuilding industry.

1957 To raise the machining efficiency of an engine bed planer at Mitsubishi Shipbuilding's Hiroshima shipyards, constructs a spare table, conducts advance setup operations on it and changes workpiece and table together. This doubles the work rate and foreshadows a crucially decisive conceptual element of SMED, that of shifting IED to EOD.

Third Period: The Institute for Management Improvement (Domestic)

1959 Leaves the Japan Management Association to found the Institute of Management Improvement.

1960 Originates the "successive inspection system" for reducing defects and implements the system at Matsushita Electric's Moriguchi plant.

1964 From Matsushita Electric's insistence that no level of defects is tolerable, realizes that although selective inspection may be a rational procedure, it is not a rational means of assuring quality.

1965 Stimulated by Toyota Motor's "foolproof" production measures, eagerly seeks to eliminate defects entirely by systematically combining the concepts of successive inspection, independent inspection, and source inspection with "foolproof" techniques.

1966 Works as a business consultant to various Taiwanese firms, including Formosa Plastic Co., Matsushita Electric (Taiwan), and China Grinding Wheel Co. Consulted annually until 1981.

1969 Improves setup change for a 1,000-ton press at Toyota Motor's main plant from four hours to one and a half. Is soon afterward asked by management to cut setup time to three minutes and in a flash of insight thinks to shift IED to OED. With this, a systematic technique for achieving SMED is born.

Notices the difference between mechanization and automation when asked by Saga Ironworks' plant manager Yaya why automatic machines needed to be manned. This observation evolves into the concept of "pre-automation" which, Shingo later realizes, is identical to Toyota Motor's "autonomation."

1970 Is awarded the Yellow Ribbon Medal for contributions to streamlining operations in the shipbuilding industry, etc.

Fourth Period: The Institute for Management Improvement (International Expansion)

1971   Participates in observation tour of the European machine industry.

1973   Participates in observation tours of the machine industries in Europe and the United States.

1974   Lectures on SMED at die-cast industry associations in West Germany and Switzerland.

On this visit, observes vacuum die-casting methods at Daimler Benz in West Germany and Buehler in Switzerland and grows eager to implement vacuum molding in die-casting and plastic molding.

1975   Grows more enthusiastic about the "zero defects" concept on the basis of the achievement of zero defects in one month at the Shizuoka plant of Matsushita Electric's Washing Machine Operations Division.

Works for improvement based on fundamental approaches including high-speed plating, instantaneous drying, and the elimination of layout marking.

1976   Consults and lectures widely to promote SMED in Europe and the United States.

1977   Treats Toyota Motor's *kanban* system as essentially a scheme of "non-stock" production and develops systematic techniques for the system.

1978   Visits America's Federal-Mogul Corporation to provide on-site advice on SMED.

The sale by the Japan Management Association of an audiovisual set of slides on SMED and pre-automation meets with considerable success.

1979   Further success is attained by the Japan Management Association's sale of "zero defects" slides.

Visits Federal-Mogul to give follow-up guidance on SMED.

The collected results of Shingo's experiences and ideas concerning improvement are published.

1981   Makes two trips, in the spring and fall, to provide plant guidance to the French automobile manufacturers Peugeot and Citroen.

Travels to Australia to observe Toyota (Australia) and Borg-Warner.

1982   Makes follow-up consulting visits to Peugeot and Citroen in France and is impressed by the considerable results achieved through the application of SMED and nonstock production.

Consults and lectures at the Siemens company in Germany.

Lectures on "The Toyota Production System — An Industrial Engineering Study" in Munich.

Gives lectures at Chalmers University in Sweden.

Lectures at the University of Chicago.

CONSULTING

Below is a list of companies where Shigeo Shingo has given a training course or lecture, or has consulted for productivity improvement.

Industry	Name of Company	
JAPAN		
Automobiles and Suppliers	Toyota Motor Car Co., Ltd.	Yamaha Motor Co., Ltd.
	Toyota Auto Body Co., Ltd.	Kanto Auto Works, Co., Ltd.
	Toyo Motor Car Co., Ltd.	Central Motor Car Co., Ltd.
	Honda Motor Co., Ltd.	Arakawa Auto Body Co., Ltd.
	Mitsubishi Heavy Industries Co., Ltd.	Koito Manufacturing Co., Ltd. (Car parts)
	Daihatsu Motor Car Co., Ltd.	Aishin Seiki Co., Ltd. (Parts of motor car, diecast)
	Bridgestone Cycle Kogyo Co., Ltd.	Hosei Brake Co., Ltd.
Electric apparatus	Matsushita Electric Industrial Co., Ltd.	Hitachi Co., Ltd.
	Tokyo Shibaura Electric Co., Ltd.	Sony Electric Co., Ltd.
	Sharp Electric Co., Ltd.	Mitsubishi Electric Co., Ltd.
	Fuji Electric Co., Ltd.	Yasukawa Electric Mfg. Co., Ltd.
	Nippon Columbia Co., Ltd. (Stereo Disk)	Kyushu Matsushita Electric Co., Ltd.
	Stanley Electric Co., Ltd.	Asahi National Lighting Co., Ltd.
	Matsushita Electric Works Co., Ltd.	Matsushita Denshi Buhin Co., Ltd. (Electric parts)
	Matsushita Jutaku Setsubi Kiki Co., Ltd. (House equipment)	Sabsga Denki Co., Ltd. (Rectifier)
	Matsushita Denchi Kogyo Co., Ltd. (Lighting parts)	
Precision machine	Nippon Optical Co., Ltd.	Olympus Optical Co., Ltd.
	Sankyo Seiki Mfg. Co., Ltd. (Music box)	
Steel, Non-ferrous Metals and Metal Products	Nippon Steel Co., Ltd.	Nisshin Steel Co., Ltd.
	Toyo Steel Plate Co., Ltd.	
	Mitsui Mining and Smelting Co., Ltd.	The Furukawa Electric Co., Ltd.
	Sumitomo Electric Industries, Ltd.	The Fujikura Cable Works, Ltd.
	Toyo Can Industry Co., Ltd.	Hokkai Can Industry Co., Ltd.
	Nippon Spring Co., Ltd.	Chuo Spring Co., Ltd.
	Togo Seisakusho Co., Ltd. (Spring)	
Machine	Amada Co., Ltd. (Metallic Press Machine)	Aida Engineering, Co., Ltd. (Metallic press machine)
	Iseki Agricultural Machinery Mfg. Co., Ltd.	Toyota Automatic Loom Works, Ltd.

Industry	Name of Company	
	Kanzaki Kokyu Koki Co., Ltd. (**Machine tools**) Nippon Seiko Co., Ltd. (Bearings) Taiho Industry Co., Ltd. (Bearings) Asian Industry Co., Ltd. (Carburetor)	Kubota Ltd. (Engine and farming machinery) Daikin Kogyo Co., Ltd. (Coolers) Nach-Fujikoshi, Co., Ltd. (**Bearings, cutters, etc.**)
Rubber	Bridgestone Tire Co., Ltd. Nippon Rubber Co., Ltd.	Toyota Gosei Co., Ltd. Tsuki-Boshi Shoemaking Co., Ltd.
Glass	Asahi Glass Co., Ltd. Yamamura Glass Bottle Co., Ltd. Noritake China Co., Ltd.	Nippon Sheet Glass Co., Ltd. Onoda Cement Co., Ltd.
Marine products	Taiyo Fishery Co., Ltd.	
Mining	Mitsui Mining Co., Ltd. Dowa Mining Co., Ltd.	Nippon Mining Co., Ltd.
Food	Morinage & Co., Ltd. (Confectionery) Hayashikane Sangyo Co., Ltd.	Snow Brand Milk Products Co., Ltd.
Textile	Katakura Industries Co., Ltd. Kanebo Co., Ltd. Daiwa Spinning Co., Ltd. Teikoku Jinken Co., Ltd.	Gunze Co., Ltd. Fuji Spinning Co., Ltd. Daido Worsted Mills Co., Ltd. Asahi Chemical Industry Co., Ltd.
Pulp and Paper	Jujyo Paper Co., Ltd. Rengo Co., Ltd.	Oji Paper Co., Ltd.
Chemicals	Showa Denko Co., Ltd. Tokuyame Soda Co., Ltd. Hitachi Chemical Co., Ltd. Shionogi Pharmaceutical Co., Ltd. Shiseido Cosmetics Co., Ltd.	Nippon Soda Co., Ltd. Ube Industries Co., Ltd. Nippon Kayaku Co., Ltd. Fujisawa Pharmaceutical Co., Ltd.
Others	Nippon Gakki Co., Ltd. (Yamaha Piano) Saga Tekkosho Co.,Ltd. Zojirushi Mahobin Co., Ltd. Iwao Jiki Kogyo Co., Ltd. Koga Kinzoku Kogyo Co., Ltd. (Metallic press) Sanei Metallic Col., Ltd. (Metallic press)	The Sailor Pen Co., Ltd. Nippon Baruka Kogyo Co., Ltd. Gihu Dai & Mold Engineering Co., Ltd. Dia Plastics Co., Ltd. Yasutaki Industrial Co., Ltd. (Metallic press)

Industry	Name of Company	
U.S.A.	Federal-Mogul Corp. Omark Industries Storage Technology Corporation (Industrial products)	Livernois Automation Co., Ltd. Hewlett-Packard
FRANCE	Automobiles Peugeot	Automobiles Citrœn
WEST GERMANY	Daimler Benz Co., Ltd. **Bayrisches Druckgusswerk** Thurner KG Co., Ltd.	Verband Deutscher Druckgiessereien Co., Ltd. Beguform-Werke
SWITZERLAND	Gebr Buhler Co., Ltd. H-Weidmann Co., Ltd.	Bucher-guyer AC Co., Ltd.
TAIWAN	Formosa Plastic Co., Ltd. Co., Ltd. Formosa Chemicals and Fiber Co.,Ltd. China Grinding Wheel Co., Ltd. Matsushita Electric (Taiwan) Co.,Ltd. Chin Fong Machine Industrial Co., Ltd. (**Metallic press**)	Nanya Plastic Fabrication Plywood and Lumber Co., Ltd. Sunrise Plywood Co., Ltd. Taiwan Fusungta Electric Co., Ltd. (Speakers) Super Metal Industry Co., Ltd.
NETHERLANDS	Philips	

Publications

Mr. Shingo's books have sold more than 40,000 copies worldwide in English translation. For convenience, all titles are given in English, although most have not yet been translated into English.

The improvement examples presented in *Shingo Sayings* were drawn from Mr. Shingo's broad experience as a consultant. Many appear in three of his earlier works (in Japanese):

Technology for Plant Improvement. Japan Management Association, 1955.

Views and Thoughts on Plant Improvement and *Plant Improvement Embodiments and Examples*. Nikkan Kōgyō Shimbun, Ltd., 1957 (2 volumes).

A Systematic Philosophy of Plant Improvement. Nikkan Kōgyō Shimbun, Ltd., 1980.

Mr. Shingo's other works include:

"Ten Strategies for Smashing Counterarguments," *Practice and Cooperation*, (*Sakken to Kyoryoku*) 1938.

A General Introduction to Industrial Engineering. Japan Management Association, 1949.

Improving Production Control. Nihon Keizai Shimbun, 1950.

Production Control Handbook (Process Control). Kawade Shobō, 1953.

Don't Discard New Ideas. Hakuto Shobō, 1959.

Key Issues in Process Control Improvement. Nikkan Kōgyō Shimbun, Ltd., 1962.

Issues in Plant Improvement. Nikkan Kōgyō Shimbun, Ltd., 1964.

Techniques of Machine Layout Improvement. Nikkan Kōgyō Shimbun Ltd., 1965.

Fundamental Approaches to Plant Improvement. Nikkan Kōgyō Shimbun, Ltd., 1976.

"The Toyota Production System — An Industrial Engineering Study," published serially in *Factory Management* Nikkan Kōgyō Shimbun, Ltd., 1979.

A Revolution in Manufacturing: The SMED System. Japan Management Association, 1983 (English edition by Productivity Press, 1985).

Zero Quality Control: Source Inspection and the Poka-yoke System. Japan Management Association, 1985 (English edition by Productivity Press, 1986).

The Sayings of Shigeo Shingo: Key Strategies for Plant Improvement. Nikkan Kōgyō Shimbun, Ltd., 1986 (English edition by Productivity Press, 1987).

Non-Stock Production: The Shingo System for Continuous Improvement. Japan Management Association, 1987 (English edition by Productivity Press, 1988).

Index

Books from Productivity Press

Productivity Press publishes books that empower individuals and companies to achieve excellence in quality, productivity, and the creative involvement of all employees. Through steadfast efforts to support the vision and strategy of continuous improvement, Productivity Press delivers today's leading-edge tools and techniques gathered directly from industry leaders around the world. Call toll-free 1-800-394-6868 for our free catalog.

5 Pillars of the Visual Workplace
The Sourcebook for 5S Implementation
Hiroyuki Hirano

In this important sourcebook, JIT expert Hiroyuki Hirano provides the most vital information available on the visual workplace. He describes the 5S's: in Japanese they are seiri, seiton, seiso, seiketsu, and shitsuke (which translate as organization, orderliness, cleanliness, standardized cleanup, and discipline). Hirano discusses how the 5S theory fosters efficiency, maintenance, and continuous improvement in all areas of the company, from the plant floor to the sales office. Presented in a thorough, detailed style, *5 Pillars of the Visual Workplace* explains why the 5S's are important and the who, what, where, and how of 5S implementation. This book includes numerous case studies, hundreds of graphic illustrations, and over forty 5S user forms and training materials.
ISBN 1-56327-047-1 / 353 pages, illustrated / $85.00 / Order FIVE-B172

Corporate Diagnosis
Meeting Global Standards for Excellence
Thomas L. Jackson with Constance E. Dyer

All too often, strategic planning neglects an essential first step- and final step-diagnosis of the organization's current state. What's required is a systematic review of the critical factors in organizational learning and growth, factors that require monitoring, measurement, and management to ensure that your company competes successfully. This executive workbook provides a step-by-step method for diagnosing an organization's strategic health and measuring its overall competitiveness against world class standards. With checklists, charts, and detailed explanations, *Corporate Diagnosis* is a practical instruction manual. The pillars of Jackson's diagnostic system are strategy, structure, and capability. Detailed diagnostic questions in each area are provided as guidelines for developing your own self-assessment survey.
ISBN 1-56327-086-2 / 100 pages / $65.00 / Order CDIAG-B172

Productivity Press, Dept. BK, P.O. Box 13390, Portland, OR 97213-0390
Telephone: 1-800-394-6868   Fax: 1-800-394-6286

Cycle Time Management
The Fast Track to Time-Based Productivity Improvement
Patrick Northey and Nigel Southway

As much as 90 percent of the operational activities in a traditional plant are nonessential or pure waste. This book presents a proven methodology for eliminating this waste within 24 to 30 months by measuring productivity in terms of time instead of revenue or people. CTM is a cohesive management strategy that integrates just-in-time (JIT) production, computer integrated manufacturing (CIM), and total quality control (TQC). From this succinct, highly focused book, you'll learn what CTM is, how to implement it, and how to manage it.

ISBN 1-56327-015-3 / 200 pages / $35.00 / Order CYCLE-B172

The Hunters and the Hunted
A Non-Linear Solution for Reengineering the Workplace
James B. Swartz

Our competitive environment changes rapidly. If you want to survive, you have to stay on top of those changes. Otherwise, you become prey to your competitors. Hunters continuously change and learn; anyone who doesn't becomes the hunted and sooner or later will be devoured. This unusual non-fiction novel provides a veritable crash course in continuous transformation. It offers lessons from real-life companies and introduces many industrial gurus as characters. *The Hunters and the Hunted* doesn't simply tell you how to change; it puts you inside the change process itself.

ISBN 1-56327-043-9 / 582 pages / $45.00 / Order HUNT-B172

JIT Factory Revolution
A Pictorial Guide to Factory Design of the Future
Hiroyuki Hirano

The first encyclopedic picture-book of Just-In-Time, using photos and diagrams to show exactly how JIT looks and functions in production and assembly plants. Unprecedented behind-the-scenes look at multiprocess handling, cell technology, quick changeovers, kanban, andon, and other visual control systems. See why a picture is worth a thousand words.

ISBN 0-915299-44-5 / 218 pages / $50.00 / Order JITFAC-B172

Kaizen for Quick Changeover
Going Beyond SMED
Kenichi Sekine and Keisuke Arai

Especially useful for manufacturing managers and engineers, this book describes exactly how to achieve faster changeover. Picking up where Shingo's SMED book left off, you'll learn how to streamline the process even further to reduce changeover time and optimize staffing at the same time.

ISBN 0-915299-38-0 / 315 pages / $75.00 / Order KAIZEN-B172

Productivity Press, Dept. BK, P.O. Box 13390, Portland, OR 97213-0390
Telephone: 1-800-394-6868   Fax: 1-800-394-6286

One-Piece Flow
Cell Design for Transforming the Production Process
Kenichi Sekine

By reconfiguring your traditional assembly lines into production cells based on one-piece flow, you can drastically reduce your lead time, staffing requirements, and number of defects. Sekine examines the basic principles of process flow building, then offers detailed case studies of how various industries designed unique one-piece flow systems to meet their particular needs.
ISBN 0-915299-33-X / 308 pages / $75.00 / Order 1PIECE-B172

Poka-Yoke
Improving Product Quality by Preventing Defects
Nikkan Kogyo Shimbun Ltd. and Factory Magazine (ed.)

If your goal is 100 percent zero defects, here is the book for you—a completely illustrated guide to poka-yoke (mistake-proofing) for supervisors and shop-floor workers. Many poka-yoke devices come from line workers and are implemented with the help of engineering staff. The result is better product quality—and greater participation by workers in efforts to improve your processes, your products, and your company as a whole.
ISBN 0-915299-31-3 / 295 pages / $65.00 / Order IPOKA-B172

A Revolution in Manufacturing
The SMED System
Shigeo Shingo

The heart of JIT is quick changeover methods. Dr. Shingo, inventor of the Single-Minute Exchange of Die (SMED) system for Toyota, shows you how to reduce your changeovers by an average of 98 percent! By applying Shingo's techniques, you'll see rapid improvements (lead time reduced from weeks to days, lower inventory and warehousing costs) that will improve quality, productivity, and profits.
ISBN 0-915299-03-8 / 383 pages / $80.00 / Order SMED-B172

Zero Quality Control
Source Inspection and the Poka-Yoke System
Shigeo Shingo

Dr. Shingo reveals his unique defect prevention system, which combines source inspection and poka-yoke (mistake-proofing) devices that provide instant feedback on errors before they can become defects. The result: 100 percent inspection that eliminates the need for SQC and produces defect-free products without fail. Includes 112 examples, most costing under $100. Two-part video program also available; call for details.
ISBN 0-915299-07-0 / 328 pages / $75.00 / Order ZQC-B172

Productivity Press, Dept. BK, P.O. Box 13390, Portland, OR 97213-0390
Telephone: 1-800-394-6868   Fax: 1-800-394-6286

The Benchmarking Workbook
Adapting Best Practices for Performance Improvement
Gregory H. Watson

Managers today need benchmarking to anticipate trends and maintain competitive advantage. This practical workbook shows you how to do your own benchmarking study. Watson's discussion includes a case study that takes you through each step of the benchmarking process, raises thought-provoking questions, and provides examples of how to use forms for a benchmarking study.
ISBN 1-56327-033-1 / 169 pages / $30.00 / Order BENCHW-B172

Introduction to TPM
Total Productive Maintenance
Seiichi Nakajima

Total Productive Maintenance (TPM) combines preventive maintenance with Japanese concepts of total quality control (TQC) and total employee involvement (TEI). The result is a new system for equipment maintenance that optimizes effectiveness, eliminates breakdowns, and promotes autonomous operator maintenance through day-to-day activities. Since it was first introduced in Japan, TPM has caused a worldwide revolution in plant maintenance. Here are the steps involved in TPM and case examples from top Japanese plants.
ISBN 0-915299-23-2 / 149 pages / $45.00 / Order ITPM-B172

Manufacturing Strategy
How to Formulate and Implement a Winning Plan
John Miltenburg

This book offers a step-by-step method for creating a strategic manufacturing plan. The key tool is a multidimensional worksheet that links the competitive analysis to manufacturing outputs, the seven basic production systems, the levels of capability and the levers for moving to a higher level. The author presents each element of the worksheet and shows you how to link them to create an integrated strategy and implementation plan. By identifying the appropriate production system for your business, you can determine what output you can expect from manufacturing, how to improve outputs, and how to change to more optimal production systems as your business needs change.
ISBN 1-56327-071-4 / 391 pages / $45.00 / Order MANST-B172

Productivity Press, Dept. BK, P.O. Box 13390, Portland, OR 97213-0390
Telephone: 1-800-394-6868   Fax: 1-800-394-6286

Toyota Production System
Beyond Large-Scale Production
Taiichi Ohno

Here's the first information ever published in Japan on the Toyota production system (known as Just-In-Time manufacturing). Here Ohno, who created JIT for Toyota, reveals the origins, daring innovations, and ceaseless evolution of the Toyota system into a full management system. You'll learn how to manage JIT from the man who invented it, and to create a winning JIT environment in your own manufacturing operation.
ISBN 0-915299-14-3 / 163 pages / $45.00 / Order OTPS-B172

TPM Case Studies
Factory Management Series
Nikkan Kogyo Shimbun (ed.)

Total Productive Maintenance (TPM) combines the best features of productive and predictive maintenance with innovative management strategies and total employee involvement. This collection of foundational articles and classic implementation case studies culled from NKS Factory Management Journal details how TPM has helped prize-winning companies in Japan achieve remarkable results. It includes in-depth explorations of the approach to loss reduction and plantwide implementation; a classic essay on the relationship between JIT and TPM by Seiichi Nakajima, the "father" of TPM; and numerous detailed examples of equipment modifications addressing specific types of losses.
ISBN 1-56327-066-8 / 200 pages / $30.00 / Order TPMCS-B172

The Right Fit
The Power of Ergonomics as a Competitive Strategy
Clifford M. Gross

Each year, poorly designed products and workplaces account for thousands of injuries and skyrocketing costs. That's why ergonomics—the human factor in product and workplace design—is fast becoming a major concern of manufacturers. Now one of the country's top experts argues that ergonomics will become the next strategic imperative for American business, the deciding factor in which companies ultimately succeed. Here's a brilliant non-technical introduction for corporate planners and strategic decision makers.
ISBN 1-56327-111-7 / 185 pages / $24.00 / Order ERGO-B172

Productivity Press, Dept. BK, P.O. Box 13390, Portland, OR 97213-0390
Telephone: 1-800-394-6868   Fax: 1-800-394-6286

TPM for America
What It Is and Why You Need It
Herbert R. Steinbacher and Norma L. Steinbacher

As much as 15 to 40 percent of manufacturing costs are attributable to maintenance. With a fully implemented TPM program, your company can eradicate all but a fraction of these costs. Co-written by an American TPM practitioner and an experienced educator, this book gives a convincing account of why American companies must adopt TPM if they are to successfully compete in world markets. Includes examples from leading American companies showing how TPM has changed them into more efficient and productive organizations.
ISBN 1-56327-044-7 / 169 pages / $25.00 / Order TPMAM-B172

Uptime
Strategies for Excellence in Maintenance Management
John Dixon Campbell

Campbell outlines a blueprint for a world class maintenance program by examining, piece by piece, its essential elements – leadership (strategy and management), control (data management, measures, tactics, planning and scheduling), continuous improvement (RCM and TPM), and quantum leaps (process reengineering). He explains each element in detail, using simple language and practical examples from a wide range of industries. This book is for every manager who needs to see the "big picture" of maintenance management. In addition to maintenance, engineering, and manufacturing managers, all business managers will benefit from this comprehensive and realistic approach to improving asset performance.
ISBN 1-56327-053-6 / 204 pages / $35.00 / Order UP-B172

Implementing a Lean Management System
Thomas L. Jackson with Karen R. Jones

Does your company think and act ahead of technological change, ahead of the customer, and ahead of the competition? Thinking strategically requires a company to face these questions with a clear future image of itself. Implementing a Lean Management System lays out a comprehensive management system for aligning the firm's vision of the future with market realities. Based on hoshin management, the Japanese strategic planning method used by top managers for driving TQM throughout an organization, Lean Management is about deploying vision, strategy, and policy to all levels of daily activity. It is an eminently practical methodology emerging out of the implementation of continuous improvement methods and employee involvement. The key tools of this book build on multiskilling, the knowledge of the worker, and an understanding of the role of the new lean manufacturer.
ISBN 1-56327-085-4 / 182 pages / $65.00 / Order ILMS-B172

Productivity Press, Dept. BK, P.O. Box 13390, Portland, OR 97213-0390
Telephone: 1-800-394-6868   Fax: 1-800-394-6286